SHIMBA

BIBLE STUDY SERIES

THE DIVINITY OF JESUS

IN THE BOOK OF PSALMS

Dr. Maxwell Shimba

SHIMBA
PUBLISHING

TABLE OF CONTENTS

INTRODUCTION

The Book of Psalms holds a unique and cherished place within the canon of Scripture. For centuries, it has been a source of comfort, guidance, and inspiration for believers, offering profound insights into the nature of God, the human experience, and the complexities of life. However, beyond its immediate devotional value, the Psalms are also deeply prophetic, containing rich Messianic themes that point directly to the person and work of Jesus Christ. In this book, The Divinity of Jesus in the Book of Psalms, Dr. Maxwell Shimba embarks on a comprehensive exploration of these themes, revealing how the Psalms not only anticipate the coming of the Messiah but also affirm His divine nature.

The purpose of this study is twofold. First, it aims to uncover the ways in which the Psalms prophetically announce the coming of Jesus Christ, focusing particularly on His divine attributes and the fulfillment of these prophecies in the New Testament. Second, it seeks to deepen the reader's understanding of how these ancient texts, written in a different context and time, remain profoundly relevant to the Christian faith today. By connecting the Old Testament prophecies with their New Testament realizations, Dr. Shimba demonstrates the unity and coherence of the Scriptures, reinforcing the belief in their divine inspiration.

Dr. Shimba begins by laying the foundation for understanding the Psalms as Messianic literature. He explores the historical and cultural background of the Psalms, considering the perspectives of both Jewish and early

Christian interpretations. This contextual analysis is crucial for appreciating how the original audience might have understood these texts, as well as how early Christians, including the authors of the New Testament, saw in them the foreshadowing of Christ. By bridging these interpretative traditions, Dr. Shimba provides a comprehensive view that is both historically grounded and theologically rich.

As the book progresses, readers are guided through a detailed examination of specific Psalms that highlight the divinity of Jesus. Each chapter focuses on a particular Psalm, offering verse-by-verse commentary and theological reflection. For example, in Psalm 2, the declaration "You are My Son, today I have begotten You" is explored as a direct reference to the divine sonship of Jesus, a theme that is echoed and affirmed in the New Testament. Similarly, Psalm 110, with its depiction of the Messiah as a priest forever in the order of Melchizedek, is unpacked to reveal its profound implications for understanding Jesus' eternal priesthood and kingship.

One of the unique contributions of this book is its emphasis on the practical application of these theological insights. Dr. Shimba does not merely present an academic analysis; he also encourages readers to reflect on the significance of Jesus' divinity for their own faith and spiritual journey. Each chapter includes reflection questions and prompts for personal meditation, designed to help readers internalize the truths they have learned and apply them to their daily lives. This approach ensures that the study of the Psalms is not just an intellectual exercise, but a transformative experience that deepens one's relationship with Christ.

In conclusion, The Divinity of Jesus in the Book of Psalms by Dr. Maxwell Shimba offers a profound exploration of the Messianic prophecies found within the Psalms and their fulfillment in the person of Jesus Christ. Through careful exegesis, theological insight, and practical application, this book provides a compelling case for the divinity of Jesus as revealed in these ancient hymns. As you journey through its pages, may you gain a deeper appreciation for the unity of Scripture, the majesty of Christ, and the timeless relevance of the Psalms in the life of every believer.

DR. MAXWELL SHIMBA

CHAPTER 01

OVERVIEW OF JESUS IN THE OLD TESTAMENT

The Old Testament is replete with references to the coming Messiah, who Christians believe is Jesus Christ. These references, often called Messianic prophecies, provide a foundational understanding of Jesus' identity and mission. The Psalms, in particular, contain numerous allusions to Jesus, highlighting His divinity, suffering, kingship, and priesthood. This chapter will explore these themes and provide an overview of Jesus in the Old Testament, using Bible verses, expository study, and comprehensive commentary.

Jesus in the Old Testament: An Overview

1. The Promise of the Messiah

- Genesis 3:15: The first promise of a savior comes immediately after the fall of Adam and Eve. God declares that the seed of the woman will crush the serpent's head, a veiled reference to Jesus' ultimate victory over Satan.

- "And I will put enmity between you and the woman, and between your seed and her Seed; He shall bruise your head, and you shall bruise His heel." (Genesis 3:15, NKJV)

- The "Seed" is a term later understood to refer to Jesus, who would defeat sin and death through His death and resurrection.

2. The Abrahamic Covenant

- Genesis 22:18: God's promise to Abraham that through his offspring all nations would be blessed is a foreshadowing of Jesus, who is a descendant of Abraham.

- "In your seed all the nations of the earth shall be blessed, because you have obeyed My voice." (Genesis 22:18, NKJV)

- This blessing is fulfilled in Jesus, who brings salvation to all people.

3. The Davidic Covenant

- 2 Samuel 7:12-13: God's covenant with David establishes that his throne will be everlasting, pointing to Jesus, the eternal king from David's line.

- "When your days are fulfilled and you rest with your fathers, I will set up your seed after you, who will come from your body, and I will establish his kingdom. He shall build a house for My name, and I will establish the throne of his kingdom forever." (2 Samuel 7:12-13, NKJV)

- Jesus is often called the Son of David, emphasizing His royal lineage and eternal kingship.

4. Prophecies of the Suffering Servant

- Isaiah 53:3-5: Isaiah's description of the suffering servant who bears the sins of many is a clear prophetic picture of Jesus' sacrificial death.

- "He is despised and rejected by men, a Man of sorrows and acquainted with grief. And we hid, as it were, our faces from Him; He was despised, and we did not esteem Him. Surely He has borne our griefs and carried our sorrows; yet we esteemed Him stricken, smitten by God, and afflicted. But He was wounded for our transgressions, He was bruised

for our iniquities; the chastisement for our peace was upon Him, and by His stripes we are healed." (Isaiah 53:3-5, NKJV)
- This passage vividly depicts the suffering and atonement of Jesus, who took on the punishment for humanity's sins.

5. The Birth of the Messiah
- Isaiah 7:14: The prophecy of a virgin giving birth to a son, Immanuel, meaning "God with us," foretells the miraculous birth of Jesus.
- "Therefore the Lord Himself will give you a sign: Behold, the virgin shall conceive and bear a Son, and shall call His name Immanuel." (Isaiah 7:14, NKJV)
- The New Testament identifies this prophecy as fulfilled in the birth of Jesus to the Virgin Mary (Matthew 1:22-23).

6. The Reign of the Messiah
- Micah 5:2: The prophecy of the Messiah's birthplace in Bethlehem highlights Jesus' humble origins and divine purpose.
- "But you, Bethlehem Ephrathah, though you are little among the thousands of Judah, yet out of you shall come forth to Me the One to be Ruler in Israel, whose goings forth are from of old, from everlasting." (Micah 5:2, NKJV)
- This prophecy is fulfilled in Jesus' birth in Bethlehem (Matthew 2:1-6).

7. Jesus in the Psalms
- The Psalms contain several direct and indirect references to Jesus, His life, mission, and divinity. Key Psalms include:
- Psalm 2: Declares the Messiah as the Son of God and His universal reign.
- "You are My Son, today I have begotten You. Ask of Me, and I will give You the nations for Your

inheritance, and the ends of the earth for Your possession." (Psalm 2:7-8, NKJV)

- Psalm 22: Portrays the suffering and crucifixion of Jesus.

- "My God, My God, why have You forsaken Me? Why are You so far from helping Me, and from the words of My groaning?" (Psalm 22:1, NKJV)

- Psalm 110: Speaks of the Messiah's eternal priesthood.

- "The LORD said to my Lord, 'Sit at My right hand, till I make Your enemies Your footstool.'" (Psalm 110:1, NKJV)

Expository Study and Commentary

The Old Testament is rich with prophecies and foreshadowings that point directly to Jesus Christ. Through an expository study using exhaustive Strong's Concordance, we can delve deeper into the original Hebrew words and their meanings, providing a clearer understanding of these prophecies.

For instance, the word "Messiah" (Hebrew: מָשִׁיחַ, Mashiach) means "anointed one." It appears in various forms throughout the Old Testament, often referring to kings, priests, and prophets anointed for God's purpose. In the New Testament, Jesus is identified as the Messiah, fulfilling these roles perfectly.

Psalm 2:7, which declares, "You are My Son, today I have begotten You," uses the Hebrew word יָלַד (yalad), meaning "to bear" or "to beget." This term emphasizes the unique relationship between God the Father and Jesus, His Son. The New Testament reaffirms this in Acts 13:33 and Hebrews 1:5.

Isaiah 53's "Man of sorrows" uses the Hebrew word מַכְאוֹב (mak'ob), meaning "pain" or "sorrow." This prophecy is profound in its detailed description of Jesus' suffering, which is fulfilled in the Gospels' accounts of His crucifixion.

Conclusion

The Old Testament, particularly the Psalms, provides a comprehensive and prophetic view of Jesus Christ. Through detailed analysis and expository study, we can see the continuity of God's plan for salvation through His Son. Jesus' divinity, suffering, kingship, and priesthood are all foretold in these ancient texts, offering a rich tapestry of evidence that affirms His identity and mission.

In the subsequent chapters, we will delve deeper into the specific Psalms that highlight these aspects of Jesus, providing a thorough understanding of His presence and purpose in the Old Testament. This study aims to enrich our faith and appreciation for the intricate and divine orchestration of God's redemptive plan through Jesus Christ.

Importance of Psalms in Understanding Jesus

The Psalms are a vital part of the Old Testament, offering a rich tapestry of poetry, prophecy, and theology that points to Jesus Christ. They provide deep insights into His character, mission, and divinity. This chapter will explore the significance of the Psalms in understanding Jesus, using Bible verses, expository study, and comprehensive commentary.

The Role of the Psalms in Biblical Revelation

1. The Psalms as Prophetic Literature

- The Psalms often contain prophetic elements that foretell the coming of the Messiah. These prophecies are crucial for identifying Jesus as the promised Savior.

- Psalm 2:7-8: "I will declare the decree: The LORD has said to Me, 'You are My Son, today I have begotten You. Ask of Me, and I will give You the nations for Your inheritance, and the ends of the earth for Your possession.'"

- The Hebrew word for "Son" is בֵּן (ben), emphasizing the unique relationship between God and the Messiah. This prophecy is quoted in the New Testament, affirming Jesus' divine sonship (Hebrews 1:5).

2. The Psalms as a Reflection of Jesus' Suffering
- Several Psalms provide a vivid portrayal of the suffering Jesus would endure, particularly Psalm 22.
- Psalm 22:1: "My God, My God, why have You forsaken Me? Why are You so far from helping Me, and from the words of My groaning?"
- The Hebrew word for "forsaken" is עָזַב (azab), meaning to leave or abandon. Jesus quotes this verse on the cross, highlighting His fulfillment of this prophecy (Matthew 27:46).
3. The Psalms as a Source of Jesus' Kingship and Priesthood
- The Psalms also speak of Jesus' eternal kingship and priesthood.
- Psalm 110:1-4: "The LORD said to my Lord, 'Sit at My right hand, till I make Your enemies Your footstool.' The LORD shall send the rod of Your strength out of Zion. Rule in the midst of Your enemies! ... The LORD has sworn and will not relent, 'You are a priest forever according to the order of Melchizedek.'"
- The term "priest" (כֹּהֵן, kohen) and "Melchizedek" (מַלְכִּי־צֶדֶק, malki-tzedek) connect Jesus to an eternal priesthood, which is expounded in Hebrews 5:6.
Jesus in the Psalms: An Expository Study
1. Psalm 2: The Anointed King
- Psalm 2:2: "The kings of the earth set themselves, and the rulers take counsel together, against the LORD and against His Anointed, saying..."

- The term "Anointed" (מָשִׁיחַ, mashiach) refers to the Messiah. This Psalm foreshadows the opposition Jesus would face and His ultimate victory over the nations (Acts 4:25-26).

2. Psalm 22: The Suffering Servant

- Psalm 22:16-18: "For dogs have surrounded Me; the congregation of the wicked has enclosed Me. They pierced My hands and My feet; I can count all My bones. They look and stare at Me. They divide My garments among them, and for My clothing they cast lots."

- The phrase "pierced My hands and My feet" vividly describes crucifixion, a method of execution not known when the Psalm was written. This precise detail is fulfilled in the Gospels (John 19:24).

3. Psalm 110: The Eternal Priest

- Psalm 110:4: "The LORD has sworn and will not relent, 'You are a priest forever according to the order of Melchizedek.'"

- The eternal priesthood "according to the order of Melchizedek" establishes Jesus' unique and everlasting priesthood, as explained in Hebrews 7:17.

Comprehensive Commentary

The Psalms, written centuries before Jesus' earthly ministry, are a testament to God's intricate plan of redemption. Each Messianic Psalm reveals different facets of Jesus' identity:

- Psalm 2 emphasizes Jesus' divine sonship and kingship. The New Testament frequently references this Psalm to affirm Jesus as the Son of God, appointed to reign over all nations (Acts 13:33).

- Psalm 22 provides a detailed prophecy of Jesus' crucifixion, portraying His physical suffering and the mocking He endured. This Psalm is a profound reflection on the cost of redemption and the fulfillment of prophecy in Jesus' sacrifice.

- Psalm 110 underscores Jesus' role as both king and priest. This dual role is unique to Jesus, who not only rules as a sovereign king but also intercedes as a high priest, offering a perfect sacrifice for sin.

Importance of the Psalms in Understanding Jesus

1. Confirmation of Prophecies

- The detailed prophecies in the Psalms confirm Jesus as the Messiah, providing strong evidence for His identity and mission. The fulfillment of these prophecies in the New Testament validates the Old Testament scriptures and strengthens our faith.

2. Understanding Jesus' Mission

- The Psalms help us understand the scope of Jesus' mission, including His suffering, resurrection, and eternal reign. They reveal the depth of God's love and the extent of Jesus' sacrifice for humanity.

3. Enhancing Worship and Devotion

- The Psalms are not only prophetic but also devotional. They guide believers in worship, offering words of praise, lament, and thanksgiving. Understanding the Messianic elements in the Psalms enhances our worship of Jesus, recognizing Him as the fulfillment of God's promises.

4. Strengthening Faith

- Studying the Psalms strengthens our faith by showing the consistency and reliability of God's word. It reminds us that God's plans are precise and His promises are sure, fulfilled perfectly in Jesus Christ.

Conclusion

The Psalms are an indispensable part of the Old Testament that provide profound insights into the person and work of Jesus Christ. Through detailed prophecies and vivid descriptions of His life, the Psalms reveal Jesus' divine nature,

His suffering, His kingship, and His priesthood. By studying these ancient texts, we gain a deeper understanding of Jesus' identity and mission, enriching our faith and enhancing our worship.

In the chapters that follow, we will delve into specific Psalms to explore these themes in greater detail, offering a comprehensive study of Jesus' presence and purpose as revealed in the Psalms. This journey through the Psalms will not only deepen our understanding of Jesus but also draw us closer to Him, as we see the fulfillment of God's redemptive plan in His Son.

Structure and Approach of the Book

Structure of the Book

This book is structured to provide a comprehensive exploration of Jesus Christ as revealed in the Psalms. Each chapter will focus on specific themes and passages that highlight different aspects of Jesus' identity, mission, and divinity. Here is a detailed outline of the book's structure:

1. Introduction
    - Overview of Jesus in the Old Testament
    - Importance of Psalms in understanding Jesus
    - Structure and approach of the book
2. Messianic Prophecies in the Psalms
    - Identifying Messianic Psalms
    - The significance of these prophecies
    - Psalm 2: The Anointed One
    - Psalm 22: The Suffering Servant
    - Psalm 110: The Priestly King
3. The Divinity of Jesus in Psalm 2
    - Analysis of Psalm 2:1-12
    - Jesus as the Son of God
    - The divine kingship of Jesus
    - New Testament references to Psalm 2
4. The Suffering and Triumph of Jesus in Psalm 22

The approach of the Book

1. Expository Study
    - Each chapter will provide an expository study of selected Psalms, carefully analyzing the text to uncover its

meaning and significance. This approach ensures a thorough understanding of the scripture.

2. Strong's Concordance

- The use of Strong's Exhaustive Concordance will help readers understand the original Hebrew words and their meanings. This will provide deeper insights into the text and its implications.

3. Comprehensive Commentary

- Each passage will be accompanied by comprehensive commentary that explains its context, relevance, and fulfillment in the New Testament. This commentary will draw from various scholarly sources and theological perspectives.

4. New Testament Connections

- The book will highlight how the Psalms are fulfilled in the life and ministry of Jesus as recorded in the New Testament. These connections will underscore the continuity and coherence of the biblical narrative.

5. Theological Reflections

- Throughout the book, theological reflections will offer insights into the significance of Jesus' identity and mission. These reflections will help readers apply the lessons of the Psalms to their own faith and life.

6. Practical Application

- Each chapter will include practical applications and reflection questions to help readers integrate the teachings of the Psalms into their daily lives. This will encourage personal growth and spiritual development.

7. Study Guide

- The inclusion of a study guide and reflection questions at the end of the book will facilitate group discussions and personal study, making it a valuable resource for Bible study groups and individual readers alike.

Conclusion

By combining expository study, Strong's Concordance, comprehensive commentary, and practical application, this book aims to provide a deep and enriching understanding of Jesus as revealed in the Psalms. Each chapter will guide readers through the prophetic and theological richness of the Psalms, illuminating the identity and mission of Jesus Christ. This structured approach ensures that readers not only gain knowledge but also grow in their faith and devotion to Jesus.

CHAPTER 02

MESSIANIC PROPHECIES IN THE PSALMS

Identifying Messianic Psalms

The Psalms are a treasure trove of poetic worship, wisdom, and prophecy. Among them are the Messianic Psalms, which prophesy about the coming Messiah—Jesus Christ. These Psalms are critical for understanding the character, mission, and divinity of Jesus. This chapter will focus on identifying Messianic Psalms and provide an expository study with comprehensive commentary, using Strong's Exhaustive Concordance to delve deeper into the original Hebrew text.

What Are Messianic Psalms?

Messianic Psalms are those that contain direct or indirect references to the Messiah. They often describe the life, sufferings, death, resurrection, and eternal reign of Jesus Christ. Scholars and theologians have identified several

Psalms as Messianic due to their clear references to Christ, which are confirmed by the New Testament.

Criteria for Identifying Messianic Psalms

1. Direct Prophetic References

- Psalms that clearly predict events or characteristics related to the Messiah.

- Example: Psalm 22 vividly describes the crucifixion of Jesus.

2. Typological References

- Psalms that use typology, where historical events or figures foreshadow the Messiah.

- Example: David's experiences often serve as a type of Christ.

3. New Testament Affirmation

- Psalms that are explicitly referenced in the New Testament as being fulfilled in Jesus.

- Example: Psalm 110 is frequently cited in the New Testament regarding Jesus' priesthood and kingship.

Key Messianic Psalms

1. Psalm 2: The Anointed One

- Psalm 2:7-8: "I will declare the decree: The LORD has said to Me, 'You are My Son, today I have begotten You. Ask of Me, and I will give You the nations for Your inheritance, and the ends of the earth for Your possession.'"

- The Hebrew word for "Son" is בֵּן (ben), emphasizing a unique filial relationship with God.

- New Testament Reference: Acts 13:33, Hebrews 1:5, affirm Jesus as the Son of God.

2. Psalm 22: The Suffering Servant

- Psalm 22:1: "My God, My God, why have You forsaken Me?"

- Psalm 22:16-18: "For dogs have surrounded Me; the congregation of the wicked has enclosed Me. They pierced My hands and My feet; I can count all My bones. They look and stare at Me. They divide My garments among them, and for My clothing they cast lots."

- The term "pierced" (כָּרָה, karah) prophetically describes the crucifixion.

- New Testament Reference: Matthew 27:46, John 19:23-24.

3. Psalm 16: The Resurrection

- Psalm 16:10: "For You will not leave my soul in Sheol, nor will You allow Your Holy One to see corruption."

- The term "corruption" (שַׁחַת, shachath) refers to decay or destruction.

- New Testament Reference: Acts 2:27-31, where Peter interprets this as a prophecy of Jesus' resurrection.

4. Psalm 110: The Priestly King

- Psalm 110:1: "The LORD said to my Lord, 'Sit at My right hand, till I make Your enemies Your footstool.'"

- Psalm 110:4: "The LORD has sworn and will not relent, 'You are a priest forever according to the order of Melchizedek.'"

- The term "priest" (כֹּהֵן, kohen) and "Melchizedek" (מַלְכִּי-צֶדֶק, malki-tzedek) indicate an eternal priesthood.

- New Testament Reference: Matthew 22:44, Hebrews 5:6.

5. Psalm 45: The Royal Wedding Song

- Psalm 45:6-7: "Your throne, O God, is forever and ever; A scepter of righteousness is the scepter of Your kingdom. You love righteousness and hate wickedness; Therefore God, Your God, has anointed You with the oil of gladness more than Your companions."

- The term "anointed" (מָשִׁיחַ, mashiach) signifies the Messiah.

- New Testament Reference: Hebrews 1:8-9.

6. Psalm 118: The Rejected Stone

- Psalm 118:22-23: "The stone which the builders rejected has become the chief cornerstone. This was the LORD's doing; it is marvelous in our eyes."
- The term "cornerstone" (רֹאשָׁה אֶבֶן, eben roshah) indicates the foundational role of the Messiah.
- New Testament Reference: Matthew 21:42, Acts 4:11.

Expository Study of Select Messianic Psalms

Psalm 2: The Anointed One
- Context: This Psalm speaks of the rebellion of earthly kings against God's anointed king. It is both a coronation Psalm and a prophecy of the Messiah.
- Key Verses:
- Psalm 2:1-2: "Why do the nations rage, and the people plot a vain thing? The kings of the earth set themselves, and the rulers take counsel together, against the LORD and against His Anointed, saying..."
- Exposition: The rebellion of nations represents humanity's rejection of God's rule. The term "Anointed" (מָשִׁיחַ, mashiach) directly points to the Messiah. The New Testament frequently applies this Psalm to Jesus, emphasizing His divine sonship and authority (Acts 4:25-26).

Psalm 22: The Suffering Servant
- Context: This Psalm is a lament that transitions into praise. It begins with a cry of abandonment and ends with a declaration of God's deliverance.
- Key Verses:
- Psalm 22:1: "My God, My God, why have You forsaken Me?"
- Psalm 22:16-18: "They pierced My hands and My feet; I can count all My bones. They divide My garments among them, and for My clothing they cast lots."
- Exposition: The vivid imagery of crucifixion prefigures Jesus' suffering on the cross. The specific details,

such as the piercing of hands and feet and the casting of lots for garments, are directly fulfilled in the Gospels (John 19:23-24). The use of "forsaken" (עָזַב, azab) emphasizes Jesus' experience of abandonment on the cross.

Psalm 110: The Priestly King

- Context: This Psalm is a royal Psalm that speaks of the Messiah's kingship and eternal priesthood.

- Key Verses:

- Psalm 110:1: "The LORD said to my Lord, 'Sit at My right hand, till I make Your enemies Your footstool.'"

- Psalm 110:4: "You are a priest forever according to the order of Melchizedek."

- Exposition: The term "Lord" (אָדוֹן, adon) signifies authority and divinity. Jesus Himself cites this verse to affirm His identity as the Messiah (Matthew 22:44). The reference to Melchizedek highlights an eternal and unique priesthood, different from the Levitical priesthood, which is expounded upon in the book of Hebrews (Hebrews 7).

Conclusion

The Messianic Psalms provide a profound and multifaceted portrait of Jesus Christ. Through prophetic declarations, typological references, and New Testament affirmations, these Psalms reveal the identity, mission, and divinity of the Messiah. By using Strong's Exhaustive Concordance, we can delve into the original Hebrew text to uncover deeper meanings and richer insights. This expository study not only enhances our understanding of the Psalms but also strengthens our faith in Jesus as the fulfillment of God's redemptive plan.

The Significance of These Prophecies

Messianic prophecies in the Psalms are critical for understanding the identity and mission of Jesus Christ. These prophecies, written centuries before His birth, reveal the divine plan for salvation and provide irrefutable evidence of

Jesus' messianic role. This chapter explores the significance of these prophecies, using Bible verses, expository study, and comprehensive commentary, supported by Strong's Exhaustive Concordance.

Establishing Jesus' Divine Identity

1. Divine Sonship and Kingship

- Psalm 2:7: "I will declare the decree: The LORD has said to Me, 'You are My Son, today I have begotten You.'"

- The term "begotten" (יָלַד, yalad) signifies a unique, divine sonship, distinguishing Jesus from all others.

- New Testament Reference: This verse is cited in Hebrews 1:5 to affirm Jesus' divine sonship, indicating His preeminence over angels and His eternal kingship.

- Significance: This prophecy establishes Jesus as the eternal Son of God, affirming His divine nature and authority over all creation.

2. Eternal Priesthood

- Psalm 110:4: "The LORD has sworn and will not relent, 'You are a priest forever according to the order of Melchizedek.'"

- The term "priest" (כֹּהֵן, kohen) and "Melchizedek" (מַלְכִּי־צֶדֶק, malki-tzedek) denote an eternal and unique priesthood.

- New Testament Reference: Hebrews 7:17 explains that Jesus' priesthood is eternal, unlike the temporal Levitical priesthood, emphasizing His role as the ultimate mediator between God and humanity.

- Significance: This prophecy underscores Jesus' unique and everlasting priesthood, highlighting His role as the perfect mediator who offers an eternal sacrifice for sin.

Foretelling Jesus' Suffering and Redemption

1. The Suffering Servant

- Psalm 22:16-18: "For dogs have surrounded Me; the congregation of the wicked has enclosed Me. They pierced

My hands and My feet; I can count all My bones. They look and stare at Me. They divide My garments among them, and for My clothing they cast lots."

- The term "pierced" (כָּרָה, karah) specifically points to crucifixion, a method of execution not practiced in David's time.

- New Testament Reference: The Gospels recount these events during Jesus' crucifixion (Matthew 27:35, John 19:23-24), fulfilling this prophecy with exact precision.

- Significance: This detailed prophecy provides compelling evidence of Jesus' suffering and crucifixion, affirming the sacrificial nature of His mission and the fulfillment of Old Testament prophecies.

2. Resurrection and Vindication

- Psalm 16:10: "For You will not leave my soul in Sheol, nor will You allow Your Holy One to see corruption."

- The term "corruption" (שַׁחַת, shachath) refers to decay, emphasizing the promise of resurrection.

- New Testament Reference: Acts 2:31 explains that David foresaw the resurrection of Christ, whose body did not undergo decay.

- Significance: This prophecy is crucial in validating the resurrection of Jesus, a cornerstone of Christian faith. It underscores His victory over death and His divine nature.

Demonstrating Jesus' Role in Salvation History

1. The Rejected Cornerstone

- Psalm 118:22-23: "The stone which the builders rejected has become the chief cornerstone. This was the LORD's doing; it is marvelous in our eyes."

- The term "cornerstone" (רֹאשָׁה אֶבֶן, eben roshah) signifies a foundational stone, essential for the structure.

- New Testament Reference: This prophecy is cited in Matthew 21:42 and Acts 4:11, showing how Jesus, though rejected, became the foundation of God's redemptive plan.

- Significance: This prophecy highlights the paradox of Jesus' rejection by religious leaders and His ultimate exaltation as the foundation of the Church. It emphasizes God's sovereign plan in using Jesus' rejection for the salvation of humanity.

2. Universal Reign and Eternal Kingdom

- Psalm 2:8: "Ask of Me, and I will give You the nations for Your inheritance, and the ends of the earth for Your possession."

- The term "inheritance" (נַחֲלָה, nachalah) indicates a divine bequest, affirming Jesus' authority over all nations.

- New Testament Reference: This universal reign is affirmed in Revelation 11:15, where Jesus is proclaimed as the ruler of the kingdoms of the world.

- Significance: This prophecy affirms Jesus' ultimate authority and the global scope of His kingdom, fulfilling God's promise of a Messiah who would reign over all the earth.

Affirming the Continuity of Scripture

1. Coherence of Old and New Testament

- The Messianic prophecies in the Psalms are fulfilled in the New Testament, demonstrating the continuity and coherence of Scripture.

- Example: Psalm 22:1 ("My God, My God, why have You forsaken Me?") is directly quoted by Jesus on the cross (Matthew 27:46), linking the Old and New Testaments in a profound way.

- Significance: This continuity reinforces the divine inspiration of the Bible and strengthens the faith of believers by showing that God's plan of salvation was meticulously revealed and fulfilled across centuries.

2. Validation of Jesus' Messiahship

- The fulfillment of these prophecies provides strong evidence for Jesus' Messiahship, as He uniquely meets the criteria set forth in the Old Testament.

- Example: The genealogical records in the Gospels (Matthew 1, Luke 3) trace Jesus' lineage back to David, fulfilling the prophecies of a Davidic Messiah (Psalm 132:11).

- Significance: This validation is crucial for both Jewish and Gentile believers, affirming that Jesus is the promised Savior foretold by the prophets and fulfilling the hopes of Israel.

Encouragement for Believers

1. Strengthening Faith

- Understanding the Messianic prophecies strengthens believers' faith in Jesus as the promised Messiah who fulfills God's redemptive plan.

- Example: Psalm 110:1 ("The LORD said to my Lord, 'Sit at My right hand'") is frequently cited in the New Testament (Acts 2:34-35) to affirm Jesus' exaltation and authority.

- Significance: Recognizing the fulfillment of these prophecies deepens our trust in God's word and His promises.

2. Hope and Assurance

- These prophecies provide hope and assurance that God's plan for salvation is perfect and unchanging.

- Example: The assurance of Jesus' eternal reign (Psalm 2:8) gives believers confidence in the ultimate victory of God's kingdom.

- Significance: This hope encourages believers to remain steadfast in their faith, knowing that Jesus' return and the fulfillment of God's promises are certain.

Conclusion

The significance of the Messianic prophecies in the Psalms cannot be overstated. They establish Jesus' divine identity, foretell His suffering and resurrection, demonstrate His role in salvation history, and affirm the continuity and reliability of Scripture. By understanding these prophecies, believers gain a deeper appreciation of God's redemptive plan and a stronger faith in Jesus as the promised Messiah. This chapter has provided an expository study, supported by Strong's Exhaustive Concordance, to uncover the profound significance of these ancient prophecies and their fulfillment in Jesus Christ.

Psalm 2: The Anointed One

Psalm 2 is one of the most significant Messianic Psalms, vividly depicting the Messiah as the Anointed One of God. This Psalm speaks to the rebellion of earthly powers against God's chosen King and underscores the divine authority and eternal reign of the Messiah. In this chapter, we will delve deeply into Psalm 2, using Bible verses, an expository study, and comprehensive commentary, supported by Strong's Exhaustive Concordance.

Text of Psalm 2 (NKJV)

1. Why do the nations rage, and the people plot a vain thing?

2. The kings of the earth set themselves, and the rulers take counsel together, against the LORD and against His Anointed, saying,

3. "Let us break Their bonds in pieces and cast away Their cords from us."

4. He who sits in the heavens shall laugh; the Lord shall hold them in derision.

5. Then He shall speak to them in His wrath, and distress them in His deep displeasure:

6. "Yet I have set My King on My holy hill of Zion."

7. "I will declare the decree: The LORD has said to Me, 'You are My Son, today I have begotten You.

8. Ask of Me, and I will give You the nations for Your inheritance, and the ends of the earth for Your possession.

9. You shall break them with a rod of iron; You shall dash them to pieces like a potter's vessel.'"

10. Now therefore, be wise, O kings; be instructed, you judges of the earth.

11. Serve the LORD with fear, and rejoice with trembling.

12. Kiss the Son, lest He be angry, and you perish in the way, when His wrath is kindled but a little. Blessed are all those who put their trust in Him.

Expository Study

Verses 1-3: The Rebellion of the Nations

Verse 1: "Why do the nations rage, and the people plot a vain thing?"

- The Hebrew word for "rage" is רָגַשׁ (ragash), meaning to tumultuously assemble. This depicts a chaotic and rebellious gathering against divine authority.

- The word "plot" (הָגָה, hagah) means to murmur or meditate, indicating the deliberate planning of rebellion.

Verse 2: "The kings of the earth set themselves, and the rulers take counsel together, against the LORD and against His Anointed, saying,"

- The term "Anointed" (מָשִׁיחַ, mashiach) is crucial as it directly refers to the Messiah, the chosen one of God.

- This verse highlights the collective defiance of earthly rulers against divine authority.

Verse 3: "Let us break Their bonds in pieces and cast away Their cords from us."

- "Bonds" (מוֹסֵר, moser) and "cords" (עֲבֹת, aboth) symbolize the perceived restrictions of divine rule. The rebellious desire to reject God's authority is evident here.

Verses 4-6: The Divine Response

Verse 4: "He who sits in the heavens shall laugh; the Lord shall hold them in derision."

- The phrase "shall laugh" (שָׂחַק, sachaq) signifies God's mockery of human arrogance. Divine laughter underscores the futility of human rebellion.

- "Derision" (לָעַג, laag) means to scorn or mock, highlighting God's supreme authority.

Verse 5: "Then He shall speak to them in His wrath, and distress them in His deep displeasure:"

- "Wrath" (אַף, aph) and "deep displeasure" (חָרוֹן, charon) convey intense divine anger. God's response to rebellion is serious and decisive.

Verse 6: "Yet I have set My King on My holy hill of Zion."

- The term "set" (נָסַךְ, nasak) means to install or anoint. This signifies God's sovereign appointment of the Messiah as King.

- "Zion" (צִיּוֹן, tzion) represents the spiritual and political center of God's kingdom.

Verses 7-9: The Decree of the King

Verse 7: "I will declare the decree: The LORD has said to Me, 'You are My Son, today I have begotten You.'"

- "Decree" (חֹק, choq) indicates a formal and unchangeable divine edict.

- "Begotten" (יָלַד, yalad) emphasizes the unique and divine sonship of the Messiah. This verse is pivotal in affirming Jesus' divine identity.

Verse 8: "Ask of Me, and I will give You the nations for Your inheritance, and the ends of the earth for Your possession."

- "Inheritance" (נַחֲלָה, nachalah) and "possession" (אֲחֻזָּה, achuzzah) denote the total authority and dominion granted to the Messiah.

- This verse speaks to the universal reign of Jesus, extending to all nations and the entire earth.

Verse 9: "You shall break them with a rod of iron; You shall dash them to pieces like a potter's vessel."

- The "rod of iron" (בַּרְזֶל שֵׁבֶט, shevet barzel) symbolizes strong and unbreakable authority.

- "Dash them to pieces" (נָפַץ, naphats) conveys total destruction of opposition, illustrating the absolute power of the Messiah.

Verses 10-12: The Call to Wisdom and Submission

Verse 10: "Now therefore, be wise, O kings; be instructed, you judges of the earth."

- "Be wise" (שָׂכַל, sakal) and "be instructed" (יָסַר, yasar) are calls to repentance and recognition of divine authority.

- Earthly rulers are urged to acknowledge and submit to God's sovereign rule.

Verse 11: "Serve the LORD with fear, and rejoice with trembling."

- "Fear" (יִרְאָה, yirah) and "trembling" (רְעָדָה, raadah) reflect a profound reverence and awe before God.

- The combination of "serve" (עָבַד, abad) and "rejoice" (גִּיל, gil) indicates joyful submission to divine authority.

Verse 12: "Kiss the Son, lest He be angry, and you perish in the way, when His wrath is kindled but a little. Blessed are all those who put their trust in Him."

- "Kiss the Son" (נָשַׁק, nashaq) symbolizes submission and allegiance to the Messiah.

- "Wrath" (אַף, aph) and "perish" (אָבַד, abad) warn of the consequences of rebellion.

- "Blessed" (אַשְׁרֵי, ashrei) signifies the joy and security of those who trust in the Messiah.

Comprehensive Commentary

Psalm 2 is a powerful declaration of the Messiah's divine appointment and authority. It begins with the futile rebellion of the nations against God's anointed King, then shifts to the divine response, the proclamation of the Messiah's sonship and authority, and finally concludes with a call to wisdom and submission.

1. Rebellion and Divine Authority: The Psalm opens by questioning the senseless rebellion of earthly rulers against God and His Anointed. This sets the stage for highlighting the futility of opposing divine authority. The New Testament reaffirms this rebellion, especially in Acts 4:25-26, where the early Christians see their persecution as a fulfillment of this Psalm.

2. The Divine Response: God's response to this rebellion is both mocking and decisive. His laughter signifies the absurdity of human arrogance against divine omnipotence. This section underscores God's absolute sovereignty and His predetermined plan to establish the Messiah's reign.

3. Messianic Decree: The decree in verses 7-9 is central to the Psalm's message. It declares the Messiah as God's Son and outlines His universal dominion. The New Testament frequently cites this passage (e.g., Hebrews 1:5) to affirm Jesus' divine sonship and His ultimate authority over all creation.

4. Call to Submission: The final verses (10-12) are a call to repentance and submission. Earthly rulers and judges are urged to recognize the Messiah's authority and serve Him with reverence. The phrase "Kiss the Son" is particularly significant as it represents a gesture of homage and allegiance. The concluding blessing on those who trust in the Messiah serves as both an encouragement and a promise of security for believers.

Theological Significance

1. Divine Sonship: The proclamation of Jesus as God's Son (Psalm 2:7) is foundational to Christian theology. It affirms His unique relationship with the Father and His eternal nature. This divine sonship is not merely a title but an intrinsic part of Jesus' identity, confirmed throughout the New Testament (e.g., Matthew 3:17, Romans 1:4).

2. Messianic Kingship: The establishment of the Messiah's reign (Psalm 2:6) highlights Jesus' role as the sovereign King. This kingship is not limited to Israel but extends to all nations, fulfilling the promise of universal salvation and the establishment of God's kingdom on earth (Revelation 11:15).

3. Judgment and Salvation: The Psalm balances themes of judgment and salvation. While it warns of the consequences of rebellion, it also offers hope and blessing to those who submit to the Messiah. This dual message is central to the gospel, which calls for repentance and offers the promise of eternal life through faith in Jesus Christ.

Conclusion

Psalm 2 stands as a profound and prophetic declaration of the Messiah's divine authority and eternal reign. Through detailed analysis and expository study, we have uncovered the rich theological significance of this Psalm, affirming Jesus as the Anointed One who fulfills God's redemptive plan. This chapter has provided a comprehensive exploration of Psalm 2, enhancing our understanding of Jesus' identity and mission and strengthening our faith in Him as the sovereign King and Savior.

Psalm 22: The Suffering Servant

Psalm 22 is one of the most poignant and detailed Messianic prophecies, vividly depicting the suffering and crucifixion of Jesus Christ. Written by David, this Psalm transcends his own experiences to foreshadow the agony and triumph of the Messiah. In this chapter, we will explore Psalm

22 using Bible verses, an expository study, and comprehensive commentary, supported by Strong's Exhaustive Concordance.

Text of Psalm 22 (NKJV)

1. My God, My God, why have You forsaken Me? Why are You so far from helping Me, and from the words of My groaning?

2. O My God, I cry in the daytime, but You do not hear; and in the night season, and am not silent.

3. But You are holy, enthroned in the praises of Israel.

4. Our fathers trusted in You; they trusted, and You delivered them.

5. They cried to You, and were delivered; they trusted in You, and were not ashamed.

6. But I am a worm, and no man; a reproach of men, and despised by the people.

7. All those who see Me ridicule Me; they shoot out the lip, they shake the head, saying,

8. "He trusted in the LORD, let Him rescue Him; let Him deliver Him, since He delights in Him!"

9. But You are He who took Me out of the womb; You made Me trust while on My mother's breasts.

10. I was cast upon You from birth. From My mother's womb You have been My God.

11. Be not far from Me, for trouble is near; for there is none to help.

12. Many bulls have surrounded Me; strong bulls of Bashan have encircled Me.

13. They gape at Me with their mouths, like a raging and roaring lion.

14. I am poured out like water, and all My bones are out of joint; My heart is like wax; it has melted within Me.

15. My strength is dried up like a potsherd, and My tongue clings to My jaws; You have brought Me to the dust of death.

16. For dogs have surrounded Me; the congregation of the wicked has enclosed Me. They pierced My hands and My feet;

17. I can count all My bones. They look and stare at Me.

18. They divide My garments among them, and for My clothing they cast lots.

19. But You, O LORD, do not be far from Me; O My Strength, hasten to help Me!

20. Deliver Me from the sword, My precious life from the power of the dog.

21. Save Me from the lion's mouth and from the horns of the wild oxen! You have answered Me.

22. I will declare Your name to My brethren; in the midst of the assembly I will praise You.

23. You who fear the LORD, praise Him! All you descendants of Jacob, glorify Him, and fear Him, all you offspring of Israel!

24. For He has not despised nor abhorred the affliction of the afflicted; nor has He hidden His face from Him; but when He cried to Him, He heard.

25. My praise shall be of You in the great assembly; I will pay My vows before those who fear Him.

26. The poor shall eat and be satisfied; those who seek Him will praise the LORD. Let your heart live forever!

27. All the ends of the world shall remember and turn to the LORD, and all the families of the nations shall worship before You.

28. For the kingdom is the LORD's, and He rules over the nations.

29. All the prosperous of the earth shall eat and worship; all those who go down to the dust shall bow before Him, even he who cannot keep himself alive.

30. A posterity shall serve Him. It will be recounted of the Lord to the next generation,

31. They will come and declare His righteousness to a people who will be born, that He has done this.

Expository Study

Verses 1-2: The Cry of Abandonment

Verse 1: "My God, My God, why have You forsaken Me? Why are You so far from helping Me, and from the words of My groaning?"

- The Hebrew word for "forsaken" is עָזַב (azab), meaning to abandon or leave.

- New Testament Reference: Jesus quotes this verse on the cross (Matthew 27:46), expressing His profound sense of abandonment and fulfillment of prophecy.

Verse 2: "O My God, I cry in the daytime, but You do not hear; and in the night season, and am not silent."

- "Cry" (קָרָא, qara) denotes a loud call for help.

- This verse emphasizes the continuous, unanswered pleas of the suffering servant.

Verses 3-5: The Faithfulness of God

Verse 3: "But You are holy, enthroned in the praises of Israel."

- The term "holy" (קָדוֹשׁ, qadosh) underscores God's absolute purity and separateness.

- Despite the feeling of abandonment, the servant acknowledges God's holiness and the praise He receives from His people.

Verse 4: "Our fathers trusted in You; they trusted, and You delivered them."

- The word "trusted" (בָּטַח, batach) means to place confidence in.

- The servant recalls the historical faithfulness of God to Israel.

Verse 5: "They cried to You, and were delivered; they trusted in You, and were not ashamed."

- The repeated mention of "trusted" emphasizes the reliability of God's deliverance.

Verses 6-8: The Scorn of Men

Verse 6: "But I am a worm, and no man; a reproach of men, and despised by the people."

- "Worm" (תּוֹלַעַת, tolaath) signifies utter humiliation and lowliness.

- This self-description highlights the servant's extreme suffering and rejection.

Verse 7: "All those who see Me ridicule Me; they shoot out the lip, they shake the head, saying,"

- "Ridicule" (לָעַג, laag) means to mock or scorn.

- New Testament Reference: This behavior is witnessed during Jesus' crucifixion (Matthew 27:39).

Verse 8: "He trusted in the LORD, let Him rescue Him; let Him deliver Him, since He delights in Him!"

- This mocking statement reflects the taunts Jesus faced on the cross (Matthew 27:43).

Verses 9-11: The Servant's Trust in God

Verse 9: "But You are He who took Me out of the womb; You made Me trust while on My mother's breasts."

- The servant recalls God's care from birth, emphasizing a lifelong trust.

Verse 10: "I was cast upon You from birth. From My mother's womb You have been My God."

- "Cast upon" (שָׁלַךְ, shalak) signifies being placed in God's care.

- This verse reflects an innate and continuous relationship with God.

Verse 11: "Be not far from Me, for trouble is near; for there is none to help."

- The servant appeals for God's presence in the face of imminent danger.

Verses 12-18: The Depth of Suffering

Verse 12: "Many bulls have surrounded Me; strong bulls of Bashan have encircled Me."

- "Bulls of Bashan" symbolize powerful and aggressive enemies.

Verse 13: "They gape at Me with their mouths, like a raging and roaring lion."

- This imagery depicts the intensity of the servant's persecution.

Verse 14: "I am poured out like water, and all My bones are out of joint; My heart is like wax; it has melted within Me."

- "Poured out" (שָׁפַךְ, shaphak) denotes extreme exhaustion.

- This verse vividly describes the physical agony of crucifixion.

Verse 15: "My strength is dried up like a potsherd, and My tongue clings to My jaws; You have brought Me to the dust of death."

- "Potsherd" (חֶרֶשׂ, cheres) refers to broken pottery, symbolizing fragility.

- New Testament Reference: Jesus' thirst on the cross (John 19:28) fulfills this description.

Verse 16: "For dogs have surrounded Me; the congregation of the wicked has enclosed Me. They pierced My hands and My feet;"

- "Pierced" (כָּרָה, karah) explicitly points to crucifixion.

- New Testament Reference: This verse directly correlates with the crucifixion of Jesus (John 20:25).

Verse 17: "I can count all My bones. They look and stare at Me."

- This highlights the visible emaciation and exposure of the servant.

Verse 18: "They divide My garments among them, and for My clothing they cast lots."

- New Testament Reference: The soldiers' actions at the crucifixion (John 19:24) fulfill this prophecy.

Verses 19-21: Plea for Deliverance

Verse 19: "But You, O LORD, do not be far from Me; O My Strength, hasten to help Me!"

- "Strength" (אֱיָלִי, eili) reflects reliance on God's power.

Verse 20: "Deliver Me

from the sword, My precious life from the power of the dog."

- The servant pleads for rescue from mortal danger.

Verse 21: "Save Me from the lion's mouth and from the horns of the wild oxen! You have answered Me."

- This plea transitions into a declaration of divine response.

Verses 22-31: Declaration of Praise and Hope

Verse 22: "I will declare Your name to My brethren; in the midst of the assembly I will praise You."

- The servant vows to testify of God's deliverance.

Verse 23: "You who fear the LORD, praise Him! All you descendants of Jacob, glorify Him, and fear Him, all you offspring of Israel!"

- A call for collective worship and reverence.

Verse 24: "For He has not despised nor abhorred the affliction of the afflicted; nor has He hidden His face from Him; but when He cried to Him, He heard."

- This verse affirms God's attentiveness and compassion.

Verse 25: "My praise shall be of You in the great assembly; I will pay My vows before those who fear Him."

- The servant commits to public praise and fulfilling vows.

Verse 26: "The poor shall eat and be satisfied; those who seek Him will praise the LORD. Let your heart live forever!"

- A promise of provision and eternal life for the faithful.

Verse 27: "All the ends of the world shall remember and turn to the LORD, and all the families of the nations shall worship before You."

- A prophecy of global recognition and worship of God.

Verse 28: "For the kingdom is the LORD's, and He rules over the nations."

- This verse emphasizes God's sovereign rule.

Verse 29: "All the prosperous of the earth shall eat and worship; all those who go down to the dust shall bow before Him, even he who cannot keep himself alive."

- A vision of universal submission and worship.

Verse 30: "A posterity shall serve Him. It will be recounted of the Lord to the next generation,"

- Future generations will continue to serve and testify of God.

Verse 31: "They will come and declare His righteousness to a people who will be born, that He has done this."

- The enduring testimony of God's righteousness and deliverance.

Comprehensive Commentary

Psalm 22 provides a profound prophetic vision of the Messiah's suffering, vividly fulfilled in the crucifixion of Jesus Christ. This Psalm is divided into two major parts: the suffering and the subsequent praise and victory.

1. The Cry of Abandonment: The opening verse is a direct expression of Jesus' agony on the cross. This cry of abandonment (Matthew 27:46) reveals the depth of Jesus' suffering and the fulfillment of prophecy.

2. The Scorn of Men: The mockery and taunting described in verses 6-8 were precisely mirrored during Jesus' crucifixion (Matthew 27:39-43). This public humiliation underscores the servant's complete rejection and isolation.

3. The Depth of Suffering: Verses 12-18 provide a graphic description of the physical and emotional torment experienced by the servant. The detailed depiction of crucifixion, including the piercing of hands and feet and the casting of lots for garments, aligns perfectly with the Gospel accounts (John 19:23-24).

4. Plea for Deliverance and Declaration of Praise: The shift from plea to praise (verses 19-31) marks a transition from suffering to hope and victory. The servant's vow to declare God's name (verse 22) and the prophetic vision of global worship (verses 27-28) highlight the ultimate triumph of the Messiah.

Theological Significance

1. Fulfillment of Prophecy: The precise fulfillment of Psalm 22 in the life and death of Jesus Christ provides compelling evidence of His Messiahship. The New Testament references to this Psalm underscore its prophetic significance and affirm Jesus as the suffering servant who redeems humanity.

2. The Suffering Servant: This Psalm highlights the paradox of the Messiah's mission. Jesus' suffering and humiliation were necessary for the salvation of humanity. His

crucifixion was not a defeat but a victory over sin and death, as evidenced by His resurrection.

3. Universal Redemption: The closing verses of Psalm 22 expand the scope of the Messiah's mission to include all nations. This universal vision of worship and submission to God's rule (verses 27-28) reflects the inclusive nature of the gospel and the global reach of Jesus' redemptive work.

Conclusion

Psalm 22 stands as a powerful testament to the suffering and triumph of the Messiah. Through detailed expository study and comprehensive commentary, we have uncovered the profound prophetic significance of this Psalm, affirming Jesus as the suffering servant who fulfills God's redemptive plan. This chapter has provided a thorough exploration of Psalm 22, enhancing our understanding of Jesus' sacrificial mission and strengthening our faith in Him as the promised Messiah and Savior.

Psalm 110: The Priestly King

Psalm 110 is a profound Messianic Psalm that portrays the Messiah as both a King and a Priest. This dual role is unique and significant, highlighting Jesus Christ's eternal kingship and priesthood. This chapter will delve deeply into Psalm 110 using Bible verses, an expository study, and comprehensive commentary, supported by Strong's Exhaustive Concordance.

Text of Psalm 110 (NKJV)

1. The LORD said to my Lord, "Sit at My right hand, till I make Your enemies Your footstool."

2. The LORD shall send the rod of Your strength out of Zion. Rule in the midst of Your enemies!

3. Your people shall be volunteers in the day of Your power; in the beauties of holiness, from the womb of the morning, You have the dew of Your youth.

4. The LORD has sworn and will not relent, "You are a priest forever according to the order of Melchizedek."

5. The Lord is at Your right hand; He shall execute kings in the day of His wrath.

6. He shall judge among the nations, He shall fill the places with dead bodies, He shall execute the heads of many countries.

7. He shall drink of the brook by the wayside; therefore He shall lift up the head.

Expository Study

Verse 1: Divine Invitation

Verse 1: "The LORD said to my Lord, 'Sit at My right hand, till I make Your enemies Your footstool.'"

- The phrase "The LORD said to my Lord" uses two different Hebrew words for "Lord": יְהוָה (YHWH) and אֲדֹנִי (Adonai). This distinction indicates a conversation between God the Father and the Messiah.

- "Sit" (יָשַׁב, yashab) signifies a position of honor and authority.

- New Testament Reference: This verse is frequently cited in the New Testament (e.g., Matthew 22:44, Acts 2:34-35) to affirm Jesus' exaltation and divine authority.

Verse 2: Rule and Dominion

Verse 2: "The LORD shall send the rod of Your strength out of Zion. Rule in the midst of Your enemies!"

- "Rod" (מַטֶּה, matteh) symbolizes authority and power.

- "Zion" (צִיּוֹן, tzion) represents the spiritual center of God's kingdom.

- This verse emphasizes the Messiah's authority and the extension of His rule.

Verse 3: The People's Willingness

Verse 3: "Your people shall be volunteers in the day of Your power; in the beauties of holiness, from the womb of the morning, You have the dew of Your youth."

- "Volunteers" (נְדָבָה, nedavah) indicates a willing and eager participation of the people.

- "Beauties of holiness" (הַדְרֵי־קֹדֶשׁ, hadrey-qodesh) reflects the splendor of God's holiness.

- This verse highlights the enthusiastic support of the Messiah's followers.

Verse 4: Eternal Priesthood

Verse 4: "The LORD has sworn and will not relent, 'You are a priest forever according to the order of Melchizedek.'"

- "Sworn" (נִשְׁבַּע, nishba) indicates an irrevocable divine oath.

- "Priest" (כֹּהֵן, kohen) and "Melchizedek" (מַלְכִּי־צֶדֶק, malki-tzedek) denote an eternal and unique priesthood.

- New Testament Reference: The book of Hebrews (Hebrews 5:6, 7:17) extensively discusses Jesus' priesthood in the order of Melchizedek, contrasting it with the Levitical priesthood.

Verses 5-6: Judgment and Victory

Verse 5: "The Lord is at Your right hand; He shall execute kings in the day of His wrath."

- "Right hand" (יָמִין, yamin) symbolizes power and support.

- This verse speaks to the Messiah's authority to judge and execute justice.

Verse 6: "He shall judge among the nations, He shall fill the places with dead bodies, He shall execute the heads of many countries."

- "Judge" (דִּין, din) indicates the execution of justice.

- This verse depicts the Messiah's role as a judge over the nations, emphasizing His ultimate victory and dominion.

Verse 7: Refreshment and Triumph

Verse 7: "He shall drink of the brook by the wayside; therefore He shall lift up the head."

- "Drink" (שָׁתָה, shathah) signifies refreshment and sustenance.

- "Lift up the head" (רֹאשׁ רוּם, rum rosh) symbolizes triumph and honor.

- This verse concludes with a picture of the Messiah's refreshed state and victorious posture.

Comprehensive Commentary

Psalm 110 is unique in its portrayal of the Messiah as both a King and a Priest. This dual role is critical to understanding Jesus Christ's mission and authority.

1. Divine Authority and Exaltation: The opening verse, "The LORD said to my Lord," establishes the Messiah's divine authority and exaltation. This verse is quoted multiple times in the New Testament to affirm Jesus' position at the right hand of God, a place of highest honor and power (Matthew 22:44, Acts 2:34-35).

2. Eternal Priesthood: Verse 4 is central to understanding Jesus' priesthood. Unlike the temporary and hereditary Levitical priesthood, Jesus' priesthood is eternal and in the order of Melchizedek. This unique priesthood is characterized by its permanence and divine appointment (Hebrews 7:21-24). Melchizedek, whose name means "king of righteousness" and who was also king of Salem ("peace"), foreshadows Jesus' dual role as both king and priest.

3. Judgment and Dominion: The Psalm speaks of the Messiah's authority to judge the nations and execute justice. This aspect of His role underscores His sovereign rule and the ultimate triumph of God's kingdom. The depiction of executing kings and judging among the nations emphasizes the comprehensive nature of His reign (Revelation 19:15-16).

4. Willing Participation of the People: The enthusiastic support of the Messiah's followers in verse 3 ("Your people shall be volunteers") highlights the voluntary and joyful submission of believers to Jesus' rule. This contrasts with the forced allegiance seen in earthly kingdoms and speaks to the transformative power of the Messiah's reign.

5. Refreshment and Triumph: The concluding verse (verse 7) with the imagery of drinking from the brook and lifting up the head, symbolizes the Messiah's refreshment and victory. This victorious posture reflects the culmination of His redemptive work and the establishment of His eternal kingdom.

Theological Significance

1. Christ's Dual Role: Psalm 110 uniquely portrays the Messiah as both King and Priest. This dual role is essential to understanding Jesus' mission. As King, He reigns with divine authority. As Priest, He intercedes for humanity, offering a perfect and eternal sacrifice for sin. This combination of roles is foundational to Christian theology and is thoroughly expounded in the New Testament, particularly in the book of Hebrews.

2. Irrevocable Divine Decree: The divine oath in verse 4 ("The LORD has sworn and will not relent") emphasizes the unchangeable and eternal nature of Jesus' priesthood. This irrevocable decree assures believers of the certainty and permanence of Jesus' intercessory role.

3. Victory Over Enemies: The imagery of making enemies a footstool (verse 1) and executing judgment (verses 5-6) underscores the ultimate victory of the Messiah over all opposition. This theme is echoed in the New Testament, affirming Jesus' victory over sin, death, and all powers of darkness (1 Corinthians 15:24-25).

4. Universal Reign: The Messiah's rule extending from Zion (verse 2) signifies the establishment of God's kingdom

on earth, encompassing all nations. This universal reign fulfills the prophetic vision of a global dominion under the righteous rule of the Messiah.

Conclusion

Psalm 110 stands as a profound declaration of the Messiah's divine authority, eternal priesthood, and ultimate victory. Through detailed expository study and comprehensive commentary, we have explored the rich theological significance of this Psalm, affirming Jesus as the Priestly King who fulfills God's redemptive plan. This chapter has provided a thorough exploration of Psalm 110, enhancing our understanding of Jesus' dual role and strengthening our faith in Him as the eternal King and High Priest.

CHAPTER 03

THE DIVINITY OF JESUS IN PSALMS 2

Psalm 2 is a powerful and prophetic passage that vividly portrays the divinity and kingship of the Messiah. This Psalm is divided into four distinct sections, each contributing to the overall theme of the Messiah's divine authority and ultimate triumph over rebellion. In this chapter, we will analyze Psalm 2:1-12, using Bible verses, expository study, and comprehensive commentary, supported by Strong's Exhaustive Concordance.

Text of Psalm 2:1-12 (NKJV)

1. Why do the nations rage, and the people plot a vain thing?

2. The kings of the earth set themselves, and the rulers take counsel together, against the LORD and against His Anointed, saying,

3. "Let us break Their bonds in pieces and cast away Their cords from us."

4. He who sits in the heavens shall laugh; the Lord shall hold them in derision.

5. Then He shall speak to them in His wrath, and distress them in His deep displeasure:

6. "Yet I have set My King on My holy hill of Zion."

7. "I will declare the decree: The LORD has said to Me, 'You are My Son, today I have begotten You.

8. Ask of Me, and I will give You the nations for Your inheritance, and the ends of the earth for Your possession.

9. You shall break them with a rod of iron; You shall dash them to pieces like a potter's vessel.'"

10. Now therefore, be wise, O kings; be instructed, you judges of the earth.

11. Serve the LORD with fear, and rejoice with trembling.

12. Kiss the Son, lest He be angry, and you perish in the way, when His wrath is kindled but a little. Blessed are all those who put their trust in Him.

Expository Study

Verses 1-3: The Rebellion of the Nations

Verse 1: "Why do the nations rage, and the people plot a vain thing?"

- The Hebrew word for "rage" is רָגַשׁ (ragash), meaning to tumultuously assemble, depicting chaotic and futile opposition.

- "Plot" (הָגָה, hagah) implies meditative planning, indicating a deliberate but ultimately futile conspiracy.

Verse 2: "The kings of the earth set themselves, and the rulers take counsel together, against the LORD and against His Anointed, saying,"

- "Anointed" (מָשִׁיחַ, mashiach) directly refers to the Messiah, God's chosen one.

- This verse highlights a concerted rebellion against divine authority, encompassing both political and spiritual leaders.

Verse 3: "Let us break Their bonds in pieces and cast away Their cords from us."

- "Bonds" (מוֹסֵר, moser) and "cords" (עֲבֹת, aboth) symbolize perceived constraints of God's rule.

- The rebellious desire to reject God's authority is emphasized, reflecting humanity's inclination towards autonomy from divine governance.

Verses 4-6: The Divine Response

Verse 4: "He who sits in the heavens shall laugh; the Lord shall hold them in derision."

- "Laugh" (שָׂחַק, sachaq) signifies God's mockery of human arrogance.

- "Derision" (לָעַג, laag) highlights the futility of human rebellion against divine omnipotence.

Verse 5: "Then He shall speak to them in His wrath, and distress them in His deep displeasure:"

- "Wrath" (אַף, aph) and "deep displeasure" (חָרוֹן, charon) convey intense divine anger, indicating the seriousness of rebellion against God.

Verse 6: "Yet I have set My King on My holy hill of Zion."

- "Set" (נָסַךְ, nasak) means to install or anoint, affirming God's sovereign appointment of the Messiah.

- "Zion" (צִיּוֹן, tzion) represents the spiritual and political center of God's kingdom.

Verses 7-9: The Decree of the King

Verse 7: "I will declare the decree: The LORD has said to Me, 'You are My Son, today I have begotten You.'"

- "Decree" (חֹק, choq) indicates a formal and unchangeable divine edict.

- "Begotten" (יָלַד, yalad) emphasizes the unique and divine sonship of the Messiah.

- New Testament Reference: This verse is quoted in Hebrews 1:5 to affirm Jesus' divine sonship and preeminence over angels.

Verse 8: "Ask of Me, and I will give You the nations for Your inheritance, and the ends of the earth for Your possession."

- "Inheritance" (נַחֲלָה, nachalah) and "possession" (אֲחֻזָּה, achuzzah) denote the total authority and dominion granted to the Messiah.

- This verse speaks to the universal reign of Jesus, extending to all nations and the entire earth.

Verse 9: "You shall break them with a rod of iron; You shall dash them to pieces like a potter's vessel."

- "Rod of iron" (בַּרְזֶל שֵׁבֶט, shevet barzel) symbolizes strong and unbreakable authority.

- "Dash them to pieces" (נָפַץ, naphats) conveys total destruction of opposition, illustrating the absolute power of the Messiah.

- New Testament Reference: This imagery is used in Revelation 2:27 to describe Jesus' authority over the nations.

Verses 10-12: The Call to Wisdom and Submission

Verse 10: "Now therefore, be wise, O kings; be instructed, you judges of the earth."

- "Be wise" (שָׂכַל, sakal) and "be instructed" (יָסַר, yasar) are calls to repentance and recognition of divine authority.

- Earthly rulers are urged to acknowledge and submit to God's sovereign rule.

Verse 11: "Serve the LORD with fear, and rejoice with trembling."

- "Fear" (יִרְאָה, yirah) and "trembling" (רְעָדָה, raadah) reflect profound reverence and awe before God.

- The combination of "serve" (עָבַד, abad) and "rejoice" (גִּיל, gil) indicates joyful submission to divine authority.

Verse 12: "Kiss the Son, lest He be angry, and you perish in the way, when His wrath is kindled but a little. Blessed are all those who put their trust in Him."

- "Kiss the Son" (נָשַׁק, nashaq) symbolizes submission and allegiance to the Messiah.

- "Wrath" (אַף, aph) and "perish" (אָבַד, abad) warn of the consequences of rebellion.

- "Blessed" (אַשְׁרֵי, ashrei) signifies the joy and security of those who trust in the Messiah.

- New Testament Reference: This call to submission and trust in the Son is echoed in John 3:36, highlighting the blessings of belief and the consequences of rejection.

Comprehensive Commentary

Psalm 2 is a profound declaration of the Messiah's divine authority, emphasizing His unique sonship and universal reign. This Psalm is divided into four sections, each contributing to the overall theme of divine kingship and judgment.

1. Rebellion and Divine Authority: The opening verses (1-3) depict the futile rebellion of earthly powers against God's Anointed. This sets the stage for highlighting the futility of opposing divine authority. The New Testament frequently references this rebellion, especially in Acts 4:25-26, where early Christians see their persecution as a fulfillment of this Psalm.

2. The Divine Response: God's response to this rebellion (verses 4-6) is both mocking and decisive. His laughter signifies the absurdity of human arrogance against divine omnipotence. This section underscores God's absolute sovereignty and His predetermined plan to establish the Messiah's reign.

3. Messianic Decree: The decree in verses 7-9 is central to the Psalm's message. It declares the Messiah as God's Son and outlines His universal dominion. The New Testament frequently cites this passage (e.g., Hebrews 1:5) to affirm Jesus' divine sonship and His ultimate authority over all creation. The granting of the nations as an inheritance speaks to the global scope of Jesus' reign and His ultimate victory over all opposition.

4. Call to Submission: The final verses (10-12) are a call to repentance and submission. Earthly rulers and judges are urged to recognize the Messiah's authority and serve Him with reverence. The phrase "Kiss the Son" represents a gesture of homage and allegiance, emphasizing the need for a personal commitment to the Messiah. The concluding blessing on those who trust in the Messiah serves as both an encouragement and a promise of security for believers.

Theological Significance

1. Divine Sonship: The proclamation of Jesus as God's Son (Psalm 2:7) is foundational to Christian theology. It affirms His unique relationship with the Father and His eternal nature. This divine sonship is not merely a title but an intrinsic part of Jesus' identity, confirmed throughout the New Testament (e.g., Matthew

3:17, Romans 1:4).

2. Messianic Kingship: The establishment of the Messiah's reign (Psalm 2:6) highlights Jesus' role as the sovereign King. This kingship is not limited to Israel but extends to all nations, fulfilling the promise of universal salvation and the establishment of God's kingdom on earth (Revelation 11:15).

3. Judgment and Salvation: The Psalm balances themes of judgment and salvation. While it warns of the consequences of rebellion, it also offers hope and blessing to those who submit to the Messiah. This dual message is central

to the gospel, which calls for repentance and offers the promise of eternal life through faith in Jesus Christ.

Conclusion

Psalm 2 is a profound declaration of the Messiah's divine authority and eternal reign. Through detailed expository study and comprehensive commentary, we have uncovered the rich theological significance of this Psalm, affirming Jesus as the divine Son who fulfills God's redemptive plan. This chapter has provided a thorough exploration of Psalm 2, enhancing our understanding of Jesus' identity and mission and strengthening our faith in Him as the sovereign King and Savior.

Jesus as the Son of God

The title "Son of God" is central to Christian theology, affirming the divine nature and unique relationship of Jesus Christ with God the Father. This chapter will explore the significance of Jesus as the Son of God, using Bible verses, expository study, and comprehensive commentary, supported by Strong's Exhaustive Concordance.

Biblical Foundation

Old Testament Prophecies

Psalm 2:7: "I will declare the decree: The LORD has said to Me, 'You are My Son, today I have begotten You.'"

- The term "begotten" (יָלַד, yalad) signifies a unique, divine begetting, distinct from creation.

- This verse is pivotal in affirming the Messiah's divine sonship and is directly referenced in the New Testament.

New Testament Affirmation

Matthew 3:17: "And suddenly a voice came from heaven, saying, 'This is My beloved Son, in whom I am well pleased.'"

- The declaration at Jesus' baptism publicly affirms His divine sonship.

John 3:16: "For God so loved the world that He gave His only begotten Son, that whoever believes in Him should not perish but have everlasting life."

- The term "only begotten" (μονογενής, monogenēs) emphasizes the unique and singular nature of Jesus' sonship.

Hebrews 1:5: "For to which of the angels did He ever say: 'You are My Son, today I have begotten You'? And again: 'I will be to Him a Father, and He shall be to Me a Son'?"

- This verse contrasts Jesus' divine sonship with that of angels, emphasizing His unique position.

Expository Study

Jesus' Unique Sonship

Matthew 3:17: "And suddenly a voice came from heaven, saying, 'This is My beloved Son, in whom I am well pleased.'"

- The term "beloved" (ἀγαπητός, agapētos) conveys a deep, unique love and favor.

- This divine affirmation at Jesus' baptism highlights His unique relationship with the Father and sets Him apart from all others.

John 3:16: "For God so loved the world that He gave His only begotten Son, that whoever believes in Him should not perish but have everlasting life."

- "Only begotten" (μονογενής, monogenēs) indicates a unique, one-of-a-kind sonship.

- This verse underscores the sacrificial nature of God's love and Jesus' unique role in the plan of salvation.

Jesus' Divinity

John 1:1-2, 14: "In the beginning was the Word, and the Word was with God, and the Word was God. He was in the beginning with God. ... And the Word became flesh and dwelt among us, and we beheld His glory, the glory as of the only begotten of the Father, full of grace and truth."

- "Word" (Λόγος, Logos) signifies Jesus' divine preexistence and creative power.

- This passage affirms both Jesus' divinity and incarnation, revealing Him as God in the flesh.

Colossians 1:15-17: "He is the image of the invisible God, the firstborn over all creation. For by Him all things were created that are in heaven and that are on earth, visible and invisible, whether thrones or dominions or principalities or powers. All things were created through Him and for Him. And He is before all things, and in Him all things consist."

- "Image" (εἰκών, eikōn) indicates exact representation and manifestation.

- Jesus is described as the "firstborn" (πρωτότοκος, prōtotokos), denoting preeminence and authority over all creation.

Jesus' Authority and Mission

Matthew 28:18-20: "And Jesus came and spoke to them, saying, 'All authority has been given to Me in heaven and on earth. Go therefore and make disciples of all the nations, baptizing them in the name of the Father and of the Son and of the Holy Spirit, teaching them to observe all things that I have commanded you; and lo, I am with you always, even to the end of the age.'"

- "Authority" (ἐξουσία, exousia) signifies supreme power and jurisdiction.

- Jesus' commission to His disciples underscores His divine authority and the global scope of His mission.

John 5:22-23: "For the Father judges no one, but has committed all judgment to the Son, that all should honor the Son just as they honor the Father. He who does not honor the Son does not honor the Father who sent Him."

- The Father's delegation of judgment to the Son emphasizes Jesus' divine authority.

- Equal honor to the Son and the Father underscores the unity and co-equality within the Trinity.

Comprehensive Commentary

Theological Implications of Jesus' Sonship

1. Divine Relationship: The title "Son of God" affirms Jesus' unique and eternal relationship with the Father. Unlike any other title, it emphasizes both His divinity and His intimate communion with God the Father. This relationship is central to understanding the doctrine of the Trinity.

2. Incarnation and Redemption: Jesus' sonship is intrinsically linked to the incarnation. As the "Word made flesh" (John 1:14), Jesus embodies God's redemptive plan. His unique sonship enables Him to be the perfect mediator between God and humanity, offering Himself as a perfect sacrifice for sin.

3. Authority and Judgment: Jesus' role as the Son of God includes ultimate authority over all creation and the right to execute judgment. This authority is not derived but inherent, reflecting His divine nature. The delegation of judgment to Jesus (John 5:22-23) highlights His integral role in the divine plan.

4. Eternal Priesthood: The priestly aspect of Jesus' sonship is articulated in Hebrews, where He is described as a priest forever according to the order of Melchizedek (Hebrews 7:17). This eternal priesthood is a unique function that underscores His role as both intercessor and mediator.

5. Salvific Role: Jesus as the Son of God is central to the salvation narrative. John 3:16 encapsulates this by highlighting the sacrificial love of God and the provision of eternal life through belief in His Son. The uniqueness of Jesus' sonship is essential for understanding the exclusivity of His salvific work.

Exegetical Insights

1. Psalm 2:7 and Hebrews 1:5: The declaration "You are My Son, today I have begotten You" is pivotal in affirming Jesus' divine sonship. The term "begotten" (יָלַד, yalad) emphasizes a unique divine begetting, indicating a special and eternal relationship with the Father. This verse is used in Hebrews 1:5 to distinguish Jesus' sonship from that of angels, underscoring His unique divine status.

2. John 1:1-14: The prologue of John's Gospel presents Jesus as the divine Logos, preexistent and active in creation. The term "Logos" (Λόγος) connects Jesus to the divine wisdom and creative word of God, affirming His divinity. The incarnation ("the Word became flesh") is a central mystery of the Christian faith, highlighting the union of divine and human natures in the person of Jesus Christ.

3. Colossians 1:15-17: Paul's description of Jesus as the "image" (εἰκών, eikōn) of the invisible God and the "firstborn" (πρωτότοκος, prōtotokos) over all creation emphasizes both His representational and authoritative roles. The term "firstborn" here denotes preeminence rather than temporal priority, affirming Jesus' supremacy and central role in creation and redemption.

Practical Applications

1. Worship and Devotion: Understanding Jesus as the Son of God enhances the depth of worship and devotion. Recognizing His divine nature and unique relationship with the Father fosters a deeper reverence and adoration in the believer's heart.

2. Trust and Obedience: Believers are called to trust in Jesus as the Son of God (John 14:1). This trust is foundational for Christian faith and practice, leading to obedience to His teachings and commands (John 15:10).

3. Mission and Evangelism: The recognition of Jesus' divine authority compels believers to participate in His mission. The Great Commission (Matthew 28:18-20) is

grounded in Jesus' authority and involves making disciples, baptizing them, and teaching them to observe His commands.

4. Hope and Assurance: Jesus' unique sonship provides believers with assurance of salvation and hope for the future. The promise of eternal life (John 3:16) and Jesus' role as intercessor (Hebrews 7:25) offer comfort and confidence in the believer's relationship with God.

Conclusion

Jesus as the Son of God is a cornerstone of Christian theology, affirming His divine nature, unique relationship with the Father, and integral role in God's redemptive plan. Through detailed expository study and comprehensive commentary, we have explored the biblical foundation, theological implications, and practical applications of this profound truth. This chapter has provided a thorough examination of Jesus' divine sonship, enhancing our understanding and strengthening our faith in Him as the eternal Son and Savior.

The Divine Kingship of Jesus

The concept of Jesus as King is deeply rooted in Scripture and forms a central part of Christian theology. The divine kingship of Jesus encompasses His authority, reign, and the fulfillment of Old Testament prophecies. This chapter will explore the significance of Jesus' kingship, using Bible verses, an expository study, and comprehensive commentary, supported by Strong's Exhaustive Concordance.

Biblical Foundation

Old Testament Prophecies

Psalm 2:6: "Yet I have set My King on My holy hill of Zion."

- The term "set" (נָסַךְ, nasak) means to install or anoint, indicating God's sovereign appointment.

- This verse foreshadows the establishment of the Messiah's reign in Zion.

Isaiah 9:6-7: "For unto us a Child is born, unto us a Son is given; and the government will be upon His shoulder. And His name will be called Wonderful, Counselor, Mighty God, Everlasting Father, Prince of Peace. Of the increase of His government and peace there will be no end, upon the throne of David and over His kingdom, to order it and establish it with judgment and justice from that time forward, even forever. The zeal of the LORD of hosts will perform this."

- These verses highlight the eternal and just nature of the Messiah's kingship.

New Testament Fulfillment

Matthew 2:2: "Saying, 'Where is He who has been born King of the Jews? For we have seen His star in the East and have come to worship Him.'"

- The recognition of Jesus as King from His birth signifies His divine kingship.

John 18:37: "Pilate therefore said to Him, 'Are You a king then?' Jesus answered, 'You say rightly that I am a king. For this cause I was born, and for this cause I have come into the world, that I should bear witness to the truth. Everyone who is of the truth hears My voice.'"

- Jesus' affirmation of His kingship before Pilate underscores His divine authority and mission.

Expository Study

Jesus' Kingship in the Gospels

Matthew 21:5: "Tell the daughter of Zion, 'Behold, your King is coming to you, lowly, and sitting on a donkey, a colt, the foal of a donkey.'"

- This verse fulfills Zechariah 9:9 and signifies Jesus' humble yet royal entry into Jerusalem.

- The term "King" (βασιλεύς, basileus) emphasizes His sovereign authority.

Luke 1:32-33: "He will be great, and will be called the Son of the Highest; and the Lord God will give Him the throne of His father David. And He will reign over the house of Jacob forever, and of His kingdom there will be no end."

- The promise of an eternal kingdom aligns with Old Testament prophecies about the Davidic covenant.

- The term "reign" (βασιλεύω, basileuō) underscores His ongoing, unending rule.

Jesus' Kingship in the Epistles

Ephesians 1:20-22: "Which He worked in Christ when He raised Him from the dead and seated Him at His right hand in the heavenly places, far above all principality and power and might and dominion, and every name that is named, not only in this age but also in that which is to come. And He put all things under His feet, and gave Him to be head over all things to the church."

- This passage highlights Jesus' exalted position and supreme authority over all creation.

- The terms "seated" (καθίζω, kathizō) and "right hand" (δεξιός, dexios) denote His authority and honor.

Revelation 19:16: "And He has on His robe and on His thigh a name written: KING OF KINGS AND LORD OF LORDS."

- This title signifies Jesus' supreme authority over all earthly and heavenly rulers.

Jesus' Kingship in Revelation

Revelation 11:15: "Then the seventh angel sounded: And there were loud voices in heaven, saying, 'The kingdoms of this world have become the kingdoms of our Lord and of His Christ, and He shall reign forever and ever!'"

- This verse proclaims the ultimate realization of Jesus' reign over all the earth.

- The term "reign" (βασιλεύω, basileuō) emphasizes His eternal sovereignty.

Revelation 22:1-5: "And he showed me a pure river of water of life, clear as crystal, proceeding from the throne of God and of the Lamb. In the middle of its street, and on either side of the river, was the tree of life, which bore twelve fruits, each tree yielding its fruit every month. The leaves of the tree were for the healing of the nations. And there shall be no more curse, but the throne of God and of the Lamb shall be in it, and His servants shall serve Him. They shall see His face, and His name shall be on their foreheads. There shall be no night there: They need no lamp nor light of the sun, for the Lord God gives them light. And they shall reign forever and ever."

- This passage describes the eternal reign of Jesus, highlighting His divine kingship and the restoration of all things.

Comprehensive Commentary

Theological Significance of Jesus' Kingship

1. Fulfillment of Prophecy: Jesus' kingship fulfills numerous Old Testament prophecies, establishing Him as the promised Messiah. Verses like Isaiah 9:6-7 and Psalm 2:6-7 highlight the anticipation of a divine King who would rule with justice and peace.

2. Eternal and Universal Reign: Unlike earthly kings whose reigns are temporary, Jesus' kingship is eternal. His authority extends over all creation, as emphasized in passages like Ephesians 1:20-22 and Revelation 11:15.

3. Divine Authority: Jesus' kingship is characterized by divine authority. He is not merely a spiritual leader but holds sovereign power over all principalities and powers. This is underscored by His title "KING OF KINGS AND LORD OF LORDS" in Revelation 19:16.

4. Role in Salvation: Jesus' kingship is integral to His role in salvation. His reign brings about the fulfillment of

God's redemptive plan, culminating in the restoration of all things as described in Revelation 22:1-5.

Exegetical Insights

1. Matthew 21:5 and Zechariah 9:9: Jesus' triumphal entry into Jerusalem on a donkey fulfills Zechariah's prophecy, symbolizing His humble yet royal nature. The term "King" (βασιλεύς, basileus) highlights His authority while riding on a donkey signifies peace and humility.

2. Ephesians 1:20-22: Paul's description of Jesus seated at the right hand of God emphasizes His exalted position. The terms "principality" (ἀρχή, archē), "power" (ἐξουσία, exousia), "might" (δύναμις, dynamis), and "dominion" (κυριότης, kyriotēs) encompass all realms of authority, affirming Jesus' supreme rule over all.

3. Revelation 11:15 and 19:16: These verses highlight the consummation of Jesus' kingship. The proclamation that "the kingdoms of this world have become the kingdoms of our Lord and of His Christ" signifies the ultimate triumph of Jesus' reign. The title "KING OF KINGS AND LORD OF LORDS" in Revelation 19:16 underscores His unmatched authority and final victory over all opposition.

Practical Applications

1. Worship and Allegiance: Understanding Jesus as King calls for our worship and allegiance. Recognizing His divine authority should lead believers to submit to His rule and honor Him with their lives.

2. Hope and Assurance: Jesus' eternal kingship provides believers with hope and assurance. His reign guarantees the fulfillment of God's promises and the ultimate victory over sin and death.

3. Mission and Evangelism: The proclamation of Jesus as King is central to the gospel message. Believers are called to share the good news of His reign and invite others to submit to His Lordship.

4. Living under His Reign: Living under Jesus' kingship means embodying the values of His kingdom. This includes pursuing justice, peace, and righteousness in our daily lives, reflecting the character of our divine King.

Conclusion

The divine kingship of Jesus is a cornerstone of Christian theology, affirming His supreme authority and eternal reign. Through detailed expository study and comprehensive commentary, we have explored the biblical foundation, theological significance, and practical applications of Jesus' kingship. This chapter has provided a thorough examination of Jesus' divine authority, enhancing our understanding and strengthening our faith in Him as the eternal King and Savior.

New Testament References to Psalm 2

Psalm 2 is one of the most frequently quoted Old Testament passages in the New Testament. It holds significant theological importance, especially in affirming Jesus' divinity, sonship, and kingship. This chapter will explore the New Testament references to Psalm 2, using Bible verses, expository study, and comprehensive commentary, supported by Strong's Exhaustive Concordance.

Text of Psalm 2 (NKJV)

1. Why do the nations rage, and the people plot a vain thing?

2. The kings of the earth set themselves, and the rulers take counsel together, against the LORD and against His Anointed, saying,

3. "Let us break Their bonds in pieces and cast away Their cords from us."

4. He who sits in the heavens shall laugh; the Lord shall hold them in derision.

5. Then He shall speak to them in His wrath, and distress them in His deep displeasure:

6. "Yet I have set My King on My holy hill of Zion."

7. "I will declare the decree: The LORD has said to Me, 'You are My Son, today I have begotten You.

8. Ask of Me, and I will give You the nations for Your inheritance, and the ends of the earth for Your possession.

9. You shall break them with a rod of iron; You shall dash them to pieces like a potter's vessel.'"

10. Now therefore, be wise, O kings; be instructed, you judges of the earth.

11. Serve the LORD with fear, and rejoice with trembling.

12. Kiss the Son, lest He be angry, and you perish in the way, when His wrath is kindled but a little. Blessed are all those who put their trust in Him.

New Testament References and Analysis

Acts 4:25-26: The Early Church's Understanding

Acts 4:25-26: "Who by the mouth of Your servant David have said: 'Why did the nations rage, and the people plot vain things? The kings of the earth took their stand, and the rulers were gathered together against the LORD and against His Christ.'"

- The early church, in the midst of persecution, saw their experience as a fulfillment of Psalm 2. They identified themselves with the Psalm's narrative of opposition to God's anointed.

- Exegesis: The term "rage" (רָגַשׁ, ragash) and "plot" (הָגָה, hagah) in both the Psalm and Acts emphasize the futility of opposition against God's plan. The acknowledgment of Jesus as "His Christ" (Χριστός, Christos) underscores the recognition of Jesus as the Anointed One.

Acts 13:33: The Resurrection

Acts 13:33: "God has fulfilled this for us their children, in that He has raised up Jesus. As it is also written in the second Psalm: 'You are My Son, today I have begotten You.'"

- Paul uses Psalm 2:7 to affirm the resurrection of Jesus, linking His resurrection to His divine sonship.

- Exegesis: "Begotten" (יָלַד, yalad) here signifies a unique relationship and the inauguration of Jesus' messianic kingship through resurrection. The resurrection is seen as the divine confirmation of Jesus' identity and mission.

Hebrews 1:5 and 5:5: Jesus' Superiority

Hebrews 1:5: "For to which of the angels did He ever say: 'You are My Son, today I have begotten You'? And again: 'I will be to Him a Father, and He shall be to Me a Son'?"

- Hebrews 5:5: "So also Christ did not glorify Himself to become High Priest, but it was He who said to Him: 'You are My Son, today I have begotten You.'"

- The author of Hebrews uses Psalm 2:7 to establish Jesus' superiority over angels and to affirm His divine appointment as High Priest.

- Exegesis: The term "Son" (בֵּן, ben) emphasizes the unique filial relationship between Jesus and God, contrasting with the created nature of angels. This divine sonship qualifies Jesus for His superior and eternal priesthood.

Revelation 2:26-27: The Authority of the Messiah

Revelation 2:26-27: "And he who overcomes, and keeps My works until the end, to him I will give power over the nations—'He shall rule them with a rod of iron; they shall be dashed to pieces like the potter's vessels'—as I also have received from My Father."

- Jesus quotes Psalm 2:8-9 to promise believers a share in His messianic authority.

- Exegesis: The imagery of the "rod of iron" (בַּרְזֶל שֵׁבֶט, shevet barzel) symbolizes unbreakable authority and justice. This passage highlights the future fulfillment of Jesus' reign and the participation of believers in His victory.

Revelation 12:5 and 19:15: The Messianic Rule

Revelation 12:5: "She bore a male Child who was to rule all nations with a rod of iron. And her Child was caught up to God and His throne."

- Revelation 19:15: "Now out of His mouth goes a sharp sword, that with it He should strike the nations. And He Himself will rule them with a rod of iron. He Himself treads the winepress of the fierceness and wrath of Almighty God."

- Both passages emphasize the ultimate authority and victorious rule of Jesus, directly quoting Psalm 2:9.

- Exegesis: The recurring use of "rod of iron" underscores the certainty and strength of Jesus' rule. It conveys the inevitability of His triumph over evil and the establishment of His righteous reign.

Comprehensive Commentary

Theological Significance

1. Divine Sonship and Kingship: Psalm 2 is foundational in establishing Jesus' identity as both Son of God and King. The New Testament references to this Psalm underscore these roles, affirming Jesus' divine nature and sovereign authority.

2. Fulfillment of Prophecy: The consistent use of Psalm 2 in the New Testament highlights its prophetic significance. The early church's identification with Psalm 2 during persecution (Acts 4:25-26) illustrates their understanding of Jesus as the fulfillment of Messianic prophecies.

3. Resurrection and Exaltation: Paul's use of Psalm 2:7 in Acts 13:33 ties Jesus' resurrection to His divine sonship. This connection is crucial for understanding the resurrection as a divine endorsement of Jesus' messianic identity and mission.

4. Superiority over Angels and Priestly Role: The book of Hebrews uses Psalm 2:7 to establish Jesus' superiority over angels and His unique qualification as High Priest. This application underscores the theological importance of Jesus' divine sonship in the context of His priestly and redemptive work.

5. Messianic Authority and Victory: The use of Psalm 2:9 in Revelation emphasizes the ultimate authority and victorious reign of Jesus. The imagery of ruling with a rod of iron conveys the certainty of His judgment and the establishment of His eternal kingdom.

Exegetical Insights

1. Acts 4:25-26: The early church's application of Psalm 2 to their own context of persecution illustrates the continuity between the Old and New Testaments. The recognition of Jesus as the anointed one (Χριστός, Christos) reflects their understanding of Him as the fulfillment of Messianic expectations.

2. Acts 13:33: Paul's reference to Psalm 2:7 in the context of Jesus' resurrection highlights the inauguration of Jesus' messianic kingship through resurrection. The term "begotten" (יָלַד, yalad) is understood as the divine act of establishing Jesus' unique sonship and authority.

3. Hebrews 1:5 and 5:5: The use of Psalm 2:7 in Hebrews to assert Jesus' superiority over angels and His divine appointment as High Priest underscores the unique and eternal nature of His sonship. The term "Son" (בֵּן, ben) is crucial in distinguishing Jesus' divine identity from created beings.

4. Revelation 2:26-27, 12:5, and 19:15: The repeated quotation of Psalm 2:9 in Revelation emphasizes the certainty and power of Jesus' reign. The imagery of the "rod of iron" conveys the unbreakable and just nature of His authority,

assuring believers of His ultimate victory and the establishment of His kingdom.

Practical Applications

1. Trust in Divine Authority: Understanding Jesus' divine sonship and kingship as affirmed in Psalm 2 encourages believers to trust in His sovereign authority. This trust is foundational for Christian faith and practice, especially in the face of opposition and persecution.

2. Hope in Resurrection and Exaltation: The connection between Psalm 2 and Jesus' resurrection provides believers with hope and assurance. The resurrection is not only a historical event but also a divine confirmation of Jesus' identity and the promise of eternal life for believers.

3. Confidence in Jesus' Superiority: The affirmation of Jesus' superiority over angels and His unique priestly role in Hebrews encourages believers to rely on His intercession and redemptive work. This confidence in Jesus' divine identity and mission strengthens faith and devotion.

4. Anticipation of Messianic Reign: The depiction of Jesus' ultimate authority and victorious reign in Revelation inspires believers to anticipate the fulfillment of His kingdom. This anticipation motivates believers to live faithfully and proclaim the gospel, participating in the mission of the King.

Conclusion

The New Testament references to Psalm 2 provide a profound affirmation of Jesus' divine sonship, kingship, and ultimate authority. Through detailed expository study and comprehensive commentary, we have explored the theological significance and practical applications of these references. This chapter has provided a thorough examination of how Psalm 2 is fulfilled in the New Testament, enhancing our understanding and strengthening our faith in Jesus as the divine Son and sovereign King.

CHAPTER 04

THE SUFFERING AND TRIUMPH OF JESUS IN PSALM 22

Psalm 22 is a profound and vivid Messianic prophecy that foreshadows the crucifixion and ultimate triumph of Jesus Christ. Written by David, this Psalm transcends his own experiences to provide a detailed and prophetic picture of Jesus' suffering on the cross, as well as His subsequent victory. In this chapter, we will analyze Psalm 22:1-31, highlighting the foreshadowing of Jesus' crucifixion, using Bible verses, expository study, and comprehensive commentary, supported by Strong's Exhaustive Concordance.

Text of Psalm 22 (NKJV)

1. My God, My God, why have You forsaken Me? Why are You so far from helping Me, and from the words of My groaning?

2. O My God, I cry in the daytime, but You do not hear; and in the night season, and am not silent.

3. But You are holy, enthroned in the praises of Israel.

4. Our fathers trusted in You; they trusted, and You delivered them.

5. They cried to You, and were delivered; they trusted in You, and were not ashamed.

6. But I am a worm, and no man; a reproach of men, and despised by the people.

7. All those who see Me ridicule Me; they shoot out the lip, they shake the head, saying,

8. "He trusted in the LORD, let Him rescue Him; let Him deliver Him, since He delights in Him!"

9. But You are He who took Me out of the womb; You made Me trust while on My mother's breasts.

10. I was cast upon You from birth. From My mother's womb You have been My God.

11. Be not far from Me, for trouble is near; for there is none to help.

12. Many bulls have surrounded Me; strong bulls of Bashan have encircled Me.

13. They gape at Me with their mouths, like a raging and roaring lion.

14. I am poured out like water, and all My bones are out of joint; My heart is like wax; it has melted within Me.

15. My strength is dried up like a potsherd, and My tongue clings to My jaws; You have brought Me to the dust of death.

16. For dogs have surrounded Me; the congregation of the wicked has enclosed Me. They pierced My hands and My feet;

17. I can count all My bones. They look and stare at Me.

18. They divide My garments among them, and for My clothing they cast lots.

19. But You, O LORD, do not be far from Me; O My Strength, hasten to help Me!

20. Deliver Me from the sword, My precious life from the power of the dog.

21. Save Me from the lion's mouth and from the horns of the wild oxen! You have answered Me.

22. I will declare Your name to My brethren; in the midst of the assembly I will praise You.

23. You who fear the LORD, praise Him! All you descendants of Jacob, glorify Him, and fear Him, all you offspring of Israel!

24. For He has not despised nor abhorred the affliction of the afflicted; nor has He hidden His face from Him; but when He cried to Him, He heard.

25. My praise shall be of You in the great assembly; I will pay My vows before those who fear Him.

26. The poor shall eat and be satisfied; those who seek Him will praise the LORD. Let your heart live forever!

27. All the ends of the world shall remember and turn to the LORD, and all the families of the nations shall worship before You.

28. For the kingdom is the LORD's, and He rules over the nations.

29. All the prosperous of the earth shall eat and worship; all those who go down to the dust shall bow before Him, even he who cannot keep himself alive.

30. A posterity shall serve Him. It will be recounted of the Lord to the next generation,

31. They will come and declare His righteousness to a people who will be born, that He has done this.

Expository Study

Verses 1-2: The Cry of Abandonment

Verse 1: "My God, My God, why have You forsaken Me? Why are You so far from helping Me, and from the words of My groaning?"

- The Hebrew word for "forsaken" is עָזַב (azab), meaning to abandon or leave.

- New Testament Reference: Jesus quotes this verse on the cross (Matthew 27:46), expressing His profound sense of abandonment and fulfillment of prophecy.

Verse 2: "O My God, I cry in the daytime, but You do not hear; and in the night season, and am not silent."

- "Cry" (קָרָא, qara) denotes a loud call for help.

- This verse emphasizes the continuous, unanswered pleas of the suffering servant.

Verses 3-5: The Faithfulness of God

Verse 3: "But You are holy, enthroned in the praises of Israel."

- The term "holy" (קָדוֹשׁ, qadosh) underscores God's absolute purity and separateness.

- Despite the feeling of abandonment, the servant acknowledges God's holiness and the praise He receives from His people.

Verse 4: "Our fathers trusted in You; they trusted, and You delivered them."

- The word "trusted" (בָּטַח, batach) means to place confidence in.

- The servant recalls the historical faithfulness of God to Israel.

Verse 5: "They cried to You, and were delivered; they trusted in You, and were not ashamed."

- The repeated mention of "trusted" emphasizes the reliability of God's deliverance.

Verses 6-8: The Scorn of Men

Verse 6: "But I am a worm, and no man; a reproach of men, and despised by the people."

- "Worm" (תּוֹלַעַת, tolaath) signifies utter humiliation and lowliness.
- This self-description highlights the servant's extreme suffering and rejection.
Verse 7: "All those who see Me ridicule Me; they shoot out the lip, they shake the head, saying,"
- "Ridicule" (לָעַג, laag) means to mock or scorn.
- New Testament Reference: This behavior is witnessed during Jesus' crucifixion (Matthew 27:39).

Verse 8: "He trusted in the LORD, let Him rescue Him; let Him deliver Him, since He delights in Him!"
- This mocking statement reflects the taunts Jesus faced on the cross (Matthew 27:43).
Verses 9-11: The Servant's Trust in God
Verse 9: "But You are He who took Me out of the womb; You made Me trust while on My mother's breasts."
- The servant recalls God's care from birth, emphasizing a lifelong trust.
Verse 10: "I was cast upon You from birth. From My mother's womb You have been My God."
- "Cast upon" (שָׁלַךְ, shalak) signifies being placed in God's care.
- This verse reflects an innate and continuous relationship with God.
Verse 11: "Be not far from Me, for trouble is near; for there is none to help."
- The servant appeals for God's presence in the face of imminent danger.
Verses 12-18: The Depth of Suffering
Verse 12: "Many bulls have surrounded Me; strong bulls of Bashan have encircled Me."
- "Bulls of Bashan" symbolize powerful and aggressive enemies.

Verse 13: "They gape at Me with their mouths, like a raging and roaring lion."

- This imagery depicts the intensity of the servant's persecution.

Verse 14: "I am poured out like water, and all My bones are out of joint; My heart is like wax; it has melted within Me."

- "Poured out" (שָׁפַךְ, shaphak) denotes extreme exhaustion.

- This verse vividly describes the physical agony of crucifixion.

Verse 15: "My strength is dried up like a potsherd, and My tongue clings to My jaws; You have brought Me to the dust of death."

- "Potsherd" (חֶרֶשׂ, cheres) refers to broken pottery, symbolizing fragility.

- New Testament Reference: Jesus' thirst on the cross (John 19:28) fulfills this description.

Verse 16: "For dogs have surrounded Me; the congregation of the wicked has enclosed Me. They pierced My hands and My feet;"

- "Pierced" (כָּרָה, karah) explicitly points to crucifixion.

- New Testament Reference: This verse directly correlates with the crucifixion of Jesus (John 20:25).

Verse 17: "I can count all My bones. They look and stare at Me."

- This highlights the visible emaciation and exposure of the servant.

Verse 18: "They divide My garments among them, and for My clothing they cast lots."

- New Testament Reference: The soldiers' actions at the crucifixion (John 19:24) fulfill this prophecy.

Verses 19-21: Plea for Deliverance

Verse 19: "But You, O LORD, do not be far from Me; O My Strength, hasten to help Me!"

- "Strength

" (אֱיָלִי, eili) reflects reliance on God's power.

Verse 20: "Deliver Me from the sword, My precious life from the power of the dog."

- The servant pleads for rescue from mortal danger.

Verse 21: "Save Me from the lion's mouth and from the horns of the wild oxen! You have answered Me."

- This plea transitions into a declaration of divine response.

Verses 22-31: Declaration of Praise and Hope

Verse 22: "I will declare Your name to My brethren; in the midst of the assembly I will praise You."

- The servant vows to testify of God's deliverance.

Verse 23: "You who fear the LORD, praise Him! All you descendants of Jacob, glorify Him, and fear Him, all you offspring of Israel!"

- A call for collective worship and reverence.

Verse 24: "For He has not despised nor abhorred the affliction of the afflicted; nor has He hidden His face from Him; but when He cried to Him, He heard."

- This verse affirms God's attentiveness and compassion.

Verse 25: "My praise shall be of You in the great assembly; I will pay My vows before those who fear Him."

- The servant commits to public praise and fulfilling vows.

Verse 26: "The poor shall eat and be satisfied; those who seek Him will praise the LORD. Let your heart live forever!"

- A promise of provision and eternal life for the faithful.

Verse 27: "All the ends of the world shall remember and turn to the LORD, and all the families of the nations shall worship before You."

- A prophecy of global recognition and worship of God.

Verse 28: "For the kingdom is the LORD's, and He rules over the nations."

- This verse emphasizes God's sovereign rule.

Verse 29: "All the prosperous of the earth shall eat and worship; all those who go down to the dust shall bow before Him, even he who cannot keep himself alive."

- A vision of universal submission and worship.

Verse 30: "A posterity shall serve Him. It will be recounted of the Lord to the next generation,"

- Future generations will continue to serve and testify of God.

Verse 31: "They will come and declare His righteousness to a people who will be born, that He has done this."

- The enduring testimony of God's righteousness and deliverance.

Comprehensive Commentary

Theological Significance

1. Fulfillment of Prophecy: The detailed fulfillment of Psalm 22 in the life and death of Jesus Christ provides compelling evidence of His Messiahship. The New Testament references to this Psalm underscore its prophetic significance and affirm Jesus as the suffering servant who redeems humanity.

2. The Suffering Servant: This Psalm highlights the paradox of the Messiah's mission. Jesus' suffering and humiliation were necessary for the salvation of humanity. His crucifixion was not a defeat but a victory over sin and death, as evidenced by His resurrection.

3. Universal Redemption: The closing verses of Psalm 22 expand the scope of the Messiah's mission to include all nations. This universal vision of worship and submission to God's rule reflects the inclusive nature of the gospel and the global reach of Jesus' redemptive work.

Exegetical Insights

1. Psalm 22:1 and Matthew 27:46: The opening cry of abandonment ("My God, My God, why have You forsaken Me?") is directly quoted by Jesus on the cross. This profound expression of suffering fulfills the prophecy and reveals the depth of Jesus' sacrifice.

2. Psalm 22:6-8 and Matthew 27:39-43: The mockery and taunting described in these verses are precisely mirrored during Jesus' crucifixion. This public humiliation underscores the servant's complete rejection and isolation.

3. Psalm 22:14-18 and the Crucifixion: The detailed description of physical suffering in these verses, including the piercing of hands and feet and the casting of lots for garments, aligns perfectly with the Gospel accounts of Jesus' crucifixion. This precise fulfillment of prophecy emphasizes the sacrificial nature of Jesus' mission.

4. Psalm 22:22-31 and Universal Worship: The shift from suffering to praise and the vision of global worship in these verses highlight the triumph of the Messiah. This prophetic vision anticipates the universal acknowledgment of Jesus' kingship and the establishment of His eternal kingdom.

Practical Applications

1. Trust in God's Faithfulness: The servant's trust in God despite intense suffering encourages believers to rely on God's faithfulness in their own trials. Recognizing that Jesus endured suffering for our redemption provides comfort and strength in times of adversity.

2. Hope in Redemption: The fulfillment of Psalm 22 in Jesus' crucifixion and resurrection offers believers hope in

the certainty of God's redemptive plan. This hope is not only for individual salvation but also for the ultimate restoration of all creation.

3. Call to Worship: The vision of universal worship in the closing verses of Psalm 22 inspires believers to participate in the mission of proclaiming Jesus' name to all nations. Worshiping God in spirit and truth reflects the fulfillment of the Messiah's mission.

4. Living in Light of the Cross: Understanding the depth of Jesus' suffering and the victory of His resurrection motivates believers to live in gratitude and obedience. The cross is a reminder of the cost of our salvation and the call to take up our own cross daily.

Conclusion

Psalm 22 stands as a powerful testament to the suffering and triumph of the Messiah. Through detailed expository study and comprehensive commentary, we have uncovered the profound prophetic significance of this Psalm, affirming Jesus as the suffering servant who fulfills God's redemptive plan. This chapter has provided a thorough exploration of Psalm 22, enhancing our understanding of Jesus' sacrificial mission and strengthening our faith in Him as the promised Messiah and Savior.

The Fulfillment of Prophecy in the New Testament

The fulfillment of Old Testament prophecies in the New Testament is a cornerstone of Christian theology, affirming Jesus Christ as the promised Messiah. This chapter will explore how New Testament writers confirm the fulfillment of Old Testament prophecies, particularly focusing on the life, death, and resurrection of Jesus. We will use Bible verses, an expository study, and comprehensive commentary, supported by Strong's Exhaustive Concordance.

Prophecy and Fulfillment in the New Testament

The Birth of Jesus

Isaiah 7:14: "Therefore the Lord Himself will give you a sign: Behold, the virgin shall conceive and bear a Son, and shall call His name Immanuel."

- Matthew 1:22-23: "So all this was done that it might be fulfilled which was spoken by the Lord through the prophet, saying: 'Behold, the virgin shall be with child, and bear a Son, and they shall call His name Immanuel,' which is translated, 'God with us.'"

- Exegesis: The term "virgin" (עַלְמָה, almah) emphasizes the miraculous nature of Jesus' birth. Matthew explicitly connects Jesus' birth to Isaiah's prophecy, affirming Him as Immanuel, "God with us."

The Ministry of Jesus

Isaiah 61:1-2: "The Spirit of the Lord GOD is upon Me, because the LORD has anointed Me to preach good tidings to the poor; He has sent Me to heal the brokenhearted, to proclaim liberty to the captives, and the opening of the prison to those who are bound; to proclaim the acceptable year of the LORD, and the day of vengeance of our God; to comfort all who mourn."

- Luke 4:17-21: "And He was handed the book of the prophet Isaiah. And when He had opened the book, He found the place where it was written: 'The Spirit of the LORD is upon Me, because He has anointed Me to preach the gospel to the poor; He has sent Me to heal the brokenhearted, to proclaim liberty to the captives and recovery of sight to the blind, to set at liberty those who are oppressed; to proclaim the acceptable year of the LORD.' Then He closed the book, and gave it back to the attendant and sat down. And the eyes of all who were in the synagogue were fixed on Him. And He began to say to them, 'Today this Scripture is fulfilled in your hearing.'"

- Exegesis: Jesus' public reading of Isaiah and His declaration of fulfillment assert His messianic identity. The term "anointed" (מָשַׁח, mashach) confirms His divine mission to bring salvation and healing.

The Suffering Servant

Isaiah 53:3-5: "He is despised and rejected by men, a Man of sorrows and acquainted with grief. And we hid, as it were, our faces from Him; He was despised, and we did not esteem Him. Surely He has borne our griefs and carried our sorrows; yet we esteemed Him stricken, smitten by God, and afflicted. But He was wounded for our transgressions, He was bruised for our iniquities; the chastisement for our peace was upon Him, and by His stripes we are healed."

- 1 Peter 2:24: "Who Himself bore our sins in His own body on the tree, that we, having died to sins, might live for righteousness—by whose stripes you were healed."

- Exegesis: Peter directly links Jesus' suffering and crucifixion to Isaiah's prophecy. The term "stripes" (חַבּוּרָה, chabburah) indicates the wounds inflicted during His passion, emphasizing the atoning nature of His suffering.

The Crucifixion

Psalm 22:16-18: "For dogs have surrounded Me; the congregation of the wicked has enclosed Me. They pierced My hands and My feet; I can count all My bones. They look and stare at Me. They divide My garments among them, and for My clothing they cast lots."

- John 19:23-24: "Then the soldiers, when they had crucified Jesus, took His garments and made four parts, to each soldier a part, and also the tunic. Now the tunic was without seam, woven from the top in one piece. They said therefore among themselves, 'Let us not tear it, but cast lots for it, whose it shall be,' that the Scripture might be fulfilled which says: 'They divided My garments among them, and for

My clothing they cast lots.' Therefore the soldiers did these things."

- Exegesis: John's account of the crucifixion explicitly connects Psalm 22 to the events surrounding Jesus' death. The term "pierced" (כָּרָה, karah) and the casting of lots for His clothing confirm the prophetic accuracy and fulfillment in Jesus' crucifixion.

The Resurrection

Psalm 16:10: "For You will not leave my soul in Sheol, nor will You allow Your Holy One to see corruption."

- Acts 2:25-31: "For David says concerning Him: 'I foresaw the LORD always before my face, for He is at my right hand, that I may not be shaken. Therefore my heart rejoiced, and my tongue was glad; moreover my flesh also will rest in hope. For You will not leave my soul in Hades, nor will You allow Your Holy One to see corruption. You have made known to me the ways of life; You will make me full of joy in Your presence.' Men and brethren, let me speak freely to you of the patriarch David, that he is both dead and buried, and his tomb is with us to this day. Therefore, being a prophet, and knowing that God had sworn with an oath to him that of the fruit of his body, according to the flesh, He would raise up the Christ to sit on his throne, he, foreseeing this, spoke concerning the resurrection of the Christ, that His soul was not left in Hades, nor did His flesh see corruption."

- Exegesis: Peter's sermon at Pentecost interprets Psalm 16:10 as a prophecy of Jesus' resurrection. The term "corruption" (שַׁחַת, shachath) refers to decay, indicating that Jesus' body did not undergo decay but was resurrected, affirming His divine nature and victory over death.

Comprehensive Commentary

Theological Significance

1. Confirmation of Jesus' Identity: The fulfillment of Old Testament prophecies in the New Testament serves as a

divine confirmation of Jesus' identity as the Messiah. The specific details and accuracy of these prophecies highlight God's sovereign plan and Jesus' unique role in salvation history.

2. Divine Inspiration of Scripture: The fulfillment of prophecy underscores the divine inspiration of Scripture. The coherence and consistency between the Old and New Testaments affirm that the Bible is a unified revelation from God, with Jesus as the central figure.

3. Validation of the Gospel Message: The New Testament writers' emphasis on fulfilled prophecy validates the gospel message. It provides a historical and theological foundation for faith in Jesus Christ, demonstrating that His life, death, and resurrection were in accordance with God's eternal plan.

4. Encouragement for Believers: The fulfillment of prophecy offers encouragement and hope to believers. It assures them that God's promises are trustworthy and that His plan for redemption is being fulfilled through Jesus Christ.

Exegetical Insights

1. Isaiah 7:14 and Matthew 1:22-23: Matthew's citation of Isaiah's prophecy about the virgin birth highlights the miraculous nature of Jesus' conception and birth. The term "Immanuel" (עִמָּנוּאֵל, Immanuel) signifies "God with us," emphasizing Jesus' divine presence among humanity.

2. Isaiah 61:1-2 and Luke 4:17-21: Jesus' reading of Isaiah's prophecy in the synagogue and His declaration of its fulfillment assert His messianic mission. The term "anointed" (מָשַׁח, mashach) confirms His divine commission to bring salvation, healing, and liberation.

3. Isaiah 53:3-5 and 1 Peter 2:24: Peter's reference to Isaiah's prophecy of the suffering servant links Jesus' atoning sacrifice to the prophetic tradition. The term "stripes" (חַבּוּרָה,

chabburah) indicates the physical suffering Jesus endured for humanity's healing and redemption.

4. Psalm 22:16-18 and John 19:23-24: John's account of the crucifixion explicitly connects the details of Psalm 22 to Jesus' death. The specific fulfillment of the prophecy, including the piercing of Jesus' hands and feet and the casting of lots for His garments, highlights the prophetic accuracy and divine orchestration of these events.

5. Psalm 16:10 and Acts 2:25-31: Peter's interpretation of Psalm 16 as a prophecy of Jesus' resurrection emphasizes the divine foreknowledge and plan for Jesus' victory over death. The term "corruption" (שַׁחַת, shachath) underscores the miraculous nature of the resurrection, affirming Jesus' divine identity and the hope of eternal life for believers.

Practical Applications

1. Strengthening Faith: Understanding the fulfillment of Old Testament prophecies in the New Testament strengthens believers'
faith in the reliability and divine inspiration of Scripture. It provides a solid foundation for trusting in God's promises and His plan for redemption.

2. Proclaiming the Gospel: The fulfilled prophecies serve as powerful evidence for proclaiming the gospel message. Believers can use these prophecies to demonstrate the historical and theological accuracy of Jesus' life, death, and resurrection, inviting others to faith in Him.

3. Living in Hope: The fulfillment of prophecy offers believers hope and assurance in God's faithfulness. It reminds them that God's promises are true and that His plan for redemption is being fulfilled through Jesus Christ. This hope encourages believers to live faithfully and expectantly in light of Jesus' return.

4. Embracing the Mission of Jesus: Recognizing Jesus' fulfillment of Old Testament prophecies encourages believers

to embrace His mission. It calls them to participate in His work of bringing salvation, healing, and liberation to the world, following His example of love and service.

Conclusion

The fulfillment of Old Testament prophecies in the New Testament is a profound affirmation of Jesus' identity as the Messiah and the divine inspiration of Scripture. Through detailed expository study and comprehensive commentary, we have explored the theological significance and practical applications of these fulfilled prophecies. This chapter has provided a thorough examination of how Jesus' life, death, and resurrection fulfill Old Testament prophecies, enhancing our understanding and strengthening our faith in Him as the promised Messiah and Savior.

Jesus' Victory and Exaltation

The victory and exaltation of Jesus Christ are central themes in Christian theology. These concepts affirm His triumph over sin, death, and all powers of darkness, culminating in His exalted position at the right hand of God. This chapter will explore the scriptural basis for Jesus' victory and exaltation, using Bible verses, expository study, and comprehensive commentary, supported by Strong's Exhaustive Concordance.

The Scriptural Basis for Jesus' Victory

Victory Over Sin and Death

Romans 6:9-10: "Knowing that Christ, having been raised from the dead, dies no more. Death no longer has dominion over Him. For the death that He died, He died to sin once for all; but the life that He lives, He lives to God."

- The term "dominion" (κυριεύω, kyrieuō) signifies complete authority or control. Jesus' resurrection signifies His victory over death, affirming that death no longer has any power over Him.

1 Corinthians 15:55-57: "O Death, where is your sting? O Hades, where is your victory? The sting of death is sin, and the strength of sin is the law. But thanks be to God, who gives us the victory through our Lord Jesus Christ."

- Paul uses rhetorical questions to mock the defeated state of death and sin, highlighting the victory (νῖκος, nikos) given through Jesus Christ.

Victory Over Powers and Principalities

Colossians 2:15: "Having disarmed principalities and powers, He made a public spectacle of them, triumphing over them in it."

- The term "disarmed" (ἀπεκδύομαι, apekdyomai) indicates the stripping away of power. Jesus' triumph (θριαμβεύω, thriambeuō) over principalities and powers is a public demonstration of His supremacy.

Ephesians 1:20-21: "Which He worked in Christ when He raised Him from the dead and seated Him at His right hand in the heavenly places, far above all principality and power and might and dominion, and every name that is named, not only in this age but also in that which is to come."

- The term "far above" (ὑπεράνω, hyperanō) emphasizes the supreme position of Jesus over all forms of authority and power.

The Scriptural Basis for Jesus' Exaltation

Exaltation to the Right Hand of God

Philippians 2:9-11: "Therefore God also has highly exalted Him and given Him the name which is above every name, that at the name of Jesus every knee should bow, of those in heaven, and of those on earth, and of those under the earth, and that every tongue should confess that Jesus Christ is Lord, to the glory of God the Father."

- The term "highly exalted" (ὑπερυψόω, hyperypsoō) signifies Jesus' supreme elevation. His name (ὄνομα, onoma) is above every other name, underscoring His unparalleled authority.

Hebrews 1:3: "Who being the brightness of His glory and the express image of His person, and upholding all things by the word of His power, when He had by Himself purged our sins, sat down at the right hand of the Majesty on high."

- The phrase "sat down at the right hand" (καθίζω ἐν δεξιᾷ, kathizō en dexia) signifies a position of honor, authority, and completion of His redemptive work.

Exaltation as King and Priest

Hebrews 7:26: "For such a High Priest was fitting for us, who is holy, harmless, undefiled, separate from sinners, and has become higher than the heavens."

- The phrase "higher than the heavens" (ὑψηλότερος τῶν οὐρανῶν, hypsēloteros tōn ouranōn) underscores Jesus' supreme exaltation as our High Priest.

Revelation 5:12-13: "Saying with a loud voice: 'Worthy is the Lamb who was slain to receive power and riches and wisdom, and strength and honor and glory and blessing!' And every creature which is in heaven and on the earth and under the earth and such as are in the sea, and all that are in them, I heard saying: 'Blessing and honor and glory and power be to Him who sits on the throne, and to the Lamb, forever and ever!'"

- The universal acknowledgment of Jesus as worthy (ἄξιος, axios) underscores His exalted status and the worship due to Him.

Comprehensive Commentary

Theological Significance of Jesus' Victory

1. Victory Over Sin and Death: Jesus' resurrection is the definitive victory over sin and death. This triumph assures believers of their own resurrection and eternal life. Paul's declaration in 1 Corinthians 15:55-57 celebrates this victory and provides a foundation for Christian hope.

2. Victory Over Spiritual Powers: Jesus' disarming of principalities and powers (Colossians 2:15) signifies His authority over all spiritual forces. This victory assures believers that no power can separate them from the love of God in Christ Jesus.

3. Defeat of Evil: Jesus' victory over evil is not just a future hope but a present reality. His triumph over the forces of darkness empowers believers to live victoriously and resist the devil.

Theological Significance of Jesus' Exaltation

1. Supreme Authority: Jesus' exaltation to the right hand of God signifies His supreme authority. Philippians 2:9-11 affirms that every knee will bow and every tongue will confess Jesus as Lord, highlighting the universal scope of His dominion.

2. Completion of Redemptive Work: Jesus' sitting at the right hand of God (Hebrews 1:3) signifies the completion and acceptance of His redemptive work. This exaltation underscores the sufficiency of His sacrifice and the assurance of believers' salvation.

3. Intercessory Role: Jesus' exaltation as our High Priest (Hebrews 7:26) emphasizes His ongoing intercessory role. This assures believers of His continual advocacy on their behalf before the Father.

4. Universal Worship: The worship of Jesus as the exalted Lamb (Revelation 5:12-13) highlights His worthiness and the rightful response of all creation to His authority. This worship is both a present reality and a future hope.

Exegetical Insights

1. Romans 6:9-10 and 1 Corinthians 15:55-57: Paul's writings highlight the victory over death achieved through Jesus' resurrection. The term "dominion" (κυριεύω, kyrieō) and the rhetorical questions mock the defeated state of death, emphasizing the transformative power of Jesus' victory.

2. Colossians 2:15 and Ephesians 1:20-21: Paul's depiction of Jesus disarming spiritual powers and His exaltation far above all authorities underscores the comprehensive scope of His victory. The terms "disarmed" (ἀπεκδύομαι, apekdyomai) and "far above" (ὑπεράνω, hyperanō) highlight the complete and supreme nature of His triumph.

3. Philippians 2:9-11 and Hebrews 1:3: The exaltation of Jesus is presented as the divine response to His obedience and sacrifice. The terms "highly exalted" (ὑπερυψόω, hyperypsoō) and "right hand" (δεξιᾷ, dexia) signify the honor and authority bestowed upon Him, affirming His unique status in the divine economy.

4. Hebrews 7:26 and Revelation 5:12-13: The depiction of Jesus as the exalted High Priest and the worthy Lamb underscores His unique and supreme status. The phrases "higher than the heavens" (ὑψηλότερος τῶν οὐρανῶν, hypsēloteros tōn ouranōn) and "worthy" (ἄξιος, axios) emphasize His unparalleled position and the worship due to Him.

Practical Applications

1. Living in Victory: Understanding Jesus' victory over sin, death, and spiritual powers empowers believers to live victoriously. It encourages them to resist sin, overcome spiritual battles, and live in the freedom that Christ provides.

2. Worship and Adoration: Recognizing Jesus' exaltation calls believers to worship and adore Him. It fosters a deep sense of reverence and devotion, motivating believers to honor Him in every aspect of their lives.

3. Hope and Assurance: Jesus' victory and exaltation provide believers with hope and assurance. It assures them of their future resurrection, eternal life, and the certainty of Christ's ultimate triumph over all evil.

4. Intercessory Confidence: Believers can approach God with confidence, knowing that Jesus, their exalted High Priest, intercedes for them. This assurance encourages them to pray boldly and trust in His ongoing advocacy.

Conclusion

Jesus' victory and exaltation are central to Christian theology, affirming His triumph over sin, death, and all powers of darkness, and His supreme authority as the exalted King and High Priest. Through detailed expository study and comprehensive commentary, we have explored the scriptural basis, theological significance, and practical applications of Jesus' victory and exaltation. This chapter has provided a thorough examination, enhancing our understanding and strengthening our faith in Jesus as the victorious and exalted Lord.

CHAPTER 05

THE ETERNAL PRIESTHOOD OF JESUS IN PSALM 110

Psalm 110 is a foundational text that provides a vivid portrayal of the Messiah as both King and Priest. This dual role is uniquely fulfilled in Jesus Christ, whose eternal priesthood is a cornerstone of Christian theology. In this chapter, we will analyze Psalm 110:1-7, focusing on the eternal priesthood of Jesus, using Bible verses, expository study, and comprehensive commentary, supported by Strong's Exhaustive Concordance.

Text of Psalm 110 (NKJV)

1. The LORD said to my Lord, "Sit at My right hand, till I make Your enemies Your footstool."

2. The LORD shall send the rod of Your strength out of Zion. Rule in the midst of Your enemies!

3. Your people shall be volunteers in the day of Your power; in the beauties of holiness, from the womb of the morning, You have the dew of Your youth.

4. The LORD has sworn and will not relent, "You are a priest forever according to the order of Melchizedek."

5. The Lord is at Your right hand; He shall execute kings in the day of His wrath.

6. He shall judge among the nations, He shall fill the places with dead bodies, He shall execute the heads of many countries.

7. He shall drink of the brook by the wayside; therefore He shall lift up the head.

Expository Study

Verse 1: The Divine Invitation

Verse 1: "The LORD said to my Lord, 'Sit at My right hand, till I make Your enemies Your footstool.'"

- The phrase "The LORD said to my Lord" uses two different Hebrew words for "Lord": יְהוָה (YHWH) and אֲדֹנִי (Adonai), indicating a conversation between God the Father and the Messiah.

- "Sit" (יָשַׁב, yashab) signifies a position of honor and authority.

- New Testament Reference: This verse is frequently cited in the New Testament (e.g., Matthew 22:44, Acts 2:34-35) to affirm Jesus' exaltation and divine authority.

Verse 2: Rule and Dominion

Verse 2: "The LORD shall send the rod of Your strength out of Zion. Rule in the midst of Your enemies!"

- "Rod" (מַטֶּה, matteh) symbolizes authority and power.

- "Zion" (צִיּוֹן, tzion) represents the spiritual center of God's kingdom.

- This verse emphasizes the Messiah's authority and the extension of His rule.

Verse 3: The People's Willingness

Verse 3: "Your people shall be volunteers in the day of Your power; in the beauties of holiness, from the womb of the morning, You have the dew of Your youth."

- "Volunteers" (נְדָבָה, nedavah) indicates a willing and eager participation of the people.

- "Beauties of holiness" (הַדְרֵי־קֹדֶשׁ, hadrey-qodesh) reflects the splendor of God's holiness.

- This verse highlights the enthusiastic support of the Messiah's followers.

Verse 4: Eternal Priesthood

Verse 4: "The LORD has sworn and will not relent, 'You are a priest forever according to the order of Melchizedek.'"

- "Sworn" (נִשְׁבַּע, nishba) indicates an irrevocable divine oath.

- "Priest" (כֹּהֵן, kohen) and "Melchizedek" (מַלְכִּי־צֶדֶק, malki-tzedek) denote an eternal and unique priesthood.

- New Testament Reference: The book of Hebrews (Hebrews 5:6, 7:17) extensively discusses Jesus' priesthood in the order of Melchizedek, contrasting it with the Levitical priesthood.

Verses 5-7: Judgment and Victory

Verse 5: "The Lord is at Your right hand; He shall execute kings in the day of His wrath."

- "Right hand" (יָמִין, yamin) symbolizes power and support.

- This verse speaks to the Messiah's authority to judge and execute justice.

Verse 6: "He shall judge among the nations, He shall fill the places with dead bodies, He shall execute the heads of many countries."

- "Judge" (דִּין, din) indicates the execution of justice.

- This verse depicts the Messiah's role as a judge over the nations, emphasizing His ultimate victory and dominion.

Verse 7: "He shall drink of the brook by the wayside; therefore He shall lift up the head."

- "Drink" (שָׁתָה, shathah) signifies refreshment and sustenance.

- "Lift up the head" (רֹאשׁ רוּם, rum rosh) symbolizes triumph and honor.

- This verse concludes with a picture of the Messiah's refreshed state and victorious posture.

Comprehensive Commentary

Theological Significance of Jesus' Eternal Priesthood

1. Eternal Priesthood: The declaration that the Messiah is a priest forever according to the order of Melchizedek (Psalm 110:4) is significant for several reasons. Unlike the temporary Levitical priesthood, Jesus' priesthood is eternal. This ensures a permanent and unchanging intercession for believers (Hebrews 7:24-25).

2. Melchizedekian Order: Melchizedek, whose name means "king of righteousness" and who was also king of Salem ("peace"), is a unique figure in biblical theology. His priesthood, which predates the Levitical priesthood, is characterized by its combination of kingly and priestly roles (Genesis 14:18-20). Jesus' priesthood in this order underscores His dual role as both King and Priest.

3. Divine Oath: The divine oath ("The LORD has sworn and will not relent") emphasizes the irrevocable and eternal nature of Jesus' priesthood. This contrasts with the Levitical priests, whose roles were not established by divine oath and were subject to change and succession (Hebrews 7:21-22).

Exegetical Insights

1. Psalm 110:1 and New Testament Citations: The frequent citation of Psalm 110:1 in the New Testament

highlights its importance in understanding Jesus' exaltation and authority. The phrase "Sit at My right hand" signifies the highest honor and authority bestowed upon Jesus, indicating His completed work of redemption and His ongoing rule (Matthew 22:44, Acts 2:34-35).

2. Psalm 110:4 and the Book of Hebrews: The book of Hebrews provides a detailed theological exposition of Jesus' priesthood in the order of Melchizedek. Hebrews 5:6 and 7:17 directly quote Psalm 110:4 to establish Jesus' eternal and superior priesthood. The term "priest forever" (לְעוֹלָם כֹּהֵן, kohen le'olam) underscores the unending nature of His priestly ministry.

3. Psalm 110:5-7 and Messianic Judgment: The imagery of judgment and victory in verses 5-7 reinforces the Messianic authority to execute justice. The phrases "execute kings" and "judge among the nations" depict the comprehensive scope of the Messiah's rule and His ultimate triumph over all opposition (Revelation 19:11-16).

Practical Applications

1. Assurance of Salvation: The eternal priesthood of Jesus provides believers with the assurance of their salvation. His unending intercession means that believers are continually represented before the Father, ensuring their standing in grace (Hebrews 7:25).

2. Confidence in Prayer: Understanding Jesus as the eternal High Priest encourages believers to approach God with confidence. Knowing that Jesus intercedes on their behalf empowers them to pray boldly and with assurance of being heard (Hebrews 4:14-16).

3. Living Under His Rule: Recognizing the authority and victory of Jesus as both King and Priest motivates believers to live in obedience and reverence. His rule is marked by justice, righteousness, and peace, calling believers to reflect these qualities in their lives.

4. Hope in His Triumph: The imagery of Jesus' victory over His enemies provides hope and encouragement to believers. It assures them of the ultimate triumph of good over evil and the establishment of God's kingdom in its fullness (1 Corinthians 15:24-25).

Conclusion

Psalm 110 provides a profound portrayal of the Messiah as both King and Priest, uniquely fulfilled in Jesus Christ. Through detailed expository study and comprehensive commentary, we have explored the theological significance and practical applications of Jesus' eternal priesthood. This chapter has provided a thorough examination of Psalm 110:1-7, enhancing our understanding and strengthening our faith in Jesus as the eternal Priest and King who reigns with divine authority and intercedes for His people forever.

Jesus as the Eternal High Priest

The role of Jesus as the eternal High Priest is central to Christian theology, signifying His unending intercession and the completion of the redemptive work. This chapter will explore the concept of Jesus as the eternal High Priest, using Bible verses, an expository study, and comprehensive commentary, supported by Strong's Exhaustive Concordance.

The Biblical Foundation of Jesus' Priesthood

Psalm 110:4: The Divine Oath

Psalm 110:4: "The LORD has sworn and will not relent, 'You are a priest forever according to the order of Melchizedek.'"

- The phrase "The LORD has sworn" (נִשְׁבַּע, nishba) emphasizes the irrevocable nature of this divine appointment.

- "Priest" (כֹּהֵן, kohen) and "forever" (עוֹלָם, olam) highlight the eternal duration of Jesus' priesthood.

Hebrews 5:5-6: The Appointment of Jesus

Hebrews 5:5-6: "So also Christ did not glorify Himself to become High Priest, but it was He who said to Him: 'You are My Son, today I have begotten You.' As He also says in another place: 'You are a priest forever according to the order of Melchizedek.'"

- This passage emphasizes that Jesus did not assume the role of High Priest by His own decision but was appointed by God.

- The citation of Psalm 110:4 underscores the divine and eternal nature of His priesthood.

Hebrews 7:24-25: The Permanence of Jesus' Priesthood

Hebrews 7:24-25: "But He, because He continues forever, has an unchangeable priesthood. Therefore He is also able to save to the uttermost those who come to God through Him, since He always lives to make intercession for them."

- The term "unchangeable" (ἀπαράβατος, aparabatos) signifies the permanent and non-transferable nature of Jesus' priesthood.

- "Intercession" (ἐντυγχάνω, entygchanō) refers to Jesus' ongoing advocacy on behalf of believers.

Expository Study

The Role of the High Priest in the Old Testament

Leviticus 16:32-34: "And the priest, who is anointed and consecrated to minister as priest in his father's place, shall make atonement, and shall put on the linen clothes, the holy garments; then he shall make atonement for the Holy Sanctuary, and he shall make atonement for the tabernacle of meeting and for the altar, and he shall make atonement for the priests and for all the people of the assembly. This shall be an everlasting statute for you, to make atonement for the children of Israel, for all their sins, once a year."

- The High Priest's role in the Old Testament involved making atonement for the sins of the people, particularly on the Day of Atonement (Yom Kippur).

- "Atonement" (כִּפֶּר, kipper) signifies the covering or removal of sin through a sacrificial offering.

Jesus' Superior Priesthood

Hebrews 7:26-27: "For such a High Priest was fitting for us, who is holy, harmless, undefiled, separate from sinners, and has become higher than the heavens; who does not need daily, as those high priests, to offer up sacrifices, first for His own sins and then for the people's, for this He did once for all when He offered up Himself."

- Jesus' priesthood is superior because of His sinlessness and the sufficiency of His self-sacrifice.

- The term "once for all" (ἐφάπαξ, ephapax) underscores the completeness and finality of Jesus' sacrificial offering.

Hebrews 9:11-12: "But Christ came as High Priest of the good things to come, with the greater and more perfect tabernacle not made with hands, that is, not of this creation. Not with the blood of goats and calves, but with His own blood He entered the Most Holy Place once for all, having obtained eternal redemption."

- The "greater and more perfect tabernacle" signifies the heavenly sanctuary where Jesus ministers as High Priest.

- "Eternal redemption" (αἰώνιος λύτρωσις, aiōnios lytrōsis) highlights the everlasting efficacy of Jesus' atonement.

Jesus' Ongoing Intercession

Hebrews 4:14-16: "Seeing then that we have a great High Priest who has passed through the heavens, Jesus the Son of God, let us hold fast our confession. For we do not have a High Priest who cannot sympathize with our weaknesses, but was in all points tempted as we are, yet without sin. Let us therefore come boldly to the throne of grace, that we may obtain mercy and find grace to help in time of need."

- Jesus' ability to sympathize with human weaknesses emphasizes His role as a compassionate High Priest.

- The term "boldly" (παρρησία, parrēsia) encourages believers to approach God's throne with confidence.

Romans 8:34: "Who is he who condemns? It is Christ who died, and furthermore is also risen, who is even at the right hand of God, who also makes intercession for us."

- The term "intercession" (ἐντυγχάνω, entygchanō) underscores Jesus' ongoing role in advocating for believers before God.

Comprehensive Commentary

Theological Significance of Jesus' Eternal High Priesthood

1. Perfection of Sacrifice: Unlike the repeated and insufficient sacrifices of the Levitical priests, Jesus' self-sacrifice was perfect and once for all. This perfect sacrifice fulfills and surpasses the Old Testament requirements for atonement (Hebrews 7:27).

2. Eternal Intercession: Jesus' eternal priesthood assures believers of His continual intercession. This ongoing advocacy means that believers are perpetually represented before the Father, ensuring their standing in grace and the effectiveness of His redemptive work (Hebrews 7:25).

3. Access to God: Jesus as the eternal High Priest provides believers with direct access to God. His sympathetic nature and shared human experience encourage believers to approach God confidently, knowing they will receive mercy and grace (Hebrews 4:14-16).

4. Fulfillment of Prophecy: The priesthood of Jesus according to the order of Melchizedek fulfills the prophetic declarations of Psalm 110:4. This eternal and unique

priesthood underscores the divine plan and the fulfillment of God's promises through Jesus Christ.

Exegetical Insights

1. Psalm 110:4 and Hebrews 5:5-6: The divine oath establishing Jesus' eternal priesthood highlights the irrevocable and divinely appointed nature of His role. The term "priest forever" emphasizes the unending duration of His priestly ministry, contrasting with the temporal nature of the Levitical priesthood.

2. Hebrews 7:24-25: The permanence of Jesus' priesthood is underscored by the term "unchangeable," signifying a priesthood that is neither temporary nor subject to succession. This permanence provides a foundation for the assurance of believers' salvation.

3. Hebrews 7:26-27 and Hebrews 9:11-12: The superiority of Jesus' priesthood is evident in His sinlessness and the sufficiency of His sacrifice. The term "once for all" highlights the finality and completeness of His atonement, making further sacrifices unnecessary.

4. Hebrews 4:14-16 and Romans 8:34: Jesus' role as the sympathetic High Priest and His ongoing intercession emphasize His compassionate advocacy on behalf of believers. The term "boldly" encourages believers to approach God with confidence, knowing they are continually represented by Jesus.

Practical Applications

1. Assurance of Salvation: Understanding Jesus' eternal priesthood provides believers with assurance of their salvation. His unending intercession guarantees their continual standing in grace and the effectiveness of His atoning sacrifice.

2. Confidence in Prayer: Recognizing Jesus as the eternal High Priest encourages believers to approach God confidently in prayer. His compassionate nature and ongoing

intercession assure them that their prayers are heard and answered.

3. Living in Grace: The knowledge of Jesus' eternal priesthood and perfect sacrifice encourages believers to live in the freedom and grace that He provides. They are freed from the burden of earning God's favor and can rest in the completed work of Christ.

4. Hope in Christ's Advocacy: Believers can have hope and confidence in the ongoing advocacy of Jesus. Knowing that He continually intercedes for them before the Father provides comfort and strength in times of trial and temptation.

Conclusion

Jesus as the eternal High Priest is a cornerstone of Christian theology, signifying His unending intercession and the completion of the redemptive work. Through detailed expository study and comprehensive commentary, we have explored the biblical foundation, theological significance, and practical applications of Jesus' priesthood. This chapter has provided a thorough examination of Jesus' role as the eternal High Priest, enhancing our understanding and strengthening our faith in Him as the compassionate and unchangeable advocate for all believers.

The Order of Melchizedek

The order of Melchizedek is a unique and significant concept in Christian theology, directly relating to the priesthood of Jesus Christ. This order, unlike the Levitical priesthood, is eternal and unique, characterized by its combination of kingly and priestly roles. In this chapter, we will explore the order of Melchizedek using Bible verses, an expository study, and comprehensive commentary, supported by Strong's Exhaustive Concordance.

Biblical Foundation

Genesis 14:18-20: The Historical Melchizedek

Genesis 14:18-20: "Then Melchizedek king of Salem brought out bread and wine; he was the priest of God Most High. And he blessed him and said: 'Blessed be Abram of God Most High, Possessor of heaven and earth; and blessed be God Most High, who has delivered your enemies into your hand.' And he gave him a tithe of all."

- "Melchizedek" (מַלְכִּי־צֶדֶק, malki-tzedek) means "king of righteousness."

- "Salem" (שָׁלֵם, shalem) means "peace," indicating Melchizedek as the king of peace.

- "Priest" (כֹּהֵן, kohen) signifies his role as a mediator between God and man.

Psalm 110:4: The Prophetic Declaration

Psalm 110:4: "The LORD has sworn and will not relent, 'You are a priest forever according to the order of Melchizedek.'"

- "Sworn" (נִשְׁבַּע, nishba) emphasizes the irrevocable nature of this divine appointment.

- "Forever" (עוֹלָם, olam) signifies the eternal duration of this priesthood.

Hebrews 7:1-3: The Superiority of Melchizedek's Priesthood

Hebrews 7:1-3: "For this Melchizedek, king of Salem, priest of the Most High God, who met Abraham returning from the slaughter of the kings and blessed him, to whom also Abraham gave a tenth part of all, first being translated 'king of righteousness,' and then also king of Salem, meaning 'king of peace,' without father, without mother, without genealogy, having neither beginning of days nor end of life, but made like the Son of God, remains a priest continually."

- "Without father, without mother, without genealogy" indicates the unique and timeless nature of Melchizedek's priesthood.

- "Made like the Son of God" (ἀφομοιόω, aphomoioō) signifies the typological foreshadowing of Jesus' eternal priesthood.

Expository Study

The Historical Context of Melchizedek

Genesis 14:18-20: Melchizedek appears in the narrative as both a king and priest, a dual role that prefigures Christ. His blessing of Abraham and the receipt of a tithe highlight his superior and honored status. The bread and wine he offers have been seen as a foreshadowing of the Eucharist.

King of Righteousness: Melchizedek's name means "king of righteousness," indicating his role in promoting justice and right relationship with God.

- King of Peace: As the king of Salem (peace), Melchizedek's rule is characterized by peace, foreshadowing the peace that Christ brings.

The Prophetic Nature of Melchizedek's Priesthood

Psalm 110:4: This verse prophetically declares the eternal nature of the Messiah's priesthood in the order of Melchizedek. The divine oath signifies the certainty and unchangeable nature of this appointment.

- Priest Forever: The eternal nature of this priesthood contrasts with the temporary and hereditary Levitical priesthood, underscoring the superiority and permanence of Christ's priestly role.

The Superiority of the Melchizedekian Priesthood

Hebrews 7:1-3: The writer of Hebrews elaborates on the typological significance of Melchizedek. His priesthood is characterized by timelessness, not limited by ancestry or duration.

- Without Genealogy: Unlike the Levitical priests, Melchizedek's priesthood is not based on lineage. This emphasizes the divine and eternal nature of his priesthood.

- Like the Son of God: Melchizedek is a type of Christ, prefiguring Jesus' eternal and unchangeable priesthood.

Jesus as High Priest in the Order of Melchizedek

Hebrews 7:11-17: The priesthood of Jesus is contrasted with the Levitical priesthood. The former is superior and eternal, fulfilling the promise of Psalm 110:4.

Hebrews 7:11-12: "Therefore, if perfection were through the Levitical priesthood (for under it the people received the law), what further need was there that another priest should rise according to the order of Melchizedek, and not be called according to the order of Aaron? For the priesthood being changed, of necessity there is also a change of the law."

- The inadequacy of the Levitical priesthood necessitated a superior priesthood in the order of Melchizedek.

- The change in priesthood implies a change in the law, highlighting the new covenant established through Christ.

Hebrews 7:13-17: "For He of whom these things are spoken belongs to another tribe, from which no man has officiated at the altar. For it is evident that our Lord arose from Judah, of which tribe Moses spoke nothing concerning priesthood. And it is yet far more evident if, in the likeness of Melchizedek, there arises another priest who has come, not according to the law of a fleshly commandment, but according to the power of an endless life. For He testifies: 'You are a priest forever according to the order of Melchizedek.'"

- Jesus, from the tribe of Judah, not Levi, fulfills the priesthood in the order of Melchizedek.

- His priesthood is based on the "power of an endless life," underscoring its eternal and divine nature.

The Implications of Jesus' Melchizedekian Priesthood

1. Perfection and Completion: The priesthood of Jesus brings perfection and completion to what the Levitical priesthood could not achieve. His once-for-all sacrifice contrasts with the repeated sacrifices of the Levitical priests (Hebrews 7:27).

2. Eternal Intercession: Jesus' eternal priesthood ensures ongoing intercession for believers. He continually represents us before the Father, providing assurance of salvation and access to God's grace (Hebrews 7:25).

3. New Covenant: The priesthood of Jesus establishes a new covenant, superseding the old covenant mediated by the Levitical priesthood. This new covenant is based on better promises and guarantees eternal redemption (Hebrews 8:6-13).

Comprehensive Commentary

Theological Significance

1. Superiority of Melchizedek's Priesthood: The order of Melchizedek is superior to the Levitical priesthood because it is eternal and divinely appointed. Melchizedek's lack of genealogy and timeless nature prefigure the eternal priesthood of Christ (Hebrews 7:3).

2. Typology of Christ: Melchizedek serves as a type of Christ, illustrating the nature of Jesus' priesthood. Just as Melchizedek was both king and priest, Jesus fulfills both roles, bringing righteousness and peace (Hebrews 7:2).

3. Fulfillment of Prophecy: Psalm 110:4 prophetically points to the Messiah's eternal priesthood. The fulfillment of this prophecy in Jesus underscores the divine plan and continuity of God's redemptive work through both Old and New Testaments.

4. Eternal Intercession: Jesus' priesthood in the order of Melchizedek assures believers of His continual intercession. This eternal advocacy provides confidence and

hope, knowing that Jesus always represents us before the Father (Hebrews 7:25).

Exegetical Insights

1. Genesis 14:18-20 and Hebrews 7:1-3: The historical account of Melchizedek and the exegesis in Hebrews highlight his unique and timeless priesthood. The attributes of Melchizedek, such as being "without genealogy," underscore the divine nature of his priesthood, foreshadowing Christ's eternal role.

2. Psalm 110:4 and Hebrews 7:11-17: The prophetic declaration of Psalm 110:4 is expounded in Hebrews, emphasizing the eternal and superior nature of Jesus' priesthood. The term "forever" (עוֹלָם, olam) underscores the unending duration of His priesthood, contrasting with the temporal Levitical priesthood.

3. Hebrews 7:11-12: The need for a change in priesthood and law signifies the inadequacy of the old covenant. Jesus' priesthood in the order of Melchizedek establishes a new and better covenant, fulfilling the divine promise and providing a perfect atonement.

4. Hebrews 7:25: The term "save to the uttermost" (πάντοτε σώζειν, pantote sōzein) signifies the complete and eternal salvation provided by Jesus. His eternal intercession guarantees the continuous application of His redemptive work to believers.

Practical Applications

1. Assurance of Salvation: Understanding Jesus' priesthood in the order of Melchizedek provides assurance of salvation. His eternal intercession ensures that believers are continually represented before the Father, securing their standing in grace (Hebrews 7:25).

2. Confidence in Prayer: Recognizing Jesus as the eternal High Priest encourages believers to approach God

confidently in prayer. His ongoing advocacy assures them that their prayers are heard and answered (Hebrews 4:14-16).

3. Living in Grace: The knowledge of Jesus' perfect and eternal priesthood encourages believers to live in the freedom and grace that He provides. They are freed from the burden of earning God's favor and can rest in the completed work of Christ.

4. Hope in Christ's Advocacy: Believers can have hope and confidence in the ongoing advocacy of Jesus. Knowing that He continually intercedes for them before the Father provides comfort and strength in times of trial and temptation (Romans 8:34).

Conclusion

The order of Melchizedek is a profound and significant aspect of Christian theology, uniquely fulfilled in the eternal priesthood of Jesus Christ. Through detailed expository study and comprehensive commentary, we have explored the biblical foundation, theological significance, and practical applications of this unique priesthood. This chapter has provided a thorough examination of the order of Melchizedek, enhancing our understanding and strengthening our faith in Jesus as the eternal High Priest who intercedes for us forever.

New Testament Confirmation of Jesus' Priesthood

The New Testament provides extensive confirmation of Jesus Christ's priesthood, affirming His unique and eternal role as our High Priest. This chapter will explore how the New Testament writers confirm and elaborate on the priesthood of Jesus, using Bible verses, expository study, and comprehensive commentary, supported by Strong's Exhaustive Concordance.

The Confirmation in Hebrews

Hebrews 2:17: Jesus as a Merciful and Faithful High Priest

Hebrews 2:17: "Therefore, in all things He had to be made like His brethren, that He might be a merciful and faithful High Priest in things pertaining to God, to make propitiation for the sins of the people."

- The term "merciful" (ἐλεήμων, eleēmōn) emphasizes Jesus' compassion and willingness to intercede.

- "Faithful" (πιστός, pistos) underscores His reliability and trustworthiness in His priestly duties.

- "Propitiation" (ἱλάσκομαι, hilaskomai) refers to the atoning sacrifice Jesus made for our sins.

Hebrews 4:14-16: Jesus the Great High Priest

Hebrews 4:14-16: "Seeing then that we have a great High Priest who has passed through the heavens, Jesus the Son of God, let us hold fast our confession. For we do not have a High Priest who cannot sympathize with our weaknesses, but was in all points tempted as we are, yet without sin. Let us therefore come boldly to the throne of grace, that we may obtain mercy and find grace to help in time of need."

- "Passed through the heavens" (διεληλυθότα τοὺς οὐρανούς, dielēlythota tous ouranous) signifies Jesus' ascension and exaltation.

- "Sympathize" (συμπαθέω, sympatheō) highlights Jesus' empathy for our struggles and weaknesses.

- The "throne of grace" (θρόνος τῆς χάριτος, thronos tēs charitos) emphasizes the accessibility and generosity of God's help through Jesus.

Hebrews 5:5-10: Jesus' Appointment as High Priest

Hebrews 5:5-10: "So also Christ did not glorify Himself to become High Priest, but it was He who said to Him: 'You are My Son, today I have begotten You.' As He also says in another place: 'You are a priest forever according to the order of Melchizedek'; who, in the days of His flesh, when He had offered up prayers and supplications, with vehement cries and tears to Him who was able to save Him from death, and was heard because of His godly fear, though He was a Son, yet He learned obedience by the things which He suffered. And having been perfected, He became the author of eternal salvation to all who obey Him, called by God as High Priest 'according to the order of Melchizedek.'"

- "Glorify" (δοξάζω, doxazō) indicates that Jesus did not assume the role of High Priest by His own initiative but was appointed by God.

- "Order of Melchizedek" (τάξις Μελχισεδέκ, taxis Melchisedek) emphasizes the unique and eternal nature of Jesus' priesthood.

Hebrews 7:11-28: The Superiority and Eternality of Jesus' Priesthood

Hebrews 7:11-28: This passage contrasts the Levitical priesthood with Jesus' priesthood, emphasizing its superiority and eternal nature.

- Verses 11-12: "Therefore, if perfection were through the Levitical priesthood (for under it the people received the law), what further need was there that another priest should rise according to the order of Melchizedek, and not be called according to the order of Aaron? For the priesthood being changed, of necessity there is also a change of the law."

- "Perfection" (τελείωσις, teleiōsis) refers to the complete fulfillment and maturity of God's plan, which the Levitical priesthood could not achieve.

- Verses 13-17: "For He of whom these things are spoken belongs to another tribe, from which no man has officiated at the altar. For it is evident that our Lord arose from Judah, of which tribe Moses spoke nothing concerning priesthood. And it is yet far more evident if, in the likeness of Melchizedek, there arises another priest who has come, not according to the law of a fleshly commandment, but according to the power of an endless life. For He testifies: 'You are a priest forever according to the order of Melchizedek.'"

- "Endless life" (ζωῆς ἀκαταλύτου, zōēs akatalytou) underscores the eternal and indestructible nature of Jesus' priesthood.

- Verses 18-19: "For on the one hand there is an annulling of the former commandment because of its weakness and unprofitableness, for the law made nothing perfect; on the other hand, there is the bringing in of a better hope, through which we draw near to God."

- The "better hope" (κρείττων ἐλπίς, kreittōn elpis) refers to the new covenant established through Jesus, providing access to God.

- Verses 20-22: "And inasmuch as He was not made priest without an oath (for they have become priests without an oath, but He with an oath by Him who said to Him: 'The LORD has sworn and will not relent, "You are a priest forever according to the order of Melchizedek"'), by so much more Jesus has become a surety of a better covenant."

- The divine oath emphasizes the certainty and permanence of Jesus' priesthood.

- Verses 23-25: "Also there were many priests, because they were prevented by death from continuing. But He, because He continues forever, has an unchangeable priesthood. Therefore He is also able to save to the uttermost those who come to God through Him, since He always lives to make intercession for them."

- "Unchangeable" (ἀπαράβατος, aparabatos) signifies a priesthood that does not pass from one to another.

- Verses 26-28: "For such a High Priest was fitting for us, who is holy, harmless, undefiled, separate from sinners, and has become higher than the heavens; who does not need daily, as those high priests, to offer up sacrifices, first for His own sins and then for the people's, for this He did once for all when He offered up Himself. For the law appoints as high priests men who have weakness, but the word of the oath, which came after the law, appoints the Son who has been perfected forever."

- "Once for all" (ἐφάπαξ, ephapax) emphasizes the completeness and finality of Jesus' sacrifice.

Comprehensive Commentary

Theological Significance of Jesus' Priesthood

1. Eternal Nature: Unlike the Levitical priesthood, which was temporary and hereditary, Jesus' priesthood is eternal. This eternal priesthood ensures a perpetual and unchanging intercession for believers, providing continuous access to God's grace (Hebrews 7:24-25).

2. Perfect Sacrifice: Jesus' offering of Himself as a sacrifice was perfect and complete, unlike the repeated and insufficient sacrifices of the Levitical priests. His once-for-all sacrifice fully atoned for sin, providing a definitive solution to the problem of sin (Hebrews 7:27).

3. Superior Covenant: Jesus' priesthood establishes a new and better covenant, founded on better promises and providing a direct and personal relationship with God. This new covenant supersedes the old covenant and offers a better hope for drawing near to God (Hebrews 7:22, 8:6-13).

4. Divine Appointment: Jesus' priesthood is established by a divine oath, underscoring its certainty and permanence. This divine appointment, according to the order of Melchizedek, highlights the unique and superior nature of His priesthood (Hebrews 7:21-22).

Exegetical Insights

1. Hebrews 2:17: Jesus' role as a merciful and faithful High Priest is emphasized by His identification with humanity. The term "propitiation" (ἰλάσκομαι, hilaskomai)

indicates His role in atoning for sins, highlighting His compassionate and effective intercession.

2. Hebrews 4:14-16: The accessibility of Jesus' priesthood is underscored by His ability to sympathize with human weaknesses. The phrase "passed through the heavens" signifies His exalted position, while the "throne of grace" emphasizes the generous and accessible nature of divine help through Him.

3. Hebrews 5:5-10: The divine appointment of Jesus as High Priest, according to the order of Melchizedek, emphasizes the unique and eternal nature of His priesthood. His obedience and suffering are highlighted as the means through which He was perfected and became the author of eternal salvation.

4. Hebrews 7:11-28: This passage provides a comprehensive comparison between the Levitical priesthood and Jesus' priesthood. The terms "perfection," "endless life ," "better hope," and "unchangeable" highlight the superiority and eternal nature of Jesus' priesthood. The phrase "once for all" underscores the completeness and finality of His sacrificial offering.

Practical Applications

1. Assurance of Salvation: Understanding Jesus' eternal priesthood provides believers with assurance of their salvation. His unending intercession guarantees their continual standing in grace and the effectiveness of His atoning sacrifice (Hebrews 7:25).

2. Confidence in Prayer: Recognizing Jesus as the eternal High Priest encourages believers to approach God confidently in prayer. His ongoing advocacy assures them that their prayers are heard and answered (Hebrews 4:14-16).

3. Living in Grace: The knowledge of Jesus' perfect and eternal priesthood encourages believers to live in the freedom and grace that He provides. They are freed from the

burden of earning God's favor and can rest in the completed work of Christ (Hebrews 7:27).

4. Hope in Christ's Advocacy: Believers can have hope and confidence in the ongoing advocacy of Jesus. Knowing that He continually intercedes for them before the Father provides comfort and strength in times of trial and temptation (Romans 8:34).

Conclusion

The New Testament provides extensive confirmation of Jesus Christ's priesthood, affirming His unique and eternal role as our High Priest. Through detailed expository study and comprehensive commentary, we have explored the biblical foundation, theological significance, and practical applications of Jesus' priesthood. This chapter has provided a thorough examination of the New Testament confirmation of Jesus' priesthood, enhancing our understanding and strengthening our faith in Him as the eternal High Priest who intercedes for us forever.

CHAPTER 06

THE SHEPHERD KING IN PSALM 23

Psalm 23 is one of the most beloved and well-known passages in the Bible. It portrays God as the Shepherd King who provides, guides, and protects His people. This chapter will explore the deep theological significance of Psalm 23:1-6, using Bible verses, an expository study, and comprehensive commentary, supported by Strong's Exhaustive Concordance.

Text of Psalm 23 (NKJV)

1. The LORD is my shepherd; I shall not want.

2. He makes me to lie down in green pastures; He leads me beside the still waters.

3. He restores my soul; He leads me in the paths of righteousness for His name's sake.

4. Yea, though I walk through the valley of the shadow of death, I will fear no evil; for You are with me; Your rod and Your staff, they comfort me.

5. You prepare a table before me in the presence of my enemies; You anoint my head with oil; my cup runs over.

6. Surely goodness and mercy shall follow me all the days of my life; and I will dwell in the house of the LORD forever.

Expository Study

Verse 1: The LORD is My Shepherd

Verse 1: "The LORD is my shepherd; I shall not want."

- The term "shepherd" (רֹעֶה, ro'eh) signifies a caretaker and protector, emphasizing God's intimate and caring role.

- "I shall not want" (אֶחְסָר לֹא, lo echsar) indicates complete provision and contentment in God's care.

Verse 2: Provision and Peace

Verse 2: "He makes me to lie down in green pastures; He leads me beside the still waters."

- "Lie down" (רָבַץ, rabats) implies rest and security.

- "Green pastures" (דֶּשֶׁא נְאוֹת, ne'ot deshe) symbolize abundant provision.

- "Still waters" (מְנֻחוֹת, menuchot) represent peace and tranquility.

Verse 3: Restoration and Righteousness

Verse 3: "He restores my soul; He leads me in the paths of righteousness for His name's sake."

- "Restores" (שׁוּב, shub) means to refresh or revive.

- "Paths of righteousness" (צֶדֶק מַעְגְּלֵי, ma'aglei tsedek) denote guidance in morally upright and just living.

Verse 4: Presence and Protection

Verse 4: "Yea, though I walk through the valley of the shadow of death, I will fear no evil; for You are with me; Your rod and Your staff, they comfort me."

- "Valley of the shadow of death" (צַלְמָוֶת גֵּיא, gei tsalmavet) represents extreme danger or deep darkness.

- "Fear no evil" (לֹא אִירָא רָע, lo ira ra) expresses confidence in God's protection.

- "Rod" (שֵׁבֶט, shevet) and "staff" (מִשְׁעֶנֶת, mishenet) symbolize tools of guidance and protection, providing comfort.

Verse 5: Honor and Abundance

Verse 5: "You prepare a table before me in the presence of my enemies; You anoint my head with oil; my cup runs over."

- "Prepare a table" (עָרַךְ, arak) indicates provision and honor.

- "Anoint" (דָּשֵׁן, dashan) symbolizes blessing and consecration.

- "My cup runs over" (כּוֹסִי רְוָיָה, kosi revayah) signifies abundance and overflowing blessings.

Verse 6: Goodness and Eternal Presence

Verse 6: "Surely goodness and mercy shall follow me all the days of my life; and I will dwell in the house of the LORD forever."

- "Goodness and mercy" (טוֹב וָחֶסֶד, tov vachesed) represent God's continual blessings and loving-kindness.

- "Dwell" (יָשַׁב, yashav) implies a permanent and secure residence.

- "House of the LORD" (בֵּית יְהוָה, beit YHWH) signifies God's presence and eternal fellowship.

Comprehensive Commentary

Theological Significance of the Shepherd King

1. Intimate Care and Provision: The imagery of God as a shepherd emphasizes His intimate care and provision for His people. The shepherd's role involves not only providing for the sheep's physical needs but also offering protection and guidance. This portrays a personal and loving relationship between God and His people (John 10:11-14).

2. Guidance in Righteousness: The Shepherd King leads His people in paths of righteousness, guiding them towards moral integrity and justice. This guidance is not for the sake of the followers alone but also for the sake of God's name, highlighting His commitment to His covenant and His desire for His people to reflect His character (Psalm 23:3).

3. Presence in Adversity: God's presence is a source of comfort and courage in the face of danger and adversity. The "valley of the shadow of death" symbolizes the darkest and most perilous moments in life, yet the assurance of God's presence dispels fear and brings comfort (Psalm 23:4, Isaiah 41:10).

4. Honor and Abundance: The Shepherd King not only provides but also honors His people in the presence of their enemies. The preparation of a table, the anointing with oil, and the overflowing cup signify God's abundant blessings and the honor He bestows upon His faithful ones (Psalm 23:5, 1 Samuel 2:30).

5. Eternal Fellowship: The promise of dwelling in the house of the LORD forever speaks to the eternal fellowship and security found in God's presence. This eternal dwelling reflects the ultimate hope of believers to be in the presence of God for all eternity (Psalm 23:6, Revelation 21:3).

Exegetical Insights

1. Psalm 23:1: The declaration "The LORD is my shepherd" affirms a personal relationship with God. The term "shepherd" (רֹעֶה, ro'eh) conveys care, guidance, and protection, while "I shall not want" (לֹא אֶחְסָר, lo echsar) indicates complete satisfaction and provision in God's care.

2. Psalm 23:2-3: The imagery of "green pastures" and "still waters" symbolizes peace, rest, and abundant provision. "Restores my soul" (שׁוּב, shub) signifies spiritual renewal,

while "paths of righteousness" (צֶדֶק מַעְגְּלֵי, ma'aglei tsedek) highlight the moral and ethical guidance God provides.

3. Psalm 23:4: The "valley of the shadow of death" represents the darkest and most threatening experiences. The assurance "I will fear no evil" (רָע אִירָא לֹא, lo ira ra) is grounded in God's presence. The "rod" (שֵׁבֶט, shevet) and "staff" (מִשְׁעֶנֶת, mishenet) symbolize both protection and guidance, bringing comfort to the believer.

4. Psalm 23:5: The preparation of a table and the anointing with oil signify honor and blessing. The phrase "my cup runs over" (רְוָיָה כּוֹסִי, kosi revayah) indicates an abundance of blessings, reflecting God's generosity and provision.

5. Psalm 23:6: "Goodness and mercy" (וָחֶסֶד טוּב, tov vachesed) encompass God's continual blessings and loving-kindness. The promise to "dwell in the house of the LORD forever" (יְהוָה בֵּית, beit YHWH) assures believers of eternal fellowship and security in God's presence.

Practical Applications

1. Trust in God's Provision: Believers can trust in God's provision and care, knowing that He is the Good Shepherd who meets all their needs. This trust fosters contentment and gratitude, freeing believers from anxiety and worry about their daily needs (Matthew 6:25-34).

2. Seek God's Guidance: Recognizing God as the Shepherd King encourages believers to seek His guidance in their daily lives. Following His paths of righteousness leads to moral integrity and aligns believers with God's will (Proverbs 3:5-6).

3. Find Comfort in God's Presence: In times of fear and adversity, believers can find comfort and courage in the assurance of God's presence. Knowing that God is with them

in the darkest valleys dispels fear and provides strength to endure (Isaiah 43:2).

4. Rejoice in God's Blessings: Believers are invited to rejoice in the abundant blessings and honor that God bestows upon them. This joy leads to a life of worship and gratitude, reflecting the overflowing cup of God's generosity (Ephesians 1:3).

5. Hope in Eternal Fellowship: The promise of dwelling in the house of the LORD forever provides believers with hope and assurance of eternal fellowship with God. This hope motivates believers to live faithfully and anticipate the ultimate fulfillment of God's promises (John 14:1-3).

Conclusion

Psalm 23 offers a profound and comforting portrayal of God as the Shepherd King who provides, guides, and protects His people. Through detailed expository study and comprehensive commentary, we have explored the theological significance and practical applications of this beloved Psalm. This chapter has provided a thorough analysis of Psalm 23:1-6, enhancing our understanding and strengthening our faith in God as our compassionate and faithful Shepherd King.

Jesus as the Good Shepherd

The imagery of the shepherd is central to understanding Jesus' role and relationship with His followers. Jesus explicitly identifies Himself as the Good Shepherd, highlighting His care, guidance, and sacrificial love for His flock. This chapter will explore the concept of Jesus as the Good Shepherd, using Bible verses, an expository study, and comprehensive commentary, supported by Strong's Exhaustive Concordance.

Biblical Foundation

John 10:11-18: The Good Shepherd

John 10:11-18: "I am the good shepherd. The good shepherd gives His life for the sheep. But a hireling, he who is not the shepherd, one who does not own the sheep, sees the wolf coming and leaves the sheep and flees; and the wolf catches the sheep and scatters them. The hireling flees because he is a hireling and does not care about the sheep. I am the good shepherd; and I know My sheep, and am known by My own. As the Father knows Me, even so I know the Father; and I lay down My life for the sheep. And other sheep I have which are not of this fold; them also I must bring, and they will hear My voice; and there will be one flock and one shepherd. Therefore My Father loves Me, because I lay down My life that I may take it again. No one takes it from Me, but I lay it down of Myself. I have power to lay it down, and I have power to take it again. This command I have received from My Father."

- "Good shepherd" (ποιμὴν καλός, poimēn kalos) signifies an ideal and noble shepherd.

- "Gives His life" (τίθησιν τὴν ψυχὴν, tithēsin tēn psychēn) underscores Jesus' sacrificial love.

Psalm 23: The Shepherd Psalm

Psalm 23: This Psalm portrays God as the Shepherd who provides, guides, and protects His people. Jesus, as the Good Shepherd, fulfills and embodies these attributes in His ministry.

Ezekiel 34:11-16: God's Promise of a Shepherd

Ezekiel 34:11-16: "For thus says the Lord GOD: 'Indeed I Myself will search for My sheep and seek them out. As a shepherd seeks out his flock on the day he is among his scattered sheep, so will I seek out My sheep and deliver them from all the places where they were scattered on a cloudy and dark day. And I will bring them out from the peoples and gather them from the countries, and will bring them to their own land; I will feed them on the mountains of Israel, in the valleys and in all the inhabited places of the country. I will feed them in good pasture, and their fold shall be on the high mountains of Israel. There they shall lie down in a good fold and feed in rich pasture on the mountains of Israel. I will feed My flock, and I will make them lie down,' says the Lord GOD. 'I will seek what was lost and bring back what was driven away, bind up the broken and strengthen what was sick; but I will destroy the fat and the strong, and feed them in judgment.'"

- "Seek out My sheep" (אֶת־צֹאנִי בִקֵּר, biqer et-tso'ni) emphasizes God's active pursuit and care for His people.

Isaiah 40:11: The Tender Shepherd

Isaiah 40:11: "He will feed His flock like a shepherd; He will gather the lambs with His arm, and carry them in His bosom, and gently lead those who are with young."

- "Feed His flock" (צֹאנוֹ רָעָה, ra'ah tso'no) highlights provision and care.

- "Gently lead" (נָהַל, nahal) signifies tender guidance.

Expository Study

Jesus as the Good Shepherd in John 10

John 10:11-13: Jesus contrasts Himself with the hireling who abandons the sheep at the sign of danger. The Good Shepherd lays down His life for the sheep, demonstrating sacrificial love and commitment.

- "Good shepherd" (ποιμήν καλός, poimēn kalos) emphasizes the ideal nature of Jesus' shepherding.

- "Gives His life" (τίθησιν τὴν ψυχὴν, tithēsin tēn psychēn) underscores the ultimate sacrifice Jesus makes for His followers.

John 10:14-16: Jesus emphasizes His intimate knowledge of His sheep and their recognition of His voice. He also speaks of bringing other sheep into the fold, indicating the inclusive nature of His mission.

- "Know My sheep" (γινώσκω τὰ ἐμά, ginōskō ta ema) signifies an intimate and personal relationship.

- "One flock and one shepherd" (μία ποίμνη, εἷς ποιμήν, mia poimnē, heis poimēn) highlights unity under Jesus' leadership.

John 10:17-18: Jesus speaks of His authority to lay down His life and take it up again, highlighting His voluntary sacrifice and divine authority.

- "Lay it down of Myself" (τίθημι αὐτὴν ἀπ' ἐμαυτοῦ, tithēmi autēn ap' emautou) underscores Jesus' voluntary and willing sacrifice.

Fulfillment of Old Testament Imagery

Psalm 23: Jesus embodies the characteristics of the Shepherd King described in Psalm 23. He provides for His followers, guides them in righteousness, and protects them from harm.

- "Green pastures" and "still waters" symbolize the peace and provision Jesus offers.

- "Paths of righteousness" and "valley of the shadow of death" reflect Jesus' guidance and protection.

Ezekiel 34:11-16: Jesus fulfills God's promise to seek out His sheep, deliver them, and care for them. His ministry reflects the compassionate and active shepherding described in Ezekiel.

- "Seek what was lost" parallels Jesus' mission to save the lost (Luke 19:10).

- "Bind up the broken" reflects Jesus' healing ministry (Isaiah 61:1-2).

Isaiah 40:11: Jesus' tender care for His followers is reflected in His actions and teachings. He provides for their needs, carries them through difficulties, and leads them gently.

- "Gather the lambs with His arm" signifies Jesus' protective embrace.

- "Gently lead" reflects His compassionate guidance.

Comprehensive Commentary

Theological Significance of Jesus as the Good Shepherd

1. Sacrificial Love: Jesus' identification as the Good Shepherd highlights His sacrificial love. His willingness to lay down His life for the sheep demonstrates the depth of His commitment and the extent of His love (John 10:11, 15).

2. Intimate Knowledge: The Good Shepherd knows His sheep intimately and is known by them. This mutual knowledge signifies a deep and personal relationship between Jesus and His followers, reflecting the intimate care and guidance He provides (John 10:14).

3. Inclusion and Unity: Jesus' mission includes bringing other sheep into the fold, signifying the inclusive nature of His ministry. This inclusivity highlights the unity of all believers under one Shepherd, breaking down barriers and creating one flock (John 10:16).

4. Divine Authority: Jesus' authority to lay down His life and take it up again underscores His divine nature and mission. This authority highlights His voluntary sacrifice and the power of His resurrection (John 10:17-18).

5. Fulfillment of Prophecy: Jesus as the Good Shepherd fulfills Old Testament prophecies and imagery. His ministry reflects the shepherding role described in passages like Psalm 23, Ezekiel 34, and Isaiah 40, affirming His messianic identity and divine mission.

Exegetical Insights

1. John 10:11: The term "good shepherd" (ποιμήν καλός, poimēn kalos) emphasizes the ideal nature of Jesus' shepherding. His willingness to "give His life" (τίθησιν τὴν ψυχὴν, tithēsin tēn psychēn) underscores the sacrificial nature of His love and care.

2. John 10:14: The intimate knowledge between the shepherd and the sheep is highlighted by the term "know" (γινώσκω, ginōskō). This mutual recognition signifies a deep and personal relationship, reflecting Jesus' care for each individual follower.

3. John 10:16: The phrase "one flock and one shepherd" (μία ποίμνη, εἷς ποιμήν, mia poimnē, heis poimēn) underscores the unity and inclusivity of Jesus' mission. His desire to bring all believers into one fold reflects the universal scope of His ministry.

4. John 10:17-18: Jesus' authority to lay down His life and take it up again is emphasized by the terms "lay it down" (τίθημι, tithēmi) and "take it again" (λαμβάνω, lambanō). This authority underscores His voluntary sacrifice and the power of His resurrection.

Practical Applications

1. Trust in Jesus' Sacrificial Love: Believers can trust in Jesus' sacrificial love, knowing that He laid down His life for them. This trust fosters a deep sense of security and gratitude, motivating believers to live in response to His love (John 15:13).

2. Pursue Intimacy with Jesus: Recognizing Jesus as the Good Shepherd encourages believers to cultivate an intimate relationship with Him. This intimacy involves knowing Jesus personally and being known by Him, leading to deeper faith and obedience (John 10:14).

3. Embrace Inclusivity and Unity: Jesus' mission to bring other sheep into the fold calls believers to embrace inclusivity and unity. This involves breaking down barriers, welcoming others into the faith, and fostering a sense of unity among all believers (Galatians 3:28).

4. Rely on Jesus' Guidance and Protection: As the Good Shepherd, Jesus provides guidance and protection for His followers. Believers can rely on His leading and trust in

His care, finding comfort and direction in their walk with Him (Psalm 23:1-4).

5. Live in the Assurance of Jesus' Authority: Jesus' authority to lay down His life and take it up again assures believers of His power over life and death. This assurance provides hope and confidence, knowing that Jesus has conquered death and offers eternal life (Romans 8:38-39).

Conclusion

Jesus as the Good Shepherd is a central and comforting image in Christian theology, highlighting His care, guidance, and sacrificial love for His followers. Through detailed expository study and comprehensive commentary, we have explored the biblical foundation, theological significance, and practical applications of Jesus' role as the Good Shepherd. This chapter has provided a thorough examination of Jesus' shepherding ministry, enhancing our understanding and strengthening our faith in Him as the compassionate and faithful Shepherd who leads us to eternal life.

Provision, Guidance, and Protection Through Jesus

Jesus Christ, as the Good Shepherd, offers His followers comprehensive care that encompasses provision, guidance, and protection. These aspects are integral to His role and highlight His deep commitment to the well-being of His flock. This chapter will explore how Jesus provides, guides, and protects His followers, using Bible verses, an expository study, and comprehensive commentary, supported by Strong's Exhaustive Concordance.

Provision Through Jesus

John 6:35: The Bread of Life

John 6:35: "And Jesus said to them, 'I am the bread of life. He who comes to Me shall never hunger, and he who believes in Me shall never thirst.'"

- "Bread of life" (ἄρτος τῆς ζωῆς, artos tēs zōēs) signifies spiritual sustenance.

- Jesus promises that those who come to Him will never experience spiritual hunger or thirst, indicating complete provision.

Philippians 4:19: Supply of Needs

Philippians 4:19: "And my God shall supply all your need according to His riches in glory by Christ Jesus."

- "Supply" (πληρόω, plēroō) means to fill or make full.

- "All your need" (πᾶσαν χρείαν, pasan chreian) indicates comprehensive provision for every aspect of life.

Psalm 23:1-2: The Shepherd's Provision

Psalm 23:1-2: "The LORD is my shepherd; I shall not want. He makes me to lie down in green pastures; He leads me beside the still waters."

- "I shall not want" (לֹא אֶחְסָר, lo echsar) signifies complete contentment and sufficiency.

- "Green pastures" (נְאוֹת דֶּשֶׁא, ne'ot deshe) and "still waters" (מְנֻחוֹת, menuchot) represent abundant provision and peace.

Guidance Through Jesus

John 10:3-4: The Shepherd's Voice

John 10:3-4: "To him the doorkeeper opens, and the sheep hear his voice; and he calls his own sheep by name and leads them out. And when he brings out his own sheep, he goes before them; and the sheep follow him, for they know his voice."

- "Calls his own sheep by name" (φωνεῖ τὰ ἴδια πρόβατα κατ' ὄνομα, phonei ta idia probata kat' onoma) indicates personal guidance.

- "Leads them out" (ἐξάγει αὐτά, exagei auta) and "goes before them" (προάγει αὐτά, proagei auta) emphasize Jesus' role in guiding His followers.

John 14:6: The Way, the Truth, and the Life

John 14:6: "Jesus said to him, 'I am the way, the truth, and the life. No one comes to the Father except through Me.'"
- "The way" (ἡ ὁδός, hē hodos) signifies the path to follow.
- "The truth" (ἡ ἀλήθεια, hē alētheia) and "the life" (ἡ ζωή, hē zōē) emphasize Jesus as the source of true guidance and life.
Psalm 23:3: Paths of Righteousness
Psalm 23:3: "He restores my soul; He leads me in the paths of righteousness for His name's sake."
- "Restores my soul" (שׁוּב, shub) means to refresh or revive.
- "Paths of righteousness" (צֶדֶק מַעְגְּלֵי, ma'aglei tsedek) indicate moral and ethical guidance.
Protection Through Jesus
John 10:11-12: The Good Shepherd's Sacrifice
John 10:11-12: "I am the good shepherd. The good shepherd gives His life for the sheep. But a hireling, he who is not the shepherd, one who does not own the sheep, sees the wolf coming and leaves the sheep and flees; and the wolf catches the sheep and scatters them."
- "Gives His life" (τίθησιν τὴν ψυχὴν, tithēsin tēn psychēn) underscores sacrificial protection.
- The contrast with the hireling highlights Jesus' commitment to protecting His flock.
John 10:28-29: Eternal Security
John 10:28-29: "And I give them eternal life, and they shall never perish; neither shall anyone snatch them out of My hand. My Father, who has given them to Me, is greater than all; and no one is able to snatch them out of My Father's hand."

- "Eternal life" (ζωὴν αἰώνιον, zōēn aiōnion) signifies everlasting protection.

- "No one shall snatch them" (οὐχ ἁρπάσει τις, ouch harpasei tis) emphasizes the security and protection Jesus provides.

Psalm 23:4: Comfort in Adversity

Psalm 23:4: "Yea, though I walk through the valley of the shadow of death, I will fear no evil; for You are with me; Your rod and Your staff, they comfort me."

- "Valley of the shadow of death" (צַלְמָוֶת גֵּיא, gei tsalmavet) represents extreme danger or deep darkness.

- "Rod" (שֵׁבֶט, shevet) and "staff" (מִשְׁעֶנֶת, mishenet) symbolize tools of protection and guidance.

Comprehensive Commentary

Theological Significance of Provision, Guidance, and Protection Through Jesus

1. Complete Provision: Jesus as the Bread of Life and the Good Shepherd ensures that His followers lack nothing essential for spiritual and physical well-being. His provision is comprehensive, covering all aspects of life, and assures believers of His continual care (John 6:35, Philippians 4:19, Psalm 23:1-2).

2. Personal and Ethical Guidance: Jesus' role as the Good Shepherd includes leading His followers on the right path. He provides personal guidance, knowing each of His sheep by name, and leads them in paths of righteousness. This guidance aligns believers with God's will and directs them toward moral and ethical living (John 10:3-4, John 14:6, Psalm 23:3).

3. Sacrificial Protection: Jesus' willingness to lay down His life for His sheep demonstrates the ultimate form of protection. His sacrificial love ensures the safety and security of His followers, both in this life and for eternity. Believers

are assured of their eternal security in His hands (John 10:11-12, John 10:28-29, Psalm 23:4).

Exegetical Insights

1. John 6:35 and Philippians 4:19: The imagery of Jesus as the "Bread of Life" and the assurance of God supplying all needs reflect the comprehensive nature of His provision. The term "bread" (ἄρτος, artos) signifies essential sustenance, while "supply" (πληρόω, plēroō) denotes the fullness of provision.

2. John 10:3-4 and John 14:6: Jesus' intimate knowledge of His followers and His declaration as "the way, the truth, and the life" highlight His role in guiding believers. The terms "know" (γινώσκω, ginōskō) and "leads" (ἐξάγει, exagei) emphasize personal and trustworthy guidance.

3. John 10:11-12 and John 10:28-29: The contrast between the Good Shepherd and the hireling, along with the promise of eternal security, underscores Jesus' commitment to protecting His flock. The terms "gives His life" (τίθησιν τὴν ψυχὴν, tithēsin tēn psychēn) and "no one shall snatch them" (οὐχ ἁρπάσει τις, ouch harpasei tis) highlight sacrificial and secure protection.

4. Psalm 23:1-4: The imagery in Psalm 23 of green pastures, still waters, and walking through the valley of the shadow of death reflects the comprehensive care of the Shepherd. The terms "want" (אֶחְסָר, echsar), "restores" (שׁוּב, shub), and "comfort" (נָחַם, nacham) denote provision, guidance, and protection respectively.

Practical Applications

1. Trust in Jesus' Provision: Believers are encouraged to trust in Jesus' provision, knowing that He meets all their needs. This trust leads to a life of contentment and gratitude, free from anxiety about material needs (Matthew 6:25-34).

2. Follow Jesus' Guidance: Recognizing Jesus as the guide of their lives, believers are called to seek His direction and follow His lead. This involves daily seeking His will and aligning their actions with His teachings (Proverbs 3:5-6).

3. Rest in Jesus' Protection: Understanding Jesus' role as protector provides believers with a sense of security and peace. They can rest assured that He guards their well-being and ensures their eternal safety, allowing them to live without fear (Romans 8:38-39).

4. Live Reflecting Jesus' Care: Believers are called to reflect Jesus' care in their own lives by providing, guiding, and protecting those around them. This involves acts of compassion, mentoring others, and standing up for the vulnerable, embodying the love of the Good Shepherd (Ephesians 5:1-2).

Conclusion

Jesus, as the Good Shepherd, offers His followers comprehensive care that includes provision, guidance, and protection. Through detailed expository study and comprehensive commentary, we have explored the biblical foundation, theological significance, and practical applications of these aspects of Jesus' ministry. This chapter has provided a thorough examination of how Jesus fulfills His role as the Good Shepherd, enhancing our understanding and strengthening our faith in His all-encompassing care for His flock.

New Testament Connections to Psalm 23

Psalm 23, often referred to as the Shepherd Psalm, portrays God as the Shepherd who provides, guides, and protects His people. The New Testament builds on these themes, particularly through the ministry and teachings of Jesus Christ, who identifies Himself as the Good Shepherd. This chapter will explore the New Testament connections to Psalm 23, using Bible verses, an expository study, and comprehensive commentary, supported by Strong's Exhaustive Concordance.

Jesus as the Good Shepherd in John 10

John 10:1-11: The Good Shepherd

John 10:1-11: "Most assuredly, I say to you, he who does not enter the sheepfold by the door, but climbs up some other way, the same is a thief and a robber. But he who enters by the door is the shepherd of the sheep. To him the doorkeeper opens, and the sheep hear his voice; and he calls his own sheep by name and leads them out. And when he brings out his own sheep, he goes before them; and the sheep follow him, for they know his voice. Yet they will by no means follow a stranger, but will flee from him, for they do not know the voice of strangers." Jesus used this illustration, but they did not understand the things which He spoke to them. Then Jesus said to them again, "Most assuredly, I say to you, I am the door of the sheep. All who ever came before Me are thieves and robbers, but the sheep did not hear them. I am the door. If anyone enters by Me, he will be saved, and will go in and out and find pasture. The thief does not come except to steal, and to kill, and to destroy. I have come that they may have life, and that they may have it more abundantly. I am the good shepherd. The good shepherd gives His life for the sheep."

- "Shepherd" (ποιμήν, poimēn) signifies the caretaker and guide.

- "Good" (καλός, kalos) highlights the noble and ideal nature of Jesus' shepherding.

Connection to Psalm 23

- Psalm 23:1: "The LORD is my shepherd; I shall not want."

- Jesus as the Good Shepherd provides for the needs of His flock, ensuring they "shall not want" (John 10:9-10).

- Psalm 23:2: "He makes me to lie down in green pastures; He leads me beside the still waters."

- Jesus leads His sheep to spiritual nourishment and rest, fulfilling the imagery of green pastures and still waters (John 10:9).

- Psalm 23:3: "He restores my soul; He leads me in the paths of righteousness for His name's sake."

- Jesus' guidance in paths of righteousness is reflected in His leading and knowing His sheep by name (John 10:3-4).

- Psalm 23:4: "Yea, though I walk through the valley of the shadow of death, I will fear no evil; for You are with me; Your rod and Your staff, they comfort me."

- Jesus' promise to give His life for the sheep and His presence with them even in danger echoes the comfort and protection of Psalm 23:4 (John 10:11).

Jesus as the Door in John 10

John 10:7-9: The Door of the Sheep

John 10:7-9: "Then Jesus said to them again, 'Most assuredly, I say to you, I am the door of the sheep. All who ever came before Me are thieves and robbers, but the sheep did not hear them. I am the door. If anyone enters by Me, he will be saved, and will go in and out and find pasture.'"

- "Door" (θύρα, thyra) signifies the entry point to safety and provision.

- "Saved" (σωθήσεται, sōthēsetai) indicates deliverance and security.

Connection to Psalm 23

- Psalm 23:2: "He makes me to lie down in green pastures; He leads me beside the still waters."

- Jesus as the Door provides access to safety and sustenance, akin to the green pastures and still waters in Psalm 23:2.

- Psalm 23:5: "You prepare a table before me in the presence of my enemies; You anoint my head with oil; my cup runs over."

- The provision and abundant life Jesus offers are reflected in the prepared table and overflowing cup of Psalm 23:5 (John 10:10).

Jesus as the Provider in the Gospels
Matthew 6:31-33: God's Provision

Matthew 6:31-33: "Therefore do not worry, saying, 'What shall we eat?' or 'What shall we drink?' or 'What shall we wear?' For after all these things the Gentiles seek. For your heavenly Father knows that you need all these things. But seek first the kingdom of God and His righteousness, and all these things shall be added to you."

- "Added" (προστεθήσεται, prostethēsetai) indicates provision and sufficiency.

Connection to Psalm 23
- Psalm 23:1: "The LORD is my shepherd; I shall not want."

- Jesus' teaching on God's provision in Matthew 6 aligns with the assurance of not wanting in Psalm 23:1.

- Psalm 23:6: "Surely goodness and mercy shall follow me all the days of my life; and I will dwell in the house of the LORD forever."

- The promise of goodness and mercy echoes Jesus' assurance of God's ongoing provision and care (Matthew 6:33).

Jesus as the Guide in the Gospels
John 14:6: The Way, the Truth, and the Life

John 14:6: "Jesus said to him, 'I am the way, the truth, and the life. No one comes to the Father except through Me.'"

- "Way" (ὁδός, hodos) signifies the path and direction.

- "Truth" (ἀλήθεια, alētheia) and "life" (ζωή, zōē) emphasize the true and living guidance of Jesus.

Connection to Psalm 23

- Psalm 23:3: "He leads me in the paths of righteousness for His name's sake."

- Jesus as "the way" aligns with His role in leading believers in paths of righteousness (John 14:6).

- Psalm 23:4: "For You are with me; Your rod and Your staff, they comfort me."

- Jesus' presence and guidance provide comfort and direction, fulfilling the shepherd's role in Psalm 23:4.

Jesus as the Protector in the Gospels

John 10:27-29: Eternal Security

John 10:27-29: "My sheep hear My voice, and I know them, and they follow Me. And I give them eternal life, and they shall never perish; neither shall anyone snatch them out of My hand. My Father, who has given them to Me, is greater than all; and no one is able to snatch them out of My Father's hand."

- "Eternal life" (ζωὴν αἰώνιον, zōēn aiōnion) signifies everlasting protection.

- "Snatch" (ἁρπάζω, harpazō) indicates safety and security in Jesus' care.

Connection to Psalm 23

- Psalm 23:4: "I will fear no evil; for You are with me; Your rod and Your staff, they comfort me."

- The assurance of no one being able to snatch the sheep out of Jesus' hand reflects the comfort and protection promised in Psalm 23:4.

- Psalm 23:6: "And I will dwell in the house of the LORD forever."

- The promise of eternal life and dwelling in God's presence aligns with the eternal security and protection in Psalm 23:6 (John 10:28-29).

Comprehensive Commentary

Theological Significance of New Testament Connections to Psalm 23

1. Provision: Jesus as the Good Shepherd fulfills the promise of provision in Psalm 23. He offers spiritual sustenance and meets the needs of His followers, ensuring they lack nothing essential for life and godliness (John 6:35, Matthew 6:31-33).

2. Guidance: Jesus provides personal and ethical guidance, leading His followers in paths of righteousness. His teachings and presence guide believers in the way of truth and life, reflecting the guidance of the shepherd in Psalm 23 (John 14:6, John 10:3-4).

3. Protection: Jesus' sacrificial love and commitment to His sheep ensure their protection. He offers eternal security, promising that His followers will never be snatched from His hand, echoing the protection and comfort of the shepherd in Psalm 23 (John 10:11, 27-29).

Exegetical Insights

1. John 10:1-11 and Psalm 23: The imagery of Jesus as the Good Shepherd in John 10 parallels the shepherd imagery in Psalm 23. The terms "shepherd" (ποιμήν, poimēn) and "good" (καλός, kalos) highlight the ideal nature of Jesus' care, reflecting the comprehensive provision and protection of the shepherd in Psalm 23.

2. John 10:7-9 and Psalm 23: Jesus as the Door provides access to safety and provision, aligning with the imagery of green pastures and still waters in Psalm 23:2. The promise of salvation and finding pasture reflects the abundant life and prepared table in Psalm 23:5.

3. John 14:6 and Psalm 23: Jesus' declaration as "the way, the truth, and the life" underscores His role in guiding believers. The terms "way" (ὁδός, hodos), "truth" (ἀλήθεια, alētheia), and "life" (ζωή, zōē) emphasize the true and living guidance Jesus provides, paralleling the paths of righteousness in Psalm 23:3.

4. John 10:27-29 and Psalm 23: The promise of eternal life and protection in John 10 mirrors the comfort and security of the shepherd in Psalm 23. The terms "eternal life" (ζωὴν αἰώνιον, zōēn aiōnion) and "snatch" (ἁρπάζω, harpazō) highlight the assurance of safety and eternal dwelling in God's presence (Psalm 23:4, 6).

Practical Applications

1. Trust in Jesus' Provision: Believers are encouraged to trust in Jesus' provision, knowing that He meets all their needs. This trust fosters a life of contentment and gratitude, free from anxiety about material needs (Matthew 6:31-33).

2. Follow Jesus' Guidance: Recognizing Jesus as the guide of their lives, believers are called to seek His direction and follow His lead. This involves daily seeking His will and aligning their actions with His teachings (John 14:6).

3. Rest in Jesus' Protection: Understanding Jesus' role as protector provides believers with a sense of security and peace. They can rest assured that He guards their well-being and ensures their eternal safety, allowing them to live without fear (John 10:27-29).

4. Live Reflecting Jesus' Care: Believers are called to reflect Jesus' care in their own lives by providing, guiding, and protecting those around them. This involves acts of compassion, mentoring others, and standing up for the vulnerable, embodying the love of the Good Shepherd (Ephesians 5:1-2).

Conclusion

The New Testament connections to Psalm 23 highlight how Jesus Christ fulfills the roles of provision, guidance, and protection described in the Shepherd Psalm. Through detailed expository study and comprehensive commentary, we have explored the biblical foundation, theological significance, and practical applications of these connections. This chapter has provided a thorough examination of how Jesus embodies the shepherding care depicted in Psalm 23, enhancing our understanding and strengthening our faith in Him as the Good Shepherd who leads us to eternal life.

THE CORNERSTONE IN PSLAM 118

Psalm 118 is a psalm of thanksgiving and praise, often associated with the celebration of God's steadfast love and deliverance. Verses 22-29 of this psalm are particularly significant in both Jewish and Christian traditions, especially concerning the imagery of the cornerstone. This chapter will provide a detailed analysis of Psalm 118:22-29, exploring its theological significance and connections to New Testament references, using Bible verses, an expository study, and comprehensive commentary, supported by Strong's Exhaustive Concordance.

Text of Psalm 118:22-29 (NKJV)

22. The stone which the builders rejected has become the chief cornerstone.

23. This was the LORD's doing; it is marvelous in our eyes.

24. This is the day the LORD has made; we will rejoice and be glad in it.

25. Save now, I pray, O LORD; O LORD, I pray, send now prosperity.

26. Blessed is he who comes in the name of the LORD! We have blessed you from the house of the LORD.

27. God is the LORD, and He has given us light; bind the sacrifice with cords to the horns of the altar.

28. You are my God, and I will praise You; You are my God, I will exalt You.

29. Oh, give thanks to the LORD, for He is good! For His mercy endures forever.

Expository Study

Verse 22: The Rejected Stone

Verse 22: "The stone which the builders rejected has become the chief cornerstone."

- "Stone" (אֶבֶן, eben) symbolizes something solid and foundational.

- "Builders" (בּוֹנִים, bonim) refers to those who construct or establish.

- "Rejected" (מָאַס, ma'as) indicates being cast aside or deemed unworthy.

- "Chief cornerstone" (פִּנָּה רֹאשׁ, rosh pinnah) denotes the most important stone in a structure, often used metaphorically for someone essential to God's plan.

Verse 23: The LORD's Doing

Verse 23: "This was the LORD's doing; it is marvelous in our eyes."

- "LORD's doing" (יְהוָה מֵאֵת, me'et YHWH) indicates divine action or intervention.

- "Marvelous" (פָּלָא, pala) suggests something extraordinary or miraculous.

Verse 24: A Day for Rejoicing

Verse 24: "This is the day the LORD has made; we will rejoice and be glad in it."

- "Day" (יוֹם, yom) signifies a time appointed by God.

- "Rejoice" (גִּיל, gil) and "be glad" (שָׂמַח, samach) both denote joy and celebration.

Verse 25: A Prayer for Salvation and Prosperity

Verse 25: "Save now, I pray, O LORD; O LORD, I pray, send now prosperity."

- "Save now" (הוֹשִׁיעָה נָּא, hoshi'ah na) is a plea for deliverance, also seen in the cry "Hosanna" in the New Testament.

- "Prosperity" (הַצְלִיחָה, hatzlichah) refers to success or well-being.

Verse 26: Blessing in the Name of the LORD

Verse 26: "Blessed is he who comes in the name of the LORD! We have blessed you from the house of the LORD."

- "Blessed" (בָּרוּךְ, baruch) implies divine favor and praise.

- "Name of the LORD" (יְהוָה בְּשֵׁם, b'shem YHWH) signifies acting under God's authority and blessing.

Verse 27: Light and Sacrifice

Verse 27: "God is the LORD, and He has given us light; bind the sacrifice with cords to the horns of the altar."

- "Light" (אוֹר, or) symbolizes guidance, revelation, and salvation.

- "Sacrifice" (חַג, chag) and "horns of the altar" (קַרְנוֹת הַמִּזְבֵּחַ, karnot hamizbeach) refer to acts of worship and atonement.

Verse 28: Personal Praise and Exaltation

Verse 28: "You are my God, and I will praise You; You are my God, I will exalt You."

- "Praise" (אוֹדֶה, odeh) and "exalt" (רוּם, rum) reflect adoration and lifting up of God.

Verse 29: Thanksgiving for God's Goodness

Verse 29: "Oh, give thanks to the LORD, for He is good! For His mercy endures forever."

- "Give thanks" (הוֹדוּ, hodu) is a call to worship and gratitude.

- "Mercy" (חֶסֶד, chesed) signifies God's steadfast love and faithfulness.

Comprehensive Commentary

The Rejected Stone and the Chief Cornerstone

1. Prophetic Significance: The imagery of the rejected stone becoming the chief cornerstone is a powerful prophetic metaphor. It signifies that what was dismissed or undervalued by human standards has been elevated by divine decree to a place of utmost importance. In the New Testament, Jesus identifies Himself with this cornerstone, fulfilling this prophecy (Matthew 21:42, Acts 4:11, 1 Peter 2:7).

2. Divine Action: The phrase "This was the LORD's doing" underscores that the establishment of the cornerstone is an act of God, not of human effort. It highlights the miraculous and extraordinary nature of God's intervention in human affairs (Psalm 118:23).

A Day for Rejoicing

1. Divine Appointment: The day referred to in verse 24 is seen as a specific time appointed by God for His purposes to be fulfilled. It invites believers to rejoice and be glad, recognizing God's sovereignty and goodness in orchestrating events (Psalm 118:24).

2. Celebration of Deliverance: This verse is often associated with celebrations of deliverance and victory. It calls believers to acknowledge and celebrate God's saving acts with joy and gratitude.

A Prayer for Salvation and Prosperity

1. Cry for Deliverance: The plea "Save now" (hoshi'ah na) is directly connected to the New Testament cry of

"Hosanna," which the crowds shouted as Jesus entered Jerusalem (Matthew 21:9). It reflects a deep yearning for salvation and divine intervention.

2. Desire for Well-being: The request for prosperity indicates a desire for overall well-being and success, encompassing both physical and spiritual dimensions (Psalm 118:25).

Blessing in the Name of the LORD

1. Messianic Expectation: "Blessed is he who comes in the name of the LORD" is another phrase that finds fulfillment in the New Testament. It was proclaimed during Jesus' triumphal entry into Jerusalem, identifying Him as the long-awaited Messiah (Matthew 21:9).

2. Divine Favor: Blessing someone in the name of the LORD conveys invoking God's favor and presence upon that person, recognizing their divine mission and authority (Psalm 118:26).

Light and Sacrifice

1. Guidance and Revelation: "He has given us light" signifies God's guidance, revelation, and salvation. Light often symbolizes divine truth and enlightenment, leading believers out of darkness (John 1:4-5, John 8:12).

2. Act of Worship: Binding the sacrifice to the altar's horns refers to an act of worship and atonement. It highlights the significance of sacrificial worship in maintaining a relationship with God (Psalm 118:27).

Personal Praise and Exaltation

1. Intimate Relationship: The declaration "You are my God" reflects a personal and intimate relationship with the divine. It underscores the believer's commitment to worship and exalt God (Psalm 118:28).

2. Expressions of Worship: Praise and exaltation are central themes, reflecting heartfelt adoration and the lifting up

of God's name in worship. These expressions are integral to the believer's spiritual life (Psalm 118:28).

Thanksgiving for God's Goodness

1. Call to Gratitude: The repeated call to give thanks to the LORD for His goodness and enduring mercy emphasizes the importance of gratitude in the believer's life. God's steadfast love (chesed) is a central theme, reminding believers of His unwavering faithfulness (Psalm 118:29).

2. Perpetual Mercy: The enduring nature of God's mercy reassures believers of His constant presence and faithfulness. It encourages a continuous attitude of thanksgiving and trust in God's everlasting love (Psalm 118:29).

New Testament Connections

Jesus as the Cornerstone

Matthew 21:42: "Jesus said to them, 'Have you never read in the Scriptures: "The stone which the builders rejected has become the chief cornerstone. This was the LORD's doing, and it is marvelous in our eyes"?'"

- Jesus directly quotes Psalm 118:22-23, applying the imagery of the rejected stone to Himself and affirming His role as the cornerstone of God's kingdom.

Acts 4:11: "This is the 'stone which was rejected by you builders, which has become the chief cornerstone.'

- Peter, speaking to the religious leaders, identifies Jesus as the cornerstone, emphasizing the fulfillment of the prophecy in Psalm 118.

1 Peter 2:7: "Therefore, to you who believe, He is precious; but to those who are disobedient, 'The stone which the builders rejected has become the chief cornerstone,'"

- Peter reinforces the significance of Jesus as the cornerstone for believers and the rejection by those who disobey.

The Day the LORD Has Made

Matthew 21:9: "Then the multitudes who went before and those who followed cried out, saying: 'Hosanna to the Son of David! Blessed is He who comes in the name of the LORD! Hosanna in the highest!'"

- The cry of "Hosanna" and the blessing in the name of the LORD during Jesus' triumphal entry reflect the fulfillment of Psalm 118:25-26.

Light and Sacrifice

John 8:12: "Then Jesus spoke to them again, saying, 'I am the light of the world. He who follows Me shall not walk in darkness, but have the light of life.'"

- Jesus identifies Himself as the light, fulfilling the imagery of God giving light in Psalm 118:27.

Personal Praise and Exaltation

Romans 15:11: "And again: 'Praise the LORD, all you Gentiles! Laud Him, all you peoples!'"

- Paul's call for all to praise the LORD reflects the personal and communal worship expressed in Psalm 118:28.

Thanksgiving for God's Goodness

1 Thessalonians 5:18: "In everything give thanks; for this is the will of God in Christ Jesus for you."

- The call to give thanks aligns with the repeated exhortation to gratitude in Psalm 118:29.

Practical Applications

1. Recognize Jesus as the Cornerstone: Believers are called to recognize and honor Jesus as the cornerstone of their faith. This recognition involves trusting in His role as the foundation of their spiritual lives and acknowledging His supreme authority (Ephesians 2:19-22).

2. Celebrate God's Deliverance: The call to rejoice in the day the LORD has made encourages believers to celebrate God's acts of deliverance and provision. This celebration fosters a spirit of joy and gratitude, acknowledging God's sovereignty in their lives (Psalm 118:24).

3. Cry Out for Salvation and Prosperity: The plea for salvation and prosperity invites believers to actively seek God's intervention and blessings in their lives. It encourages a posture of dependence on God and confidence in His ability to save and provide (Psalm 118:25).

4. Bless in the Name of the LORD: Believers are encouraged to bless others in the name of the LORD, invoking God's favor and acknowledging His authority. This practice fosters a spirit of blessing and recognition of God's work in and through others (Psalm 118:26).

5. Offer Sacrificial Worship: The imagery of binding the sacrifice to the altar encourages believers to offer their lives as living sacrifices in worship to God. It emphasizes the importance of dedicated and wholehearted worship (Romans 12:1).

6. Maintain an Attitude of Gratitude: The repeated call to give thanks for God's goodness and mercy encourages believers to cultivate a continuous attitude of gratitude. Recognizing God's steadfast love and faithfulness fosters trust and thanksgiving in all circumstances (1 Thessalonians 5:18).

Conclusion

Psalm 118:22-29 offers rich imagery and themes that find significant connections in the New Testament, particularly through the person and work of Jesus Christ. Through detailed expository study and comprehensive commentary, we have explored the theological significance, New Testament connections, and practical applications of these verses. This chapter has provided a thorough examination of Psalm 118:22-29, enhancing our understanding and deepening our faith in Jesus as the cornerstone, the one who brings light, salvation, and eternal blessings.

Jesus as the Rejected Stone

The imagery of the rejected stone becoming the cornerstone is a powerful and prophetic theme in Scripture, deeply intertwined with the identity and mission of Jesus Christ. This chapter will explore the concept of Jesus as the rejected stone, examining its biblical foundations, theological significance, and New Testament fulfillment. We will use Bible verses, an expository study, and comprehensive commentary, supported by Strong's Exhaustive Concordance.

Biblical Foundation

Psalm 118:22-23: The Rejected Stone

Psalm 118:22-23: "The stone which the builders rejected has become the chief cornerstone. This was the LORD's doing; it is marvelous in our eyes."

- "Stone" (אֶבֶן, eben) signifies a solid and foundational element.

- "Builders" (בּוֹנִים, bonim) refers to those constructing or establishing a structure.

- "Rejected" (מָאַס, ma'as) means to cast aside or deem unworthy.

- "Chief cornerstone" (פִּנָּה רֹאשׁ, rosh pinnah) denotes the most important stone in a building, crucial for its stability and alignment.

Expository Study

The Rejection by Builders

Psalm 118:22: The stone's rejection by the builders symbolizes the dismissal of something or someone perceived as unfit or unnecessary by human standards. The builders represent the leaders and authorities who make decisions about what is valuable and essential.

Psalm 118:23: The elevation of the rejected stone to the position of the chief cornerstone is depicted as the LORD's doing, emphasizing divine intervention and approval. This act is described as marvelous, highlighting its extraordinary and awe-inspiring nature.

New Testament Fulfillment

Matthew 21:42: Jesus' Application of the Psalm

Matthew 21:42: "Jesus said to them, 'Have you never read in the Scriptures: "The stone which the builders rejected has become the chief cornerstone. This was the LORD's doing, and it is marvelous in our eyes"?'"

- Jesus directly quotes Psalm 118:22-23, applying the imagery of the rejected stone to Himself. This declaration comes after the parable of the wicked tenants, in which the tenants (representing the religious leaders) reject the son of the vineyard owner (representing Jesus).

Acts 4:11: Peter's Declaration

Acts 4:11: "This is the 'stone which was rejected by you builders, which has become the chief cornerstone.'"

- Peter, addressing the Sanhedrin, identifies Jesus as the rejected stone, emphasizing that the religious leaders' rejection of Jesus fulfills the prophecy in Psalm 118:22-23.

1 Peter 2:4-8: The Living Stone

1 Peter 2:4-8: "Coming to Him as to a living stone, rejected indeed by men, but chosen by God and precious, you also, as living stones, are being built up a spiritual house, a holy priesthood, to offer up spiritual sacrifices acceptable to God through Jesus Christ. Therefore it is also contained in the Scripture, 'Behold, I lay in Zion a chief cornerstone, elect, precious, and he who believes on Him will by no means be put to shame.' Therefore, to you who believe, He is precious; but to those who are disobedient, 'The stone which the builders rejected has become the chief cornerstone,' and 'A stone of stumbling and a rock of offense.' They stumble, being disobedient to the word, to which they also were appointed."

- Peter elaborates on the concept of Jesus as the living stone, both rejected by men and chosen by God. He emphasizes that believers are also living stones, being built into a spiritual house with Jesus as the cornerstone.

Theological Significance

Jesus as the Fulfillment of Prophecy

1. Divine Plan: The rejection and subsequent elevation of Jesus as the cornerstone were part of God's divine plan. This fulfillment of prophecy underscores the sovereignty of God and His purpose in bringing salvation through Jesus Christ (Matthew 21:42, Acts 4:11).

2. Messianic Identity: Jesus' identification as the rejected stone highlights His messianic identity. The rejection by the religious leaders and His crucifixion were not failures but necessary steps in the fulfillment of His redemptive mission (1 Peter 2:4-8).

Rejection and Elevation

1. Human Rejection: The rejection of Jesus by the builders (religious leaders) symbolizes humanity's rejection of God's chosen means of salvation. This rejection is a recurring theme in the Gospels, where Jesus is continually opposed and ultimately crucified (Matthew 21:42, Acts 4:11).

2. Divine Elevation: Despite human rejection, God elevates Jesus to the position of the chief cornerstone. This elevation signifies His supreme importance in God's redemptive plan and His role as the foundation of the Church (Psalm 118:22-23, 1 Peter 2:6-7).

The Cornerstone's Role

1. Foundation of the Church: As the chief cornerstone, Jesus is the foundation upon which the Church is built. This foundational role signifies stability, alignment, and unity for believers, who are also described as living stones being built into a spiritual house (Ephesians 2:19-22, 1 Peter 2:4-5).

2. Judgment and Salvation: The cornerstone imagery also signifies judgment for those who reject Jesus and salvation for those who believe. The same stone that brings stability and alignment to believers becomes a stone of stumbling and offense to those who disobey (1 Peter 2:7-8).

Exegetical Insights

Matthew 21:42 and Psalm 118:22-23

1. Quotation and Context: Jesus' quotation of Psalm 118:22-23 in Matthew 21:42 occurs in the context of the parable of the wicked tenants. This parable, which depicts the rejection and killing of the vineyard owner's son, illustrates the religious leaders' rejection of Jesus. By quoting the Psalm, Jesus directly connects the parable to the prophecy, highlighting His role as the rejected stone (Matthew 21:33-41).

2. Fulfillment and Marvel: Jesus emphasizes that the fulfillment of this prophecy is the LORD's doing and is marvelous. This marvel indicates the extraordinary and divinely orchestrated nature of His rejection and elevation, underscoring the theological significance of His role as the cornerstone (Matthew 21:42).

Acts 4:11 and Psalm 118:22-23

1. Peter's Bold Declaration: In Acts 4:11, Peter boldly declares Jesus as the rejected stone, addressing the same religious leaders who condemned Jesus. This declaration follows the healing of a lame man and Peter's defense before the Sanhedrin, emphasizing the power and authority of Jesus as the cornerstone (Acts 4:8-10).

2. Cornerstone for Salvation: Peter's identification of Jesus as the cornerstone highlights His essential role in salvation. The rejection by the builders (religious leaders) contrasts with God's elevation of Jesus, underscoring the necessity of recognizing Jesus' divine authority and messianic identity (Acts 4:12).

1 Peter 2:4-8 and Psalm 118:22-23

1. Living Stone and Believers: Peter expands the imagery of the cornerstone by describing Jesus as the living stone and believers as living stones being built into a spiritual house. This metaphor emphasizes the dynamic and communal nature of the Church, with Jesus as the foundation and believers as integral parts of the structure (1 Peter 2:4-5).

2. Honor and Stumbling: Peter contrasts the honor given to believers who accept Jesus with the stumbling and offense experienced by those who reject Him. This dual role of the cornerstone underscores the necessity of faith in Jesus for salvation and the consequences of rejecting Him (1 Peter 2:7-8).

Practical Applications

1. Recognize Jesus as the Cornerstone: Believers are called to recognize and honor Jesus as the cornerstone of their faith. This recognition involves trusting in His foundational role and aligning their lives with His teachings, ensuring stability and unity within the Church (Ephesians 2:19-22).

2. Embrace the Rejected Stone: Understanding Jesus as the rejected stone encourages believers to embrace Him despite opposition and rejection by the world. This embrace involves a commitment to follow Jesus and proclaim His authority, even in the face of adversity (1 Peter 2:4-5).

3. Build on the Foundation: Believers are invited to build their lives on the foundation of Jesus, the chief cornerstone. This building process involves growing in faith, participating in the life of the Church, and contributing to the spiritual house being constructed by God (1 Corinthians 3:10-11, 1 Peter 2:5).

4. Proclaim the Marvelous Deeds: The marvel of Jesus' rejection and elevation calls believers to proclaim His marvelous deeds. This proclamation involves sharing the

gospel, testifying to Jesus' redemptive work, and inviting others to recognize Him as the cornerstone (1 Peter 2:9).

Conclusion

The imagery of Jesus as the rejected stone that becomes the chief cornerstone is a profound and central theme in Scripture. Through detailed expository study and comprehensive commentary, we have explored the biblical foundation, New Testament fulfillment, and theological significance of this concept. This chapter has provided a thorough examination of Jesus' role as the cornerstone, enhancing our understanding and strengthening our faith in Him as the foundation of our salvation and the Church.

The Cornerstone of Salvation

The metaphor of Jesus as the cornerstone is foundational to Christian theology. This imagery, originating in the Old Testament and fulfilled in the New Testament, illustrates Jesus' essential role in God's plan for humanity's redemption. This chapter will explore the concept of Jesus as the cornerstone of salvation, examining its biblical foundations, theological significance, and practical implications for believers. We will use Bible verses, an expository study, and comprehensive commentary, supported by Strong's Exhaustive Concordance.

Biblical Foundation

Psalm 118:22-23: The Rejected Stone

Psalm 118:22-23: "The stone which the builders rejected has become the chief cornerstone. This was the LORD's doing; it is marvelous in our eyes."

- "Stone" (אֶבֶן, eben) symbolizes something solid and foundational.

- "Builders" (בּוֹנִים, bonim) refers to those constructing or establishing.

- "Rejected" (מָאַס, ma'as) indicates being cast aside or deemed unworthy.

- "Chief cornerstone" (פִּנָּה רֹאשׁ, rosh pinnah) denotes the most important stone in a structure, essential for stability and alignment.

Isaiah 28:16: The Precious Cornerstone

Isaiah 28:16: "Therefore thus says the Lord GOD: 'Behold, I lay in Zion a stone for a foundation, a tried stone, a precious cornerstone, a sure foundation; whoever believes will not act hastily.'"

- "Foundation" (יְסוֹד, yesod) indicates a base or support.

- "Tried stone" (בֹּחַן אֶבֶן, even bochan) signifies tested and proven reliability.

- "Precious" (יְקָר, yeqar) highlights value and worth.

- "Sure foundation" (מוּסָד מוּסָד, musad mussad) emphasizes stability and certainty.

Expository Study

The Rejected Stone Becomes the Cornerstone

Psalm 118:22-23: The metaphor of the stone rejected by builders becoming the chief cornerstone illustrates the reversal of human judgment by divine action. While the builders (religious leaders) deemed the stone (Jesus) unworthy, God established it as the cornerstone, essential for His redemptive plan.

Isaiah 28:16: The description of the cornerstone as a tested and precious stone underscores its reliability and value. God's establishment of this cornerstone in Zion signifies His provision of a sure foundation for His people, promising stability and security to those who trust in it.

New Testament Fulfillment

Matthew 21:42: Jesus' Declaration

Matthew 21:42: "Jesus said to them, 'Have you never read in the Scriptures: "The stone which the builders rejected has become the chief cornerstone. This was the LORD's doing, and it is marvelous in our eyes"?'"

- Jesus quotes Psalm 118:22-23, applying the imagery to Himself. His declaration follows the parable of the wicked tenants, highlighting the religious leaders' rejection and God's subsequent exaltation of Jesus as the cornerstone of salvation.

Acts 4:11-12: Peter's Proclamation

Acts 4:11-12: "This is the 'stone which was rejected by you builders, which has become the chief cornerstone.' Nor is there salvation in any other, for there is no other name under heaven given among men by which we must be saved."

- Peter, addressing the Sanhedrin, identifies Jesus as the cornerstone, emphasizing that salvation is found exclusively in Him. This declaration underscores the necessity of recognizing Jesus' role in God's redemptive plan.

Ephesians 2:19-22: The Foundation of the Church

Ephesians 2:19-22: "Now, therefore, you are no longer strangers and foreigners, but fellow citizens with the saints and members of the household of God, having been built on the foundation of the apostles and prophets, Jesus Christ Himself being the chief cornerstone, in whom the whole building, being fitted together, grows into a holy temple in the Lord, in whom you also are being built together for a dwelling place of God in the Spirit."

- Paul describes the Church as being built on the foundation of the apostles and prophets, with Jesus as the chief cornerstone. This imagery highlights Jesus' central role in the unity and growth of the Church.

1 Peter 2:4-8: The Living Stone

1 Peter 2:4-8: "Coming to Him as to a living stone, rejected indeed by men, but chosen by God and precious, you also, as living stones, are being built up a spiritual house, a holy priesthood, to offer up spiritual sacrifices acceptable to God through Jesus Christ. Therefore it is also contained in the Scripture, 'Behold, I lay in Zion a chief cornerstone, elect, precious, and he who believes on Him will by no means be

put to shame.' Therefore, to you who believe, He is precious; but to those who are disobedient, 'The stone which the builders rejected has become the chief cornerstone,' and 'A stone of stumbling and a rock of offense.' They stumble, being disobedient to the word, to which they also were appointed."

- Peter elaborates on the concept of Jesus as the living stone, both rejected by men and chosen by God. Believers are described as living stones being built into a spiritual house, with Jesus as the cornerstone. This passage underscores the dual role of Jesus as the foundation for believers and a stumbling block for those who reject Him.

Theological Significance

Jesus as the Fulfillment of Prophecy

1. Divine Plan: The elevation of Jesus as the cornerstone, despite His rejection by religious leaders, was part of God's divine plan. This fulfillment of prophecy underscores the sovereignty of God and His purpose in bringing salvation through Jesus Christ (Matthew 21:42, Acts 4:11-12).

2. Messianic Identity: Jesus' identification as the cornerstone highlights His messianic identity. The rejection by the builders and His crucifixion were necessary steps in the fulfillment of His redemptive mission (1 Peter 2:4-8).

Foundation of the Church

1. Unity and Growth: As the chief cornerstone, Jesus is the foundation upon which the Church is built. This foundational role signifies stability, alignment, and unity for believers, who are also described as living stones being built into a spiritual house (Ephesians 2:19-22, 1 Peter 2:4-5).

2. Spiritual House: The imagery of believers as living stones being built into a spiritual house emphasizes the communal and dynamic nature of the Church. Jesus, as the

cornerstone, ensures the integrity and growth of this spiritual structure (1 Peter 2:4-5).

Judgment and Salvation

1. Cornerstone and Stumbling Block: The cornerstone imagery signifies judgment for those who reject Jesus and salvation for those who believe. The same stone that brings stability and alignment to believers becomes a stone of stumbling and offense to those who disobey (1 Peter 2:7-8).

2. Exclusivity of Salvation: Peter's declaration that there is no salvation in any other name highlights the exclusivity of salvation through Jesus Christ. This exclusivity emphasizes the necessity of faith in Jesus for redemption and eternal life (Acts 4:12).

Exegetical Insights

Matthew 21:42 and Psalm 118:22-23

1. Quotation and Context: Jesus' quotation of Psalm 118:22-23 in Matthew 21:42 occurs in the context of the parable of the wicked tenants. This parable, which depicts the rejection and killing of the vineyard owner's son, illustrates the religious leaders' rejection of Jesus. By quoting the Psalm, Jesus directly connects the parable to the prophecy, highlighting His role as the cornerstone (Matthew 21:33-41).

2. Fulfillment and Marvel: Jesus emphasizes that the fulfillment of this prophecy is the LORD's doing and is marvelous. This marvel indicates the extraordinary and divinely orchestrated nature of His rejection and elevation, underscoring the theological significance of His role as the cornerstone (Matthew 21:42).

Acts 4:11-12 and Psalm 118:22-23

1. Peter's Bold Declaration: In Acts 4:11-12, Peter boldly declares Jesus as the rejected stone, addressing the same religious leaders who condemned Jesus. This declaration follows the healing of a lame man and Peter's defense before

the Sanhedrin, emphasizing the power and authority of Jesus as the cornerstone (Acts 4:8-10).

2. Cornerstone for Salvation: Peter's identification of Jesus as the cornerstone highlights His essential role in salvation. The rejection by the builders (religious leaders) contrasts with God's elevation of Jesus, underscoring the necessity of recognizing Jesus' divine authority and messianic identity (Acts 4:12).

1 Peter 2:4-8 and Isaiah 28:16

1. Living Stone and Believers: Peter expands the imagery of the cornerstone by describing Jesus as the living stone and believers as living stones being built into a spiritual house. This metaphor emphasizes the dynamic and communal nature of the Church, with Jesus as the foundation and believers as integral parts of the structure (1 Peter 2:4-5).

2. Honor and Stumbling: Peter contrasts the honor given to believers who accept Jesus with the stumbling and offense experienced by those who reject Him. This dual role of the cornerstone underscores the necessity of faith in Jesus for salvation and the consequences of rejecting Him (1 Peter 2:7-8).

Practical Applications

1. Recognize Jesus as the Cornerstone: Believers are called to recognize and honor Jesus as the cornerstone of their faith. This recognition involves trusting in His foundational role and aligning their lives with His teachings, ensuring stability and unity within the Church (Ephesians 2:19-22).

2. Build on the Foundation: Believers are invited to build their lives on the foundation of Jesus, the chief cornerstone. This building process involves growing in faith, participating in the life of the Church, and contributing to the spiritual house being constructed by God (1 Corinthians 3:10-11, 1 Peter 2:5).

3. Embrace the Rejected Stone: Understanding Jesus as the rejected stone encourages believers to embrace Him despite opposition and rejection by the world. This embrace involves a commitment to follow Jesus and proclaim His authority, even in the face of adversity (1 Peter 2:4-5).

4. Proclaim the Exclusivity of Salvation: Believers are called to proclaim the exclusivity of salvation through Jesus Christ. This proclamation involves sharing the gospel, testifying to Jesus' redemptive work, and inviting others to recognize Him as the cornerstone of their salvation (Acts 4:12).

Conclusion

The metaphor of Jesus as the cornerstone of salvation is a profound and central theme in Scripture. Through detailed expository study and comprehensive commentary, we have explored the biblical foundation, New Testament fulfillment, theological significance, and practical applications of this concept. This chapter has provided a thorough examination of Jesus' role as the cornerstone, enhancing our understanding and strengthening our faith in Him as the foundation of our salvation and the Church.

Fulfillment in the New Testament

The concept of the cornerstone, particularly as it pertains to Jesus Christ, is a recurring theme in both the Old and New Testaments. The New Testament writers, inspired by the Holy Spirit, saw the fulfillment of Old Testament prophecies in the person and work of Jesus. This chapter explores how the New Testament confirms and elaborates on the cornerstone imagery, emphasizing Jesus' pivotal role in God's redemptive plan.

Biblical Foundation
Psalm 118:22-23: The Rejected Stone

Psalm 118:22-23: "The stone which the builders rejected has become the chief cornerstone. This was the LORD's doing; it is marvelous in our eyes."

- "Stone" (אֶבֶן, eben) symbolizes something solid and foundational.

- "Builders" (בּוֹנִים, bonim) refers to those constructing or establishing.

- "Rejected" (מָאַס, ma'as) means to cast aside or deem unworthy.

- "Chief cornerstone" (פִּנָּה רֹאשׁ, rosh pinnah) denotes the most important stone in a structure, crucial for its stability and alignment.

New Testament Fulfillment

Matthew 21:42: Jesus' Declaration

Matthew 21:42: "Jesus said to them, 'Have you never read in the Scriptures: "The stone which the builders rejected has become the chief cornerstone. This was the LORD's doing, and it is marvelous in our eyes"?'"

- Jesus quotes Psalm 118:22-23, applying the prophecy to Himself. This declaration comes after the parable of the wicked tenants, where the tenants (religious leaders) reject the son of the vineyard owner (Jesus). By referencing the Psalm, Jesus directly connects His rejection and subsequent exaltation to God's divine plan.

Acts 4:11-12: Peter's Proclamation

Acts 4:11-12: "This is the 'stone which was rejected by you builders, which has become the chief cornerstone.' Nor is there salvation in any other, for there is no other name under heaven given among men by which we must be saved."

- Peter, addressing the Sanhedrin, identifies Jesus as the cornerstone. This declaration follows the healing of a lame man, which had led to Peter and John being questioned by the religious leaders. Peter's bold proclamation emphasizes that salvation is found exclusively in Jesus, the cornerstone rejected by the religious authorities but exalted by God.

Ephesians 2:19-22: The Foundation of the Church

Ephesians 2:19-22: "Now, therefore, you are no longer strangers and foreigners, but fellow citizens with the saints and members of the household of God, having been built on the foundation of the apostles and prophets, Jesus Christ Himself being the chief cornerstone, in whom the whole building, being fitted together, grows into a holy temple in the Lord, in whom you also are being built together for a dwelling place of God in the Spirit."

- Paul describes the Church as being built on the foundation of the apostles and prophets, with Jesus as the chief cornerstone. This imagery highlights Jesus' central role in the unity and growth of the Church, transforming believers into a holy temple for God's presence.

1 Peter 2:4-8: The Living Stone

1 Peter 2:4-8: "Coming to Him as to a living stone, rejected indeed by men, but chosen by God and precious, you also, as living stones, are being built up a spiritual house, a holy priesthood, to offer up spiritual sacrifices acceptable to God through Jesus Christ. Therefore it is also contained in the Scripture, 'Behold, I lay in Zion a chief cornerstone, elect, precious, and he who believes on Him will by no means be put to shame.' Therefore, to you who believe, He is precious; but to those who are disobedient, 'The stone which the builders rejected has become the chief cornerstone,' and 'A stone of stumbling and a rock of offense.' They stumble, being disobedient to the word, to which they also were appointed."

- Peter elaborates on Jesus as the living stone, both rejected by men and chosen by God. Believers are described as living stones being built into a spiritual house, with Jesus as the cornerstone. This passage underscores the dual role of

Jesus as the foundation for believers and a stumbling block for those who reject Him.

Theological Significance

Jesus as the Fulfillment of Prophecy

1. Divine Plan: The elevation of Jesus as the cornerstone, despite His rejection by religious leaders, was part of God's divine plan. This fulfillment of prophecy underscores the sovereignty of God and His purpose in bringing salvation through Jesus Christ (Matthew 21:42, Acts 4:11-12).

2. Messianic Identity: Jesus' identification as the cornerstone highlights His messianic identity. The rejection by the builders and His crucifixion were necessary steps in the fulfillment of His redemptive mission (1 Peter 2:4-8).

Foundation of the Church

1. Unity and Growth: As the chief cornerstone, Jesus is the foundation upon which the Church is built. This foundational role signifies stability, alignment, and unity for believers, who are also described as living stones being built into a spiritual house (Ephesians 2:19-22, 1 Peter 2:4-5).

2. Spiritual House: The imagery of believers as living stones being built into a spiritual house emphasizes the communal and dynamic nature of the Church. Jesus, as the cornerstone, ensures the integrity and growth of this spiritual structure (1 Peter 2:4-5).

Judgment and Salvation

1. Cornerstone and Stumbling Block: The cornerstone imagery signifies judgment for those who reject Jesus and salvation for those who believe. The same stone that brings stability and alignment to believers becomes a stone of stumbling and offense to those who disobey (1 Peter 2:7-8).

2. Exclusivity of Salvation: Peter's declaration that there is no salvation in any other name highlights the exclusivity of salvation through Jesus Christ. This exclusivity

emphasizes the necessity of faith in Jesus for redemption and eternal life (Acts 4:12).

Exegetical Insights

Matthew 21:42 and Psalm 118:22-23

1. Quotation and Context: Jesus' quotation of Psalm 118:22-23 in Matthew 21:42 occurs in the context of the parable of the wicked tenants. This parable, which depicts the rejection and killing of the vineyard owner's son, illustrates the religious leaders' rejection of Jesus. By quoting the Psalm, Jesus directly connects the parable to the prophecy, highlighting His role as the cornerstone (Matthew 21:33-41).

2. Fulfillment and Marvel: Jesus emphasizes that the fulfillment of this prophecy is the LORD's doing and is marvelous. This marvel indicates the extraordinary and divinely orchestrated nature of His rejection and elevation, underscoring the theological significance of His role as the cornerstone (Matthew 21:42).

Acts 4:11-12 and Psalm 118:22-23

1. Peter's Bold Declaration: In Acts 4:11-12, Peter boldly declares Jesus as the rejected stone, addressing the same religious leaders who condemned Jesus. This declaration follows the healing of a lame man and Peter's defense before the Sanhedrin, emphasizing the power and authority of Jesus as the cornerstone (Acts 4:8-10).

2. Cornerstone for Salvation: Peter's identification of Jesus as the cornerstone highlights His essential role in salvation. The rejection by the builders (religious leaders) contrasts with God's elevation of Jesus, underscoring the necessity of recognizing Jesus' divine authority and messianic identity (Acts 4:12).

Ephesians 2:19-22 and Isaiah 28:16

1. Foundation of the Church: Paul's description of the Church being built on the foundation of the apostles and prophets, with Jesus as the cornerstone, emphasizes the

integral role of Jesus in the Church's unity and growth. The reference to Isaiah 28:16 underscores the security and stability provided by Jesus as the cornerstone (Ephesians 2:19-22).

2. Holy Temple: The imagery of believers being built into a holy temple for the Lord emphasizes the sacred and communal nature of the Church. Jesus as the cornerstone ensures the cohesion and sanctity of this spiritual structure (Ephesians 2:21-22).

1 Peter 2:4-8 and Isaiah 28:16

1. Living Stone and Believers: Peter expands the imagery of the cornerstone by describing Jesus as the living stone and believers as living stones being built into a spiritual house. This metaphor emphasizes the dynamic and communal nature of the Church, with Jesus as the foundation and believers as integral parts of the structure (1 Peter 2:4-5).

2. Honor and Stumbling: Peter contrasts the honor given to believers who accept Jesus with the stumbling and offense experienced by those who reject Him. This dual role of the cornerstone underscores the necessity of faith in Jesus for salvation and the consequences of rejecting Him (1 Peter 2:7-8).

Practical Applications

1. Recognize Jesus as the Cornerstone: Believers are called to recognize and honor Jesus as the cornerstone of their faith. This recognition involves trusting in His foundational role and aligning their lives with His teachings, ensuring stability and unity within the Church (Ephesians 2:19-22).

2. Build on the Foundation: Believers are invited to build their lives on the foundation of Jesus, the chief cornerstone. This building process involves growing in faith, participating in the life of the Church, and contributing to the spiritual house being constructed by God (1 Corinthians 3:10-11, 1 Peter 2:5).

3. Embrace the Rejected Stone: Understanding Jesus as the rejected stone encourages believers to embrace Him despite opposition and rejection by the world. This embrace involves a commitment to follow Jesus and proclaim His authority, even in the face of adversity (1 Peter 2:4-5).

4. Proclaim the Exclusivity of Salvation: Believers are called to proclaim the exclusivity of salvation through Jesus Christ. This proclamation involves sharing the gospel, testifying to Jesus' redemptive work, and inviting others to recognize Him as the cornerstone of their salvation (Acts 4:12).

Conclusion

The New Testament provides extensive confirmation of Jesus Christ as the cornerstone, fulfilling the Old Testament prophecies and highlighting His essential role in God's redemptive plan. Through detailed expository study and comprehensive commentary, we have explored the biblical foundation, New Testament fulfillment, theological significance, and practical applications of this concept. This chapter has provided a thorough examination of Jesus' role as the cornerstone, enhancing our understanding and strengthening our faith in Him as the foundation of our salvation and the Church.

CHAPTER 08

LESSONS OF TRUST AND FAITH IN PSALM 27

Psalm 27 is a powerful and comforting psalm that expresses profound trust and faith in God amidst life's challenges. David, the author, eloquently conveys his confidence in God's protection, guidance, and salvation. This chapter will provide a detailed analysis of Psalm 27:1-14, exploring its theological significance and practical applications. We will use Bible verses, an expository study, and comprehensive commentary, supported by Strong's Exhaustive Concordance.

Text of Psalm 27 (NKJV)

1. The LORD is my light and my salvation; whom shall I fear? The LORD is the strength of my life; of whom shall I be afraid?

2. When the wicked came against me to eat up my flesh, my enemies and foes, they stumbled and fell.

3. Though an army may encamp against me, my heart shall not fear; though war may rise against me, in this I will be confident.

4. One thing I have desired of the LORD, that will I seek: that I may dwell in the house of the LORD all the days of my life, to behold the beauty of the LORD, and to inquire in His temple.

5. For in the time of trouble He shall hide me in His pavilion; in the secret place of His tabernacle He shall hide me; He shall set me high upon a rock.

6. And now my head shall be lifted up above my enemies all around me; therefore I will offer sacrifices of joy in His tabernacle; I will sing, yes, I will sing praises to the LORD.

7. Hear, O LORD, when I cry with my voice! Have mercy also upon me, and answer me.

8. When You said, "Seek My face," my heart said to You, "Your face, LORD, I will seek."

9. Do not hide Your face from me; do not turn Your servant away in anger; You have been my help; do not leave me nor forsake me, O God of my salvation.

10. When my father and my mother forsake me, then the LORD will take care of me.

11. Teach me Your way, O LORD, and lead me in a smooth path, because of my enemies.

12. Do not deliver me to the will of my adversaries; for false witnesses have risen against me, and such as breathe out violence.

13. I would have lost heart, unless I had believed that I would see the goodness of the LORD in the land of the living.

14. Wait on the LORD; be of good courage, and He shall strengthen your heart; wait, I say, on the LORD!

Expository Study

Verse 1: The LORD as Light and Salvation

Verse 1: "The LORD is my light and my salvation; whom shall I fear? The LORD is the strength of my life; of whom shall I be afraid?"

- "Light" (אוֹר, or) symbolizes guidance, truth, and divine presence.

- "Salvation" (יְשׁוּעָה, yeshuah) indicates deliverance and safety.

- "Strength" (מָעוֹז, ma'oz) signifies protection and refuge.

David begins by affirming the LORD as his light and salvation, dispelling fear and instilling confidence. The imagery of light represents God's guidance and presence, while salvation underscores His role as deliverer. David's rhetorical questions emphasize the security he finds in God.

Verses 2-3: Confidence in the Face of Adversity

Verses 2-3: "When the wicked came against me to eat up my flesh, my enemies and foes, they stumbled and fell. Though an army may encamp against me, my heart shall not fear; though war may rise against me, in this I will be confident."

- "Stumbled and fell" (וְנָפְלוּ כָּשְׁלוּ, kashalu v'nafalu) indicates divine intervention causing the enemies' downfall.

- "Encamp" (חָנָה, chanah) implies a sustained siege or threat.

David recounts past experiences where God protected him from his enemies, reinforcing his confidence. Even in the face of overwhelming odds, such as an encamped army or war, David's trust in God remains unshaken.

Verse 4: Desire for God's Presence

Verse 4: "One thing I have desired of the LORD, that will I seek: that I may dwell in the house of the LORD all the days of my life, to behold the beauty of the LORD, and to inquire in His temple."

- "Dwell" (שָׁכַן, shakan) suggests a permanent residence.

- "Beauty" (נֹעַם, noam) signifies pleasantness and delight.

- "Inquire" (בָּקַר, baqar) means to seek or investigate.

David expresses his singular desire to dwell in God's presence, finding delight in His beauty and seeking guidance in His temple. This verse underscores the centrality of worship and communion with God in David's life.

Verses 5-6: Divine Protection and Praise

Verses 5-6: "For in the time of trouble He shall hide me in His pavilion; in the secret place of His tabernacle He shall hide me; He shall set me high upon a rock. And now my head shall be lifted up above my enemies all around me; therefore I will offer sacrifices of joy in His tabernacle; I will sing, yes, I will sing praises to the LORD."

- "Pavilion" (סֻכָּה, sukkah) and "tabernacle" (אֹהֶל, ohel) denote places of divine protection.

- "Set me high upon a rock" (עַל־צוּר יְרוֹמְמֵנִי, yeromemeni al-tsur) implies stability and safety.

David is confident in God's protection during times of trouble, symbolized by hiding in His pavilion and tabernacle. The imagery of being set high upon a rock conveys security and victory over enemies. In response, David commits to offering joyful sacrifices and singing praises to God.

Verses 7-10: Seeking God's Face

Verses 7-10: "Hear, O LORD, when I cry with my voice! Have mercy also upon me, and answer me. When You said, 'Seek My face,' my heart said to You, 'Your face, LORD, I will seek.' Do not hide Your face from me; do not turn Your servant away in anger; You have been my help; do not leave me nor forsake me, O God of my salvation. When my father

and my mother forsake me, then the LORD will take care of
me."

- "Seek My face" (פְּנָי בַּקְּשׁוּ, bakshu fanai) indicates
pursuing a personal relationship with God.

- "Do not hide Your face" (פָּנֶיךָ אַל־תַּסְתֵּר, al-taster
panecha) expresses a plea for God's continual presence and
favor.

David's prayer shifts to seeking God's face,
emphasizing his desire for an intimate relationship with Him.
He acknowledges God's past help and pleads for His
continued presence, even in times of abandonment by close
family.

Verses 11-12: Guidance and Deliverance

Verses 11-12: "Teach me Your way, O LORD, and
lead me in a smooth path, because of my enemies. Do not
deliver me to the will of my adversaries; for false witnesses
have risen against me, and such as breathe out violence."

- "Teach me Your way" (דַּרְכֶּךָ יְהוָה הוֹרֵנִי, horeni
YHWH darkecha) signifies a desire for divine instruction.

- "Smooth path" (מִישׁוֹר אֹרַח, orach mishor) represents
a path of righteousness and safety.

David seeks God's guidance to navigate the threats
posed by his enemies. His plea for a smooth path reflects his
desire for righteousness and protection from those who
falsely accuse and seek violence against him.

Verses 13-14: Hope and Patience

Verses 13-14: "I would have lost heart, unless I had
believed that I would see the goodness of the LORD in the
land of the living. Wait on the LORD; be of good courage,
and He shall strengthen your heart; wait, I say, on the LORD!"

- "Goodness of the LORD" (יְהוָה בְּטוּב, betuv YHWH)
denotes God's benevolence and blessings.

- "Wait on the LORD" (אֶל־יְהוָה קַוֵּה, kavveh el-
YHWH) implies trust and patience in God's timing.

David concludes with a declaration of hope and encouragement to wait on the LORD. His belief in witnessing God's goodness sustains him, urging others to be courageous and trust in God's strengthening presence.

Comprehensive Commentary

Theological Significance of Trust and Faith in Psalm 27

1. Confidence in God's Protection: David's unwavering trust in God's protection, even in the face of overwhelming adversity, serves as a powerful example for believers. His confidence is rooted in God's past faithfulness and the assurance of His continual presence (Psalm 27:1-3).

2. Desire for God's Presence: David's singular desire to dwell in

God's house and behold His beauty underscores the importance of prioritizing communion with God. This desire reflects a deep longing for an intimate relationship with the divine (Psalm 27:4).

3. Assurance of Divine Protection: The imagery of being hidden in God's pavilion and set high upon a rock illustrates the assurance of divine protection. Believers can find refuge and security in God's presence, knowing that He lifts them above their adversaries (Psalm 27:5-6).

4. Seeking God's Face: David's commitment to seeking God's face highlights the importance of pursuing an ongoing, personal relationship with Him. This pursuit involves a heartfelt desire for God's presence and favor (Psalm 27:7-10).

5. Guidance in Righteousness: David's plea for divine guidance and a smooth path emphasizes the need for God's instruction in navigating life's challenges. Believers are encouraged to seek God's ways and rely on His direction (Psalm 27:11-12).

6. Hope and Patience: David's declaration of hope and encouragement to wait on the LORD reinforces the importance of trust and patience in God's timing. This trust is grounded in the belief that believers will experience God's goodness in their lives (Psalm 27:13-14).

Exegetical Insights

1. Psalm 27:1: The terms "light" (אוֹר, or), "salvation" (יְשׁוּעָה, yeshuah), and "strength" (מָעוֹז, ma'oz) emphasize God's role as a guiding, saving, and protecting force. David's rhetorical questions highlight his confidence in God's all-encompassing care.

2. Psalm 27:2-3: The imagery of enemies stumbling and falling, and the assurance of not fearing an encamped army, illustrate David's trust in God's intervention. These verses underscore the security found in relying on God's protection.

3. Psalm 27:4: David's desire to dwell in God's house and behold His beauty emphasizes the centrality of worship and communion with God. The terms "dwell" (שָׁכַן, shakan), "beauty" (נֹעַם, noam), and "inquire" (בָּקַר, baqar) reflect a deep longing for God's presence.

4. Psalm 27:5-6: The references to God's pavilion and tabernacle as places of refuge, and the imagery of being set high upon a rock, convey the assurance of divine protection. David's response of offering joyful sacrifices and singing praises underscores the importance of worship.

5. Psalm 27:7-10: David's plea to seek God's face and his acknowledgment of God's past help highlight the importance of pursuing an intimate relationship with God. The assurance of God's care even in times of abandonment underscores His faithfulness.

6. Psalm 27:11-12: The request for God's guidance and protection from adversaries emphasizes the need for divine instruction and deliverance. The terms "teach" (הוֹרָה,

horah) and "smooth path" (מִישׁוֹר אֹרַח, orach mishor) reflect a desire for righteous living and safety.

7. Psalm 27:13-14: David's declaration of hope in witnessing God's goodness and his encouragement to wait on the LORD highlight the importance of trust and patience. The terms "goodness" (טוּב, tuv) and "wait" (קַוֵּה, kavvah) emphasize the assurance of God's benevolence and timing.

Practical Applications

1. Trust in God's Protection: Believers are encouraged to trust in God's protection, even in the face of overwhelming challenges. This trust is grounded in the assurance of God's past faithfulness and His continual presence (Psalm 27:1-3).

2. Pursue God's Presence: The desire to dwell in God's house and behold His beauty underscores the importance of prioritizing worship and communion with God. Believers are encouraged to seek an intimate relationship with the divine (Psalm 27:4).

3. Find Refuge in God: The imagery of being hidden in God's pavilion and set high upon a rock illustrates the assurance of divine protection. Believers can find refuge and security in God's presence, knowing that He lifts them above their adversaries (Psalm 27:5-6).

4. Seek God's Face: David's commitment to seeking God's face highlights the importance of pursuing an ongoing, personal relationship with Him. Believers are encouraged to seek God's presence and favor continually (Psalm 27:7-10).

5. Rely on God's Guidance: David's plea for divine guidance and a smooth path emphasizes the need for God's instruction in navigating life's challenges. Believers are encouraged to seek God's ways and rely on His direction (Psalm 27:11-12).

6. Hope in God's Timing: David's declaration of hope and encouragement to wait on the LORD reinforces the importance of trust and patience in God's timing. Believers

are encouraged to trust in God's goodness and wait for His perfect timing (Psalm 27:13-14).

Conclusion

Psalm 27 offers profound lessons of trust and faith in God, emphasizing His protection, guidance, and salvation. Through detailed expository study and comprehensive commentary, we have explored the theological significance and practical applications of this psalm. This chapter has provided a thorough examination of Psalm 27:1-14, enhancing our understanding and strengthening our faith in God as our light, salvation, and strength.

Jesus' Teachings on Trust and Faith

Jesus Christ, throughout His earthly ministry, emphasized the importance of trust and faith. His teachings provide profound insights into how believers should place their confidence in God and live out their faith daily. This chapter will explore Jesus' teachings on trust and faith, using Bible verses, an expository study, and comprehensive commentary supported by Strong's Exhaustive Concordance.

Faith and Trust Defined

Hebrews 11:1: Definition of Faith

Hebrews 11:1: "Now faith is the substance of things hoped for, the evidence of things not seen."

- "Substance" (ὑπόστασις, hypostasis) signifies assurance or confidence.

- "Evidence" (ἔλεγχος, elegchos) denotes conviction or proof.

Faith, as defined in Hebrews, involves a confident assurance in what is hoped for and a firm conviction in what is not seen. This definition underpins Jesus' teachings on faith and trust, highlighting the necessity of believing in God's promises and His unseen hand at work.

Jesus' Teachings on Trust

Matthew 6:25-34: Trust in God's Provision

Matthew 6:25-34: "Therefore I say to you, do not worry about your life, what you will eat or what you will drink; nor about your body, what you will put on. Is not life more than food and the body more than clothing? Look at the birds of the air, for they neither sow nor reap nor gather into barns; yet your heavenly Father feeds them. Are you not of more value than they? Which of you by worrying can add one cubit to his stature? So why do you worry about clothing? Consider the lilies of the field, how they grow: they neither toil nor spin; and yet I say to you that even Solomon in all his glory was not arrayed like one of these. Now if God so clothes the grass of the field, which today is, and tomorrow is thrown into the oven, will He not much more clothe you, O you of little faith? Therefore do not worry, saying, 'What shall we eat?' or 'What shall we drink?' or 'What shall we wear?' For after all these things the Gentiles seek. For your heavenly Father knows that you need all these things. But seek first the kingdom of God and His righteousness, and all these things shall be added to you. Therefore do not worry about tomorrow, for tomorrow will worry about its own things. Sufficient for the day is its own trouble."

- "Worry" (μεριμνάω, merimnaō) means to be anxious or distracted.

- "Seek" (ζητέω, zēteō) denotes a continuous pursuit or striving.

Jesus teaches His followers not to worry about their material needs, emphasizing that God, who provides for the birds and the lilies, will certainly care for them. He urges them to prioritize seeking God's kingdom and righteousness, trusting that their needs will be met.

John 14:1: Trust in God and Jesus

John 14:1: "Let not your heart be troubled; you believe in God, believe also in Me."

- "Troubled" (ταράσσω, tarassō) means to be agitated or disturbed.

- "Believe" (πιστεύω, pisteuō) signifies trust or confidence.

Jesus comforts His disciples by encouraging them to trust in God and in Himself. This exhortation underscores the importance of placing unwavering trust in both the Father and the Son, especially during times of uncertainty and distress.

Jesus' Teachings on Faith

Matthew 17:20: Faith as a Mustard Seed

Matthew 17:20: "So Jesus said to them, 'Because of your unbelief; for assuredly, I say to you, if you have faith as a mustard seed, you will say to this mountain, "Move from here to there," and it will move; and nothing will be impossible for you.'"

- "Mustard seed" (σίνεπι, sinapi) represents something very small.

- "Unbelief" (ἀπιστία, apistia) means lack of faith or trust.

Jesus emphasizes that even a small amount of faith, comparable to a mustard seed, can accomplish great things. This teaching highlights the power and potential of genuine faith, no matter how small it may seem.

Mark 9:23: All Things Are Possible

Mark 9:23: "Jesus said to him, 'If you can believe, all things are possible to him who believes.'"

- "Believe" (πιστεύω, pisteuō) indicates trust and confidence.

Jesus assures a father seeking healing for his son that everything is possible for those who believe. This statement reinforces the boundless potential of faith and encourages believers to trust in God's ability to work miracles.

Luke 17:5-6: Faith and Obedience

Luke 17:5-6: "And the apostles said to the Lord, 'Increase our faith.' So the Lord said, 'If you have faith as a mustard seed, you can say to this mulberry tree, "Be pulled up by the roots and be planted in the sea," and it would obey you.'"

- "Increase" (προστίθημι, prostithēmi) means to add or augment.

- "Obey" (ὑπακούω, hypakouō) signifies submission or compliance.

In response to the apostles' request for greater faith, Jesus teaches that even a small amount of faith can lead to extraordinary outcomes. This teaching underscores the significance of faith coupled with obedience to God's commands.

Matthew 8:5-13: The Centurion's Faith

Matthew 8:5-13: "Now when Jesus had entered Capernaum, a centurion came to Him, pleading with Him, saying, 'Lord, my servant is lying at home paralyzed, dreadfully tormented.' And Jesus said to him, 'I will come and heal him.' The centurion answered and said, 'Lord, I am not worthy that You should come under my roof. But only speak a word, and my servant will be healed. For I also am a man under authority, having soldiers under me. And I say to this one, "Go," and he goes; and to another, "Come," and he comes; and to my servant, "Do this," and he does it.' When Jesus heard it, He marveled, and said to those who followed, 'Assuredly, I say to you, I have not found such great faith, not even in Israel! And I say to you that many will come from east and west, and sit down with Abraham, Isaac, and Jacob in the kingdom of heaven. But the sons of the kingdom will be cast out into outer darkness. There will be weeping and gnashing of teeth.' Then Jesus said to the centurion, 'Go your way; and as you have believed, so let it be done for you.' And his servant was healed that same hour."

- "Marveled" (θαυμάζω, thaumazō) means to be amazed or astonished.

- "Authority" (ἐξουσία, exousia) signifies power or control.

The centurion's faith impresses Jesus, as it demonstrates a profound understanding of authority and trust in Jesus' power to heal. This account highlights the importance of recognizing and trusting in Jesus' authority.

Practical Applications

1. Trust in God's Provision: Jesus' teaching in Matthew 6:25-34 encourages believers to trust in God's provision and not to worry about material needs. This trust involves prioritizing seeking God's kingdom and righteousness, confident that God will provide for their needs.

2. Cultivate a Deep Faith: Jesus' statements about faith, such as those in Matthew 17:20 and Mark 9:23, emphasize the power of even a small amount of genuine faith. Believers are encouraged to cultivate their faith, trusting in God's ability to accomplish the impossible.

3. Demonstrate Faith Through Obedience: The teaching in Luke 17:5-6 underscores the relationship between faith and obedience. Believers are encouraged to act in faith, trusting that their obedience to God's commands will lead to extraordinary outcomes.

4. Recognize Jesus' Authority: The account of the centurion's faith in Matthew 8:5-13 highlights the importance of recognizing and trusting in Jesus' authority. Believers are called to trust in Jesus' power and submit to His lordship in every aspect of their lives.

5. Maintain Faith in Difficult Times: Jesus' exhortation in John 14:1 to believe in God and Himself during times of trouble encourages believers to maintain their faith even in

challenging circumstances. This trust provides comfort and assurance in the midst of uncertainty.

Comprehensive Commentary

Theological Significance of Trust and Faith in Jesus' Teachings

1. God's Provision and Care: Jesus' teachings on not worrying about material needs (Matthew 6:25-34) highlight God's provision and care for His creation. This teaching reassures believers of God's attentiveness to their needs and encourages them to trust in His providence.

2. Power of Faith: Jesus' statements about the power of faith (Matthew 17:20, Mark 9:23) underscore the significant impact that even a small amount of genuine faith can have. This teaching inspires believers to develop and exercise their faith, trusting in God's ability to work miracles.

3. Faith and Authority: The account of the centurion's faith (Matthew 8:5-13) illustrates the connection between faith and recognizing Jesus' authority. This recognition is crucial for understanding the nature of faith and its implications for believers' lives.

4. Faith in Action: Jesus' teaching on faith and obedience (Luke 17:5-6) highlights the practical outworking of faith through actions. Believers are encouraged to demonstrate their faith by obeying God's commands, trusting that their obedience will lead to significant outcomes.

5. Trust During Trials: Jesus' exhortation to trust in God and Himself during times of trouble (John 14:1) provides comfort and assurance for believers facing difficult circumstances. This trust is foundational for maintaining peace and confidence in God's care.

Exegetical Insights

1. Matthew 6:25-34: The repeated use of "do not worry" (μεριμνάω, merimnaō) emphasizes Jesus' command to avoid anxiety about material needs. The examples of the birds

and lilies highlight God's provision and care for His creation, underscoring the greater value of human beings to God.

2. John 14:1: The terms "troubled" (ταράσσω, tarassō) and "believe" (πιστεύω, pisteuō) underscore the importance of maintaining peace and trust in God and Jesus. This teaching provides reassurance and encourages unwavering trust in the divine.

3. Matthew 17:20: The imagery of the mustard seed (σίνεπι, sinapi) represents the potential of even small faith to accomplish great things. Jesus' use of hyperbole in moving mountains emphasizes the boundless possibilities available through faith.

4. Mark 9:23: The statement "all things are possible" (πάντα δυνατά, panta dynata) highlights the limitless potential of faith. Jesus' assurance encourages believers to trust in God's ability to work beyond human limitations.

5. Luke 17:5-6: The apostles' request to "increase our faith" (προστίθημι, prostithēmi) reflects a desire for greater faith, while Jesus' response emphasizes the power of even small faith when combined with obedience. The imagery of the mulberry tree obeying underscores the significance of faith in action.

6. Matthew 8:5-13: The centurion's understanding of "authority" (ἐξουσία, exousia) and Jesus' "marvel" (θαυμάζω, thaumazō) at his faith highlight the connection between faith and recognizing Jesus' power. This account underscores the importance of acknowledging and trusting in Jesus' authority.

Conclusion

Jesus' teachings on trust and faith provide profound insights and practical guidance for believers. Through detailed expository study and comprehensive commentary, we have explored the biblical foundation, theological significance, and practical applications of Jesus' teachings. This chapter has provided a thorough examination of Jesus' instructions on trust and faith, enhancing our understanding and strengthening our commitment to live out these principles in our daily lives.

Overcoming Fear and Adversity Through Faith in Jesus

Fear and adversity are inevitable parts of life. However, Jesus Christ provides profound teachings and examples on how to overcome these challenges through faith. This chapter explores Jesus' teachings on overcoming fear and adversity, using Bible verses, expository study, and comprehensive commentary supported by Strong's Exhaustive Concordance.

The Nature of Fear and Adversity

Definition of Fear

Fear (φόβος, phobos) is an emotional response to a perceived threat or danger, often causing anxiety, worry, and avoidance behaviors. In the Bible, fear can be both a natural human reaction and a spiritual challenge to trust in God.

Definition of Adversity

Adversity (θλίψις, thlipsis) refers to trials, difficulties, and hardships that test one's faith and resilience. In the New Testament, adversity often relates to persecution, suffering, and challenges faced by believers.

Jesus' Teachings on Overcoming Fear

Matthew 14:22-33: Jesus Walks on Water

Matthew 14:22-33: "Immediately Jesus made His disciples get into the boat and go before Him to the other side, while He sent the multitudes away. And when He had sent the multitudes away, He went up on the mountain by Himself to pray. Now when evening came, He was alone there. But the boat was now in the middle of the sea, tossed by the waves, for the wind was contrary. Now in the fourth watch of the night Jesus went to them, walking on the sea. And when the disciples saw Him walking on the sea, they were troubled, saying, 'It is a ghost!' And they cried out for fear. But immediately Jesus spoke to them, saying, 'Be of good cheer! It is I; do not be afraid.' And Peter answered Him and said, 'Lord, if it is You, command me to come to You on the water.' So He said, 'Come.' And when Peter had come down out of the boat, he walked on the water to go to Jesus. But when he saw that the wind was boisterous, he was afraid; and beginning to sink he cried out, saying, 'Lord, save me!' And immediately Jesus stretched out His hand and caught him, and said to him, 'O you of little faith, why did you doubt?' And when they got into the boat, the wind ceased. Then those who were in the boat came and worshiped Him, saying, 'Truly You are the Son of God.'"

- "Troubled" (ταράσσω, tarassō) means to be disturbed or frightened.

- "Afraid" (φοβέομαι, phobeomai) signifies fear or terror.

- "Little faith" (ὀλιγόπιστος, oligopistos) indicates a lack of sufficient trust.

Jesus' appearance walking on water and His command, "Be of good cheer! It is I; do not be afraid," illustrate His authority over natural elements and His ability to calm fears. Peter's initial faith and subsequent doubt highlight the challenge of maintaining faith amidst adversity.

Mark 4:35-41: Jesus Calms the Storm

Mark 4:35-41: "On the same day, when evening had come, He said to them, 'Let us cross over to the other side.' Now when they had left the multitude, they took Him along in the boat as He was. And other little boats were also with Him. And a great windstorm arose, and the waves beat into the boat, so that it was already filling. But He was in the stern, asleep on a pillow. And they awoke Him and said to Him, 'Teacher, do You not care that we are perishing?' Then He arose and rebuked the wind, and said to the sea, 'Peace, be still!' And the wind ceased and there was a great calm. But He said to them, 'Why are you so fearful? How is it that you have no faith?' And they feared exceedingly, and said to one another, 'Who can this be, that even the wind and the sea obey Him!'"

- "Fearful" (δειλός, deilos) means timid or cowardly.

- "No faith" (οὐδένα πίστιν, oudena pistin) indicates a complete lack of trust.

In calming the storm, Jesus demonstrates His divine authority and power. His rebuke, "Why are you so fearful? How is it that you have no faith?" challenges the disciples to trust Him even in dire circumstances.

Jesus' Teachings on Overcoming Adversity

John 16:33: Peace in the Midst of Tribulation

John 16:33: "These things I have spoken to you, that in Me you may have peace. In the world you will have tribulation; but be of good cheer, I have overcome the world."

- "Tribulation" (θλίψις, thlipsis) refers to distress or suffering.

- "Overcome" (νικάω, nikaō) means to conquer or prevail.

Jesus assures His disciples that although they will face tribulation in the world, they can find peace in Him because He has overcome the world. This statement provides hope and encouragement to believers facing adversity.

Matthew 5:10-12: Blessed Are the Persecuted

Matthew 5:10-12: "Blessed are those who are persecuted for righteousness' sake, for theirs is the kingdom of heaven. Blessed are you when they revile and persecute you, and say all kinds of evil against you falsely for My sake. Rejoice and be exceedingly glad, for great is your reward in heaven, for so they persecuted the prophets who were before you."

- "Persecuted" (διώκω, diōkō) means to be harassed or oppressed.

- "Revile" (ὀνειδίζω, oneidizō) signifies to insult or defame.

Jesus pronounces blessings on those who face persecution for righteousness' sake, encouraging them to rejoice despite adversity. This teaching emphasizes the eternal rewards for enduring hardship for Christ's sake.

James 1:2-4: Joy in Trials

James 1:2-4: "My brethren, count it all joy when you fall into various trials, knowing that the testing of your faith produces patience. But let patience have its perfect work, that you may be perfect and complete, lacking nothing."

- "Joy" (χαρά, chara) means gladness or delight.

- "Trials" (πειρασμός, peirasmos) refers to tests or temptations.

James encourages believers to consider trials as opportunities for joy because they produce patience and spiritual maturity. This perspective transforms adversity into a means for growth and deeper faith.

Practical Applications

1. Faith Over Fear: Jesus' teachings and examples, such as walking on water and calming the storm, illustrate the importance of faith over fear. Believers are encouraged to trust in Jesus' authority and presence, even in terrifying circumstances (Matthew 14:22-33, Mark 4:35-41).

2. Peace Amidst Tribulation: Jesus assures His followers of peace despite tribulation, emphasizing His victory over the world. Believers can find comfort and strength in His words, knowing that He has conquered all adversities (John 16:33).

3. Rejoicing in Persecution: Jesus' teaching on the blessedness of the persecuted encourages believers to rejoice

despite suffering for righteousness. This perspective shifts the focus from present pain to future rewards (Matthew 5:10-12).

4. Joy in Trials: James' exhortation to find joy in trials highlights the spiritual growth that adversity can produce. Believers are encouraged to view trials as opportunities for developing patience and maturity (James 1:2-4).

Comprehensive Commentary

Theological Significance of Overcoming Fear and Adversity Through Faith

1. Divine Authority: Jesus' authority over natural elements and His rebuke of fear underscore His divine power. Believers are called to recognize and trust in His sovereign control over all circumstances (Matthew 14:22-33, Mark 4:35-41).

2. Promise of Peace: Jesus' promise of peace in the midst of tribulation offers a profound assurance to believers. This peace is rooted in His victory over the world, providing a secure foundation for overcoming adversity (John 16:33).

3. Eternal Perspective: Jesus' teaching on persecution emphasizes the eternal perspective needed to endure suffering. Believers are encouraged to focus on the eternal rewards and blessings promised to those who suffer for His sake (Matthew 5:10-12).

4. Transformative Trials: James' perspective on trials highlights their transformative potential. Adversity is seen as a means of producing patience and spiritual maturity, encouraging believers to embrace trials with joy (James 1:2-4).

Exegetical Insights

1. Matthew 14:22-33: The terms "troubled" (ταράσσω, tarassō) and "afraid" (φοβέομαι, phobeomai) reflect the disciples' fear in the face of perceived danger. Jesus' command to "be of good cheer" and His identification, "It is I," emphasize His calming and reassuring presence.

2. Mark 4:35-41: The terms "fearful" (δειλός, deilos) and "no faith" (οὐδένα πίστιν, oudena pistin) highlight the disciples' lack of trust. Jesus' rebuke and calming of the storm demonstrate His authority and call for faith in His power.

3. John 16:33: The term "tribulation" (θλίψις, thlipsis) signifies the expected challenges believers will face. Jesus' assurance of peace and His victory ("overcome," νικάω, nikaō) provide a foundation for enduring adversity with confidence.

4. Matthew 5:10-12: The terms "persecuted" (διώκω, diōkō) and "revile" (ὀνειδίζω, oneidizō) describe the hardships faced for righteousness. Jesus' call to "rejoice and be exceedingly glad" emphasizes the heavenly rewards awaiting those who endure persecution.

5. James 1:2-4: The terms "joy" (χαρά, chara) and "trials" (πειρασμός, peirasmos) highlight the counterintuitive response to adversity. James' exhortation to consider trials as opportunities for growth underscores the spiritual benefits of enduring hardships.

Practical Applications

1. Trust in Jesus' Presence: Believers are encouraged to trust in Jesus' presence and authority, especially in fearful circumstances. This trust dispels fear and fosters confidence in His ability to protect and guide (Matthew 14:22-33, Mark 4:35-41).

2. Embrace Peace in Tribulation: Jesus' promise of peace amidst tribulation invites believers to embrace His peace, even when facing adversity. This peace is rooted in the assurance of His victory and sovereign control (John 16:33).

3. Rejoice in Suffering for Righteousness: Jesus' teaching on persecution calls believers to rejoice in suffering for righteousness. This rejoicing is based on the promise of eternal rewards and the recognition of shared experiences with the prophets (Matthew 5:10-12).

4. Find Joy in Trials: James' exhortation to find joy in trials encourages believers to view adversity as an opportunity for growth. This perspective fosters resilience and spiritual maturity, transforming trials into blessings (James 1:2-4).

Conclusion

Jesus' teachings on overcoming fear and adversity through faith provide profound guidance and encouragement for believers. Through detailed expository study and comprehensive commentary, we have explored the biblical foundation, theological significance, and practical applications of Jesus' teachings. This chapter has provided a thorough examination of how faith in Jesus enables believers to overcome fear and adversity, enhancing our understanding and strengthening our commitment to live out these principles in our daily lives.

Parallels in the Gospels

The Gospels—Matthew, Mark, Luke, and John—each present a unique perspective on the life and teachings of Jesus Christ. Despite their distinct approaches, these four accounts often present parallel narratives and teachings that reinforce key themes in Jesus' ministry. This chapter explores some of the significant parallels in the Gospels, focusing on how they collectively convey essential lessons about Jesus' identity, mission, and the call to trust and faith in Him.

The Feeding of the Five Thousand

Matthew 14:13-21, Mark 6:30-44, Luke 9:10-17, John 6:1-14

Matthew 14:13-21: "When Jesus heard it, He departed from there by boat to a deserted place by Himself. But when the multitudes heard it, they followed Him on foot from the cities. And when Jesus went out He saw a great multitude; and He was moved with compassion for them, and healed their sick. When it was evening, His disciples came to Him, saying, 'This is a deserted place, and the hour is already late. Send the multitudes away, that they may go into the villages and buy themselves food.' But Jesus said to them, 'They do not need to go away. You give them something to eat.' And they said to Him, 'We have here only five loaves and two fish.' He said, 'Bring them here to Me.' Then He commanded the multitudes to sit down on the grass. And He took the five loaves and the two fish, and looking up to heaven, He blessed and broke and gave the loaves to the disciples; and the disciples gave to the multitudes. So they all ate and were filled, and they took up twelve baskets full of the fragments that remained. Now those who had eaten were about five thousand men, besides women and children."

Mark 6:30-44, Luke 9:10-17, John 6:1-14 provide similar accounts with slight variations in details, emphasizing Jesus' compassion, the disciples' doubts, and the miraculous provision.

Key Themes and Insights

1. Compassion of Jesus: All four Gospels highlight Jesus' compassion for the crowd, who followed Him despite being in a deserted place. This compassion leads to His miraculous provision, demonstrating His care for both physical and spiritual needs.

2. Miraculous Provision: The miracle of feeding the five thousand with five loaves and two fish underscores Jesus' divine power to provide abundantly. The collection of twelve baskets of leftovers signifies the completeness and abundance of His provision.

3. Involvement of Disciples: Jesus involves His disciples in the miracle, instructing them to distribute the food. This participation teaches them about reliance on His power and the importance of serving others.

4. Trust and Faith: The disciples' initial doubt about feeding the multitude contrasts with Jesus' unwavering trust in God's provision. This event challenges believers to trust in

Jesus' ability to meet their needs, even when circumstances seem impossible.

Jesus Calms the Storm

Matthew 8:23-27, Mark 4:35-41, Luke 8:22-25

Matthew 8:23-27: "Now when He got into a boat, His disciples followed Him. And suddenly a great tempest arose on the sea, so that the boat was covered with the waves. But He was asleep. Then His disciples came to Him and awoke Him, saying, 'Lord, save us! We are perishing!' But He said to them, 'Why are you fearful, O you of little faith?' Then He arose and rebuked the winds and the sea, and there was a great calm. So the men marveled, saying, 'Who can this be, that even the winds and the sea obey Him?'"

Mark 4:35-41 and Luke 8:22-25 provide similar accounts, emphasizing the disciples' fear and Jesus' authority over nature.

Key Themes and Insights

1. Authority of Jesus: All three Gospels emphasize Jesus' authority over the natural elements. His ability to calm the storm with a command demonstrates His divine power and control over creation.

2. Fear and Faith: The disciples' fear and Jesus' rebuke, "Why are you fearful, O you of little faith?" highlight the tension between fear and faith. This narrative challenges believers to trust in Jesus' power and presence, even in the midst of life's storms.

3. Revelation of Jesus' Identity: The disciples' reaction, marveling and questioning, "Who can this be, that even the winds and the sea obey Him?" points to a deeper revelation of Jesus' divine nature. This event strengthens their understanding of His identity as the Son of God.

The Healing of a Paralytic

Matthew 9:1-8, Mark 2:1-12, Luke 5:17-26

Matthew 9:1-8: "So He got into a boat, crossed over, and came to His own city. Then behold, they brought to Him a paralytic lying on a bed. When Jesus saw their faith, He said to the paralytic, 'Son, be of good cheer; your sins are forgiven you.' And at once some of the scribes said within themselves, 'This Man blasphemes!' But Jesus, knowing their thoughts, said, 'Why do you think evil in your hearts? For which is easier, to say, "Your sins are forgiven you," or to say, "Arise and walk"? But that you may know that the Son of Man has power on earth to forgive sins'—then He said to the paralytic, 'Arise, take up your bed, and go to your house.' And he arose and departed to his house. Now when the multitudes saw it, they marveled and glorified God, who had given such power to men."

Mark 2:1-12 and Luke 5:17-26 provide similar accounts with additional details, such as the paralytic being lowered through the roof due to the crowd.

Key Themes and Insights

1. Faith and Forgiveness: Jesus' response to the faith of those who brought the paralytic—"your sins are forgiven"—highlights the connection between faith and forgiveness. This narrative underscores the priority of spiritual healing over physical healing.

2. Authority to Forgive Sins: Jesus' ability to forgive sins, challenged by the scribes as blasphemy, is validated by His miraculous healing of the paralytic. This dual demonstration of authority reveals Jesus' divine prerogative to forgive sins and perform miracles.

3. Public Recognition of Divine Power: The crowd's reaction, marveling and glorifying God, underscores the public recognition of Jesus' divine power. This event strengthens the believers' faith and expands their understanding of His mission.

The Transfiguration

Matthew 17:1-9, Mark 9:2-9, Luke 9:28-36

Matthew 17:1-9: "Now after six days Jesus took Peter, James, and John his brother, led them up on a high mountain by themselves; and He was transfigured before them. His face shone like the sun, and His clothes became as white as the light. And behold, Moses and Elijah appeared to them, talking with Him. Then Peter answered and said to Jesus, 'Lord, it is good for us to be here; if You wish, let us make here three tabernacles: one for You, one for Moses, and one for Elijah.' While he was still speaking, behold, a bright cloud overshadowed them; and suddenly a voice came out of the cloud, saying, 'This is My beloved Son, in whom I am well pleased. Hear Him!' And when the disciples heard it, they fell on their faces and were greatly afraid. But Jesus came and touched them and said, 'Arise, and do not be afraid.' When they had lifted up their eyes, they saw no one but Jesus only. Now as they came down from the mountain, Jesus commanded them, saying, 'Tell the vision to no one until the Son of Man is risen from the dead.'"

Mark 9:2-9 and Luke 9:28-36 provide similar accounts with additional details, such as the conversation about Jesus' departure and the disciples' reactions.

Key Themes and Insights

1. Revelation of Divine Glory: The transfiguration reveals Jesus' divine glory, with His face shining like the sun and His clothes becoming white as light. This event provides a glimpse of His heavenly majesty and prefigures His resurrection glory.

2. Affirmation of Jesus' Sonship: The voice from the cloud—"This is My beloved Son, in whom I am well pleased. Hear Him!"—affirms Jesus' divine sonship and authority. This divine endorsement emphasizes the importance of listening to and obeying Jesus.

3. Witnesses to the Glory: Peter, James, and John, as witnesses to the transfiguration, are given a unique revelation of Jesus' glory and identity. This experience strengthens their faith and prepares them for the challenges ahead.

4. Connection to the Law and the Prophets: The presence of Moses and Elijah represents the Law and the Prophets, indicating that Jesus is the fulfillment of both. This connection highlights the continuity and fulfillment of God's redemptive plan in Jesus.

Practical Applications

1. Recognize Jesus' Compassion and Provision: The feeding of the five thousand teaches believers to trust in Jesus' compassion and provision. Despite limited resources, Jesus provides abundantly, demonstrating His care for both physical and spiritual needs (Matthew 14:13-21, Mark 6:30-44, Luke 9:10-17, John 6:1-14).

2. Trust in Jesus' Authority Over Nature: The calming of the storm illustrates Jesus' authority over natural elements, encouraging believers to trust in His power and presence during life's storms. His rebuke of fear and call to faith challenge believers to rely on His sovereignty (Matthew 8:23-27, Mark 4:35-41, Luke 8:22-25).

3. Value Spiritual Healing: The healing of the paralytic emphasizes the importance of spiritual healing and forgiveness. Believers are encouraged to prioritize their relationship with God and trust in Jesus' authority to forgive sins and heal (Matthew 9:1-8, Mark 2:1-12, Luke 5:17-26).

4. Embrace Jesus' Glory and Listen to Him: The transfiguration reveals Jesus' divine glory and affirms His sonship. Believers are called to listen to and obey Jesus, recognizing His fulfillment of the Law and the Prophets and His central role in God's redemptive plan (Matthew 17:1-9, Mark 9:2-9, Luke 9:28-36).

Comprehensive Commentary

Theological Significance of Gospel Parallels

1. Unity and Diversity: The parallels in the Gospels demonstrate the unity and diversity of the Gospel accounts. Each Gospel presents a unique perspective, yet they collectively reinforce key themes about Jesus' identity, mission, and teachings.

2. Revelation of Jesus' Identity: The parallel narratives consistently reveal Jesus' identity as the Son of God, the Messiah, and the fulfillment of God's redemptive plan. These accounts provide a multifaceted understanding of who Jesus is and what He came to accomplish.

3. Faith and Trust: The parallels emphasize the importance of faith and trust in Jesus. Whether facing physical needs, natural disasters, spiritual challenges, or witnessing divine glory, believers are called to place their trust in Jesus and rely on His power and presence.

4. Continuity and Fulfillment: The presence of Old Testament figures and themes in the Gospel parallels highlights the continuity and fulfillment of God's promises. Jesus is presented as the culmination of God's redemptive work, fulfilling the Law and the Prophets and establishing a new covenant.

Exegetical Insights

1. Matthew 14:13-21, Mark 6:30-44, Luke 9:10-17, John 6:1-14: The consistent themes of compassion, miraculous provision, and the involvement of the disciples highlight Jesus' care for the multitudes and His ability to provide abundantly. The collection of leftovers underscores the completeness of His provision.

2. Matthew 8:23-27, Mark 4:35-41, Luke 8:22-25: The disciples' fear and Jesus' authority over the storm emphasize the need for faith in His power. The question, "Who can this be, that even the winds and the sea obey Him?" points to a deeper revelation of Jesus' divine nature.

3. Matthew 9:1-8, Mark 2:1-12, Luke 5:17-26: The healing of the paralytic and the forgiveness of sins highlight Jesus' authority over both physical and spiritual realms. The reaction of the scribes and the crowd underscores the public recognition of His divine power.

4. Matthew 17:1-9, Mark 9:2-9, Luke 9:28-36: The transfiguration reveals Jesus' divine glory and affirms His sonship. The presence of Moses and Elijah connects Jesus to the Law and the Prophets, highlighting His role as the fulfillment of God's redemptive plan.

Conclusion

The parallels in the Gospels provide a rich and multifaceted understanding of Jesus' life, teachings, and mission. Through detailed expository study and comprehensive commentary, we have explored key parallel narratives and their theological significance. This chapter has provided a thorough examination of how the Gospel parallels collectively convey essential lessons about Jesus' identity, mission, and the call to trust and faith in Him, enhancing our understanding and strengthening our commitment to live out these principles in our daily lives.

CHAPTER 09

THE RIGHTEOUS KING IN PSALM 45

Psalm 45 is a royal psalm that celebrates the majesty and righteousness of the king. Traditionally understood as a wedding song for a king's marriage, it has also been interpreted as a messianic psalm, pointing to the ultimate fulfillment in Jesus Christ, the Righteous King. This chapter will provide a detailed analysis of Psalm 45:1-17, exploring its theological significance and practical applications. We will use Bible verses, an expository study, and comprehensive commentary, supported by Strong's Exhaustive Concordance.

Text of Psalm 45 (NKJV)

1. My heart is overflowing with a good theme; I recite my composition concerning the King; my tongue is the pen of a ready writer.

2. You are fairer than the sons of men; grace is poured upon Your lips; therefore God has blessed You forever.

3. Gird Your sword upon Your thigh, O Mighty One, with Your glory and Your majesty.

4. And in Your majesty ride prosperously because of truth, humility, and righteousness; and Your right hand shall teach You awesome things.

5. Your arrows are sharp in the heart of the King's enemies; the peoples fall under You.

6. Your throne, O God, is forever and ever; a scepter of righteousness is the scepter of Your kingdom.

7. You love righteousness and hate wickedness; therefore God, Your God, has anointed You with the oil of gladness more than Your companions.

8. All Your garments are scented with myrrh and aloes and cassia, out of the ivory palaces, by which they have made You glad.

9. Kings' daughters are among Your honorable women; at Your right hand stands the queen in gold from Ophir.

10. Listen, O daughter, consider and incline your ear; forget your own people also, and your father's house;

11. So the King will greatly desire your beauty; because He is your Lord, worship Him.

12. And the daughter of Tyre will come with a gift; the rich among the people will seek your favor.

13. The royal daughter is all glorious within the palace; her clothing is woven with gold.

14. She shall be brought to the King in robes of many colors; the virgins, her companions who follow her, shall be brought to You.

15. With gladness and rejoicing they shall be brought; they shall enter the King's palace.

16. Instead of Your fathers shall be Your sons, whom You shall make princes in all the earth.

17. I will make Your name to be remembered in all generations; therefore the people shall praise You forever and ever.

Expository Study

Verses 1-2: Introduction and Praise of the King

Verses 1-2: "My heart is overflowing with a good theme; I recite my composition concerning the King; my tongue is the pen of a ready writer. You are fairer than the sons of men; grace is poured upon Your lips; therefore God has blessed You forever."

- "Overflowing" (רָחַשׁ, rachash) indicates an abundant and enthusiastic outpouring.

- "Fairer" (יָפְיָפִיתָ, yaphyapita) suggests surpassing beauty and grace.

- "Grace" (חֵן, chen) signifies favor and charm.

The psalmist begins with an enthusiastic declaration, expressing his overflowing heart with praise for the king. The king is described as exceptionally fair and gracious, indicating both physical beauty and the charm of speech. God's blessing upon the king is eternal, emphasizing divine favor and approval.

Verses 3-5: The Warrior King

Verses 3-5: "Gird Your sword upon Your thigh, O Mighty One, with Your glory and Your majesty. And in Your majesty ride prosperously because of truth, humility, and righteousness; and Your right hand shall teach You awesome things. Your arrows are sharp in the heart of the King's enemies; the peoples fall under You."

- "Sword" (חֶרֶב, chereb) symbolizes military power and readiness for battle.

- "Mighty One" (גִּבּוֹר, gibbor) denotes strength and valor.

- "Truth" (אֱמֶת, emeth), "humility" (עֲנָוָה, anavah), and "righteousness" (צֶדֶק, tsedeq) are virtues that characterize the king's rule.

The psalmist portrays the king as a mighty warrior, ready for battle and adorned with glory and majesty. The king's prosperity and success are attributed to his commitment to truth, humility, and righteousness. His military prowess is depicted through the imagery of sharp arrows that defeat his enemies.

Verses 6-7: The Divine Throne

Verses 6-7: "Your throne, O God, is forever and ever; a scepter of righteousness is the scepter of Your kingdom. You love righteousness and hate wickedness; therefore God, Your God, has anointed You with the oil of gladness more than Your companions."

- "Throne" (כִּסֵּא, kisse) signifies authority and enduring rule.

- "Scepter" (שֵׁבֶט, shevet) symbolizes the king's rule and authority.

- "Anointed" (מָשַׁח, mashach) refers to the ceremonial act of consecration.

The psalmist acknowledges the divine nature of the king's throne, declaring it eternal. The scepter of righteousness signifies the just and fair governance of the king. The king's love for righteousness and hatred of wickedness result in divine anointing and exaltation above his peers.

Verses 8-9: The Royal Splendor

Verses 8-9: "All Your garments are scented with myrrh and aloes and cassia, out of the ivory palaces, by which they have made You glad. Kings' daughters are among Your honorable women; at Your right hand stands the queen in gold from Ophir."

- "Myrrh" (מֹר, mor), "aloes" (אֲהָלוֹת, ahaloth), and "cassia" (קְצִיעָה, qetsi'ah) are aromatic spices signifying wealth and luxury.

- "Ivory palaces" (שֵׁן הֵיכְלֵי, heykle shen) suggest opulence and grandeur.

The psalmist describes the king's royal splendor with vivid imagery of luxurious garments and fragrant spices. The presence of kings' daughters and the queen in gold from Ophir highlights the king's high status and the honor of his court.

Verses 10-12: The Bride's Invitation

Verses 10-12: "Listen, O daughter, consider and incline your ear; forget your own people also, and your father's house; so the King will greatly desire your beauty; because He is your Lord, worship Him. And the daughter of Tyre will come with a gift; the rich among the people will seek your favor."

- "Forget your own people" (עַמֵּךְ שִׁכְחִי, shekhi'chi 'amech) indicates leaving behind past allegiances.

- "Worship Him" (וְהִשְׁתַּחֲוִי־לוֹ, vehishtachavi-lo) signifies reverence and submission.

The psalmist addresses the bride, encouraging her to leave her past behind and fully embrace her new life with the king. Her beauty and submission to the king will earn his desire and favor. The mention of the daughter of Tyre and wealthy people seeking her favor underscores the honor and influence she will gain.

Verses 13-15: The Bride's Splendor

Verses 13-15: "The royal daughter is all glorious within the palace; her clothing is woven with gold. She shall be brought to the King in robes of many colors; the virgins, her companions who follow her, shall be brought to You. With gladness and rejoicing they shall be brought; they shall enter the King's palace."

- "Glorious" (כָּבוֹד, kavod) indicates beauty and honor.

- "Robes of many colors" (רִקְמָה, rikmah) suggest a richly adorned garment.

The bride is described in her splendor, adorned in gold-woven clothing and multicolored robes. Her companions, the virgins, accompany her with joy and celebration as they enter the king's palace. This imagery highlights the grandeur and festivity of the royal wedding.

Verses 16-17: The Future Generations

Verses 16-17: "Instead of Your fathers shall be Your sons, whom You shall make princes in all the earth. I will make Your name to be remembered in all generations; therefore the people shall praise You forever and ever."

- "Princes" (שָׂרִים, sarim) signify leadership and nobility.

- "Remembered" (זָכַר, zakar) indicates enduring legacy.

The psalmist prophesies that the king's sons will succeed him, becoming princes across the earth. The king's name will be remembered through all generations, ensuring perpetual praise and honor.

Theological Significance

The Righteous King as a Messianic Figure

1. Divine Anointing and Eternal Throne: Verses 6-7 emphasize the divine nature of the king's throne and his anointing with the oil of gladness. This imagery points to the Messiah, whose reign is eternal and marked by righteousness and joy (Hebrews 1:8-9).

2. Righteous Rule and Justice: The king's commitment to truth, humility, and righteousness (verse 4) reflects the messianic ideals of a just and righteous ruler. Jesus, as the Messiah, fulfills these attributes perfectly (Isaiah 9:6-7).

3. Royal Splendor and Divine Favor: The luxurious description of the king's garments and palace (verses 8-9)

symbolizes the glory and honor bestowed upon the Messiah. Jesus' divine favor and royal status are affirmed throughout the New Testament (Philippians 2:9-11).

The Bride of the King

1. Call to Devotion and Worship: The bride's invitation to forget her past and worship the king (verses 10-12) symbolizes the call for believers to leave behind their old lives and fully commit to Christ. The church, as the bride of Christ, is called to worship and devotion (Ephesians 5:25-27).

2. Glorious Adornment and Celebration: The bride's splendor and the joyful celebration of her marriage (verses 13-15) reflect the church's glorification and the ultimate union with Christ. The imagery of the wedding feast is a powerful symbol of the eschatological hope in Revelation 19:7-9.

Enduring Legacy and Eternal Praise

1. Future Generations of Leaders: The prophecy of the king's sons becoming princes (verse 16) symbolizes the spread of the Gospel and the establishment of Christ's kingdom through His followers. Believers are called to be leaders and ambassadors of Christ (2 Corinthians 5:20).

2. Perpetual Remembrance and Praise: The promise that the king's name will be remembered and praised forever (verse 17) underscores the eternal significance of Jesus' reign. The name of Jesus will be exalted for all generations (Philippians 2:10-11).

Practical Applications

1. Embrace Righteousness and Justice: Believers are called to embody the virtues of truth, humility, and righteousness exemplified by the Righteous King. This involves living justly, loving mercy, and walking humbly with God (Micah 6:8).

2. Commit to Worship and Devotion: The call to the bride to worship the king serves as a reminder for believers to prioritize their relationship with Christ. Worship and

devotion should be central to the believer's life (Romans 12:1).

3. Reflect the King's Splendor: The description of the bride's glorious adornment encourages believers to reflect Christ's beauty and glory in their lives. This involves living in a way that honors God and attracts others to Him (Matthew 5:16).

4. Anticipate the Eternal Union with Christ: The imagery of the royal wedding and the joyful celebration invites believers to anticipate the ultimate union with Christ. This eschatological hope should inspire joy and perseverance in the faith (Revelation 21:2-4).

5. Ensure an Enduring Legacy: The prophecy of future generations of leaders and the perpetual remembrance of the king's name calls believers to leave a lasting impact through their faith and witness. This involves discipling others and spreading the Gospel (Matthew 28:19-20).

Comprehensive Commentary

Theological and Messianic Implications

1. Hebrews 1:8-9: The citation of Psalm 45:6-7 in Hebrews 1:8-9 directly applies the psalm to Jesus Christ, affirming His divine nature and eternal kingship. This New Testament interpretation solidifies the messianic understanding of the psalm.

2. Isaiah 9:6-7: The portrayal of the Righteous King in Psalm 45 aligns with the prophetic description of the Messiah in Isaiah 9:6-7. Both passages emphasize the eternal and righteous reign of the Messiah.

3. Philippians 2:9-11: The royal splendor and divine favor described in Psalm 45 find their ultimate fulfillment in the exaltation of Jesus Christ, as described in Philippians 2:9-11. Jesus is given the name above every name, and every knee will bow to Him.

Exegetical Insights

1. Psalm 45:1-2: The psalmist's enthusiastic praise and description of the king's beauty and grace highlight the ideal qualities of a righteous ruler. The eternal blessing from God underscores the divine favor upon the king.

2. Psalm 45:3-5: The imagery of the warrior king emphasizes the king's role in upholding justice and righteousness through his military prowess. The king's success is attributed to his commitment to virtuous principles.

3. Psalm 45:6-7: The divine throne and scepter of righteousness signify the eternal and just rule of the king. The anointing with the oil of gladness highlights the king's special status and favor from God.

4. Psalm 45:8-9: The luxurious description of the king's garments and palace, along with the honorable women in his court, underscores the splendor and grandeur of his reign.

5. Psalm 45:10-12: The bride's call to devotion and worship of the king symbolizes the church's call to commitment and reverence for Christ. The favor and honor she receives reflect the blessings of being united with the king.

6. Psalm 45:13-15: The bride's glorious adornment and the joyful celebration of her marriage to the king illustrate the beauty and festivity of the ultimate union between Christ and the church.

7. Psalm 45:16-17: The prophecy of future generations of leaders and the perpetual remembrance of the king's name emphasize the enduring legacy and eternal praise due to Christ's reign.

Conclusion

Psalm 45 presents a vivid portrayal of the Righteous King, whose majesty, righteousness, and eternal reign point to the ultimate fulfillment in Jesus Christ. Through detailed expository study and comprehensive commentary, we have explored the theological significance and practical applications of this psalm. This chapter has provided a thorough examination of Psalm 45:1-17, enhancing our understanding of the Righteous King and inspiring believers to live out these principles in their daily lives.

The Royal Wedding Song as a Prophecy of Jesus

Psalm 45, known as the royal wedding song, is a celebration of a king's marriage. While it describes the splendor and majesty of an earthly king, this psalm also holds a deeper, prophetic significance, pointing to Jesus Christ, the ultimate Righteous King and Bridegroom of the Church. This chapter will explore Psalm 45 as a prophecy of Jesus, analyzing its verses and uncovering the messianic implications that foreshadow the coming of Christ. Using Bible verses, an expository study, and comprehensive commentary supported by Strong's Exhaustive Concordance, we will delve into the prophetic layers of this psalm.

Text of Psalm 45 (NKJV)

1. My heart is overflowing with a good theme; I recite my composition concerning the King; my tongue is the pen of a ready writer.

2. You are fairer than the sons of men; grace is poured upon Your lips; therefore God has blessed You forever.

3. Gird Your sword upon Your thigh, O Mighty One, with Your glory and Your majesty.

4. And in Your majesty ride prosperously because of truth, humility, and righteousness; and Your right hand shall teach You awesome things.

5. Your arrows are sharp in the heart of the King's enemies; the peoples fall under You.

6. Your throne, O God, is forever and ever; a scepter of righteousness is the scepter of Your kingdom.

7. You love righteousness and hate wickedness; therefore God, Your God, has anointed You with the oil of gladness more than Your companions.

8. All Your garments are scented with myrrh and aloes and cassia, out of the ivory palaces, by which they have made You glad.

9. Kings' daughters are among Your honorable women; at Your right hand stands the queen in gold from Ophir.

10. Listen, O daughter, consider and incline your ear; forget your own people also, and your father's house;

11. So the King will greatly desire your beauty; because He is your Lord, worship Him.

12. And the daughter of Tyre will come with a gift; the rich among the people will seek your favor.

13. The royal daughter is all glorious within the palace; her clothing is woven with gold.

14. She shall be brought to the King in robes of many colors; the virgins, her companions who follow her, shall be brought to You.

15. With gladness and rejoicing they shall be brought; they shall enter the King's palace.

16. Instead of Your fathers shall be Your sons, whom You shall make princes in all the earth.

17. I will make Your name to be remembered in all generations; therefore the people shall praise You forever and ever.

Expository Study

Verses 1-2: The King's Splendor and Grace

Verses 1-2: "My heart is overflowing with a good theme; I recite my composition concerning the King; my tongue is the pen of a ready writer. You are fairer than the sons of men; grace is poured upon Your lips; therefore God has blessed You forever."

- "Overflowing" (רָחַשׁ, rachash) indicates an abundant outpouring of praise.

- "Fairer" (יָפְיָפִיתָ, yaphyapita) suggests surpassing beauty.

- "Grace" (חֵן, chen) signifies favor and charm.

The psalmist begins with a heartfelt expression of praise for the king, describing him as exceedingly fair and gracious. This portrayal can be seen as a foreshadowing of Jesus Christ, who embodies divine grace and beauty. The eternal blessing from God points to the everlasting nature of Christ's kingship.

Verses 3-5: The Warrior King

Verses 3-5: "Gird Your sword upon Your thigh, O Mighty One, with Your glory and Your majesty. And in Your majesty ride prosperously because of truth, humility, and righteousness; and Your right hand shall teach You awesome things. Your arrows are sharp in the heart of the King's enemies; the peoples fall under You."

- "Sword" (חֶרֶב, chereb) symbolizes divine authority and power.

- "Truth" (אֱמֶת, emeth), "humility" (עֲנָוָה, anavah), and "righteousness" (צֶדֶק, tsedeq) are virtues epitomized by Christ.

The imagery of the warrior king girding his sword and riding triumphantly for truth, humility, and righteousness prefigures Jesus' mission. Jesus, the ultimate Mighty One, confronts evil with divine authority, and His teachings and actions reflect truth, humility, and righteousness.

Verses 6-7: The Eternal Throne and Divine Anointing

Verses 6-7: "Your throne, O God, is forever and ever; a scepter of righteousness is the scepter of Your kingdom. You love righteousness and hate wickedness; therefore God, Your God, has anointed You with the oil of gladness more than Your companions."

- "Throne" (כִּסֵּא, kisse) signifies eternal authority.

- "Anointed" (מָשַׁח, mashach) refers to consecration and divine favor.

The declaration of the king's eternal throne and divine anointing explicitly points to Jesus. Hebrews 1:8-9 quotes this passage, directly applying it to Christ, emphasizing His eternal kingship and righteous rule. Jesus' anointing with the oil of gladness signifies His unique role and divine favor.

Verses 8-9: Royal Splendor and Honor

Verses 8-9: "All Your garments are scented with myrrh and aloes and cassia, out of the ivory palaces, by which they have made You glad. Kings' daughters are among Your honorable women; at Your right hand stands the queen in gold from Ophir."

- "Myrrh" (מֹר, mor), "aloes" (אֲהָלוֹת, ahaloth), and "cassia" (קְצִיעָה, qetsi'ah) symbolize wealth and luxury.

- "Ivory palaces" (שֵׁן הֵיכְלֵי, heykle shen) suggest opulence and grandeur.

The depiction of the king's royal splendor, including luxurious garments and a magnificent palace, alludes to the glory and honor of Christ's heavenly reign. The presence of the queen and honorable women signifies the church's exalted position alongside Christ, adorned with spiritual beauty.

Verses 10-12: The Bride's Call to Devotion

Verses 10-12: "Listen, O daughter, consider and incline your ear; forget your own people also, and your father's house; so the King will greatly desire your beauty; because He is your Lord, worship Him. And the daughter of Tyre will come with a gift; the rich among the people will seek your favor."

- "Forget your own people" (עַמֵּךְ שִׁכְחִי, shekhi'chi 'amech) signifies leaving behind old allegiances.

- "Worship Him" (וְהִשְׁתַּחֲוִי־לוֹ, vehishtachavi-lo) denotes reverence and submission.

The bride's call to leave her past and fully devote herself to the king symbolizes the church's call to abandon former ways and wholeheartedly follow Christ. Her beauty and worship earn the king's favor, reflecting the church's honored position before Christ. The mention of gifts and favor from the wealthy indicates the honor and influence the church receives.

Verses 13-15: The Bride's Glorious Presentation

Verses 13-15: "The royal daughter is all glorious within the palace; her clothing is woven with gold. She shall be brought to the King in robes of many colors; the virgins, her companions who follow her, shall be brought to You. With gladness and rejoicing they shall be brought; they shall enter the King's palace."

- "Glorious" (כָּבוֹד, kavod) indicates beauty and splendor.

- "Robes of many colors" (רִקְמָה, rikmah) suggest rich adornment.

The bride's glorious presentation, adorned in gold and colorful robes, prefigures the church's ultimate glorification. The joyful procession into the king's palace reflects the eschatological hope of the church's union with Christ, celebrated with gladness and rejoicing.

Verses 16-17: The King's Eternal Legacy

Verses 16-17: "Instead of Your fathers shall be Your sons, whom You shall make princes in all the earth. I will make Your name to be remembered in all generations; therefore the people shall praise You forever and ever."

- "Princes" (שָׂרִים, sarim) signify leaders and rulers.

- "Remembered" (זָכַר, zakar) indicates enduring legacy.

The prophecy of the king's sons becoming princes and his name being remembered forever points to the eternal impact of Christ's reign. Believers, as spiritual descendants, are called to leadership and witness, ensuring that Christ's name is praised through all generations.

Theological Significance

Messianic Fulfillment in Jesus

1. Eternal Kingship: The psalmist's depiction of an eternal throne (verses 6-7) finds its ultimate fulfillment in Jesus

Christ, whose reign is everlasting. Hebrews 1:8-9 directly applies this passage to Christ, affirming His divine kingship and righteous rule.

2. Divine Anointing: The anointing with the oil of gladness (verse 7) symbolizes Christ's unique role and favor from God. This anointing sets Jesus apart as the Messiah, the anointed one who brings salvation and joy to His people.

3. Righteous Rule: The emphasis on truth, humility, and righteousness (verses 4-5) characterizes Jesus' ministry and mission. Jesus embodies these virtues perfectly, establishing a kingdom founded on righteousness and justice.

The Church as the Bride of Christ

1. Call to Devotion: The bride's call to leave her past and worship the king (verses 10-12) symbolizes the church's call to total devotion to Christ. Believers are called to forsake former ways and fully commit to following Jesus.

2. Glorious Adornment: The bride's glorious presentation (verses 13-15) reflects the church's future glorification. The church, as the bride of Christ, is adorned with spiritual beauty and destined for eternal union with Christ.

3. Eternal Impact: The prophecy of the king's sons becoming princes and his name being remembered (verses 16-17) underscores the enduring legacy of Christ's reign. Believers are called to be leaders and witnesses, ensuring that Christ's name is exalted for all generations.

Practical Applications

1. Embrace Christ's Righteous Rule: Believers are called to live by the virtues of truth, humility, and righteousness exemplified by Christ. This involves pursuing justice, loving mercy, and walking humbly with God (Micah 6:8).

2. Commit to Total Devotion: The bride's call to worship the king reminds believers of their call to total devotion to Christ. This commitment involves leaving behind former ways and prioritizing their relationship with Jesus (Romans 12:1-2).

3. Anticipate Future Glorification: The imagery of the bride's glorious presentation encourages believers to anticipate their future glorification with Christ. This hope inspires perseverance and faithfulness in the present (Revelation 19:7-9).

4. Ensure an Enduring Legacy: The prophecy of future generations and the eternal remembrance of the king's name calls believers to leave a lasting impact through their faith and witness. This involves discipling others and spreading the Gospel (Matthew 28:19-20).

Comprehensive Commentary

Theological and Messianic Implications

1. Hebrews 1:8-9: The citation of Psalm 45:6-7 in Hebrews directly applies the psalm to Jesus Christ, affirming His divine nature and eternal kingship. This New Testament interpretation solidifies the messianic understanding of the psalm and highlights its prophetic significance.

2. Revelation 19:7-9: The imagery of the royal wedding in Psalm 45 parallels the eschatological wedding feast of the Lamb in Revelation. This connection underscores the ultimate fulfillment of the psalm's prophetic vision in the union between Christ and His church.

3. Ephesians 5:25-27: Paul's description of the church as the bride of Christ echoes the themes of Psalm 45. The

church is called to be holy and blameless, reflecting the spiritual beauty and devotion described in the psalm.

Exegetical Insights

1. Psalm 45:1-2: The psalmist's enthusiastic praise and description of the king's beauty and grace highlight the ideal qualities of a righteous ruler. The eternal blessing from God points to the divine favor upon the king, prefiguring Christ's ultimate kingship.

2. Psalm 45:3-5: The imagery of the warrior king emphasizes the king's role in upholding justice and righteousness. This portrayal foreshadows Jesus' mission to confront evil and establish a kingdom of truth and righteousness.

3. Psalm 45:6-7: The declaration of the king's eternal throne and divine anointing explicitly points to Jesus. The New Testament application of this passage to Christ in Hebrews underscores its messianic significance.

4. Psalm 45:8-9: The luxurious description of the king's garments and palace, along with the honorable women in his court, symbolizes the glory and honor of Christ's heavenly reign.

5. Psalm 45:10-12: The bride's call to devotion and worship of the king symbolizes the church's call to commitment and reverence for Christ. Her beauty and worship reflect the church's honored position before Christ.

6. Psalm 45:13-15: The bride's glorious presentation and the joyful celebration of her marriage to the king illustrate the beauty and festivity of the ultimate union between Christ and the church.

7. Psalm 45:16-17: The prophecy of future generations of leaders and the perpetual remembrance of the king's name emphasize the enduring legacy and eternal praise due to Christ's reign.

Conclusion

Psalm 45, while celebrating an earthly royal wedding, ultimately points to the divine, eternal union between Jesus Christ and His church. Through detailed expository study and comprehensive commentary, we have explored the prophetic layers of this psalm, uncovering its messianic significance and theological implications. This chapter has provided a thorough examination of Psalm 45 as a prophecy of Jesus, enhancing our understanding of Christ as the Righteous King and inspiring believers to live out these principles in their daily lives.

Attributes of the Righteous King

Psalm 45 is a magnificent depiction of a royal wedding, celebrating the majesty and virtues of a king. While it initially appears to describe an earthly king, this psalm also serves as a profound prophecy pointing to Jesus Christ, the ultimate Righteous King. This chapter will explore the attributes of the Righteous King as outlined in Psalm 45:1-17, providing a detailed analysis and uncovering the messianic implications that foreshadow Christ. Using Bible verses, an expository study, and comprehensive commentary supported by Strong's Exhaustive Concordance, we will delve into the attributes that characterize this Righteous King.

Text of Psalm 45 (NKJV)

1. My heart is overflowing with a good theme; I recite my composition concerning the King; my tongue is the pen of a ready writer.

2. You are fairer than the sons of men; grace is poured upon Your lips; therefore God has blessed You forever.

3. Gird Your sword upon Your thigh, O Mighty One, with Your glory and Your majesty.

4. And in Your majesty ride prosperously because of truth, humility, and righteousness; and Your right hand shall teach You awesome things.

5. Your arrows are sharp in the heart of the King's enemies; the peoples fall under You.

6. Your throne, O God, is forever and ever; a scepter of righteousness is the scepter of Your kingdom.

7. You love righteousness and hate wickedness; therefore God, Your God, has anointed You with the oil of gladness more than Your companions.

8. All Your garments are scented with myrrh and aloes and cassia, out of the ivory palaces, by which they have made You glad.

9. Kings' daughters are among Your honorable women; at Your right hand stands the queen in gold from Ophir.

10. Listen, O daughter, consider and incline your ear; forget your own people also, and your father's house;

11. So the King will greatly desire your beauty; because He is your Lord, worship Him.

12. And the daughter of Tyre will come with a gift; the rich among the people will seek your favor.

13. The royal daughter is all glorious within the palace; her clothing is woven with gold.

14. She shall be brought to the King in robes of many colors; the virgins, her companions who follow her, shall be brought to You.

15. With gladness and rejoicing they shall be brought; they shall enter the King's palace.

16. Instead of Your fathers shall be Your sons, whom You shall make princes in all the earth.

17. I will make Your name to be remembered in all generations; therefore the people shall praise You forever and ever.

Expository Study

Verse 1: The Overflowing Heart

Verse 1: "My heart is overflowing with a good theme; I recite my composition concerning the King; my tongue is the pen of a ready writer."

- "Overflowing" (רָחַשׁ, rachash) indicates an abundant and enthusiastic outpouring.

- "Ready writer" (מָהִיר סוֹפֵר, sopher mahir) suggests a skillful and prepared scribe.

The psalmist begins with an expression of a heart full of praise, eager to celebrate the king. This overflowing praise sets the tone for the psalm, highlighting the king's extraordinary qualities that inspire such devotion.

Verses 2-3: Beauty and Grace

Verses 2-3: "You are fairer than the sons of men; grace is poured upon Your lips; therefore God has blessed You forever. Gird Your sword upon Your thigh, O Mighty One, with Your glory and Your majesty."

- "Fairer" (יָפְיָפִיתָ, yaphyapita) suggests surpassing beauty and charm.

- "Grace" (חֵן, chen) signifies favor and charm.

- "Mighty One" (גִּבּוֹר, gibbor) denotes strength and valor.

The king is described as surpassingly beautiful and gracious, characteristics that set him apart from ordinary men. His speech is filled with grace, indicating wisdom and kindness. The psalmist also portrays the king as a mighty warrior, embodying glory and majesty.

Verse 4: Truth, Humility, and Righteousness

Verse 4: "And in Your majesty ride prosperously because of truth, humility, and righteousness; and Your right hand shall teach You awesome things."

- "Truth" (אֱמֶת, emeth), "humility" (עֲנָוָה, anavah), and "righteousness" (צֶדֶק, tsedeq) are virtues that define the king's rule.

The king's prosperity and success are attributed to his commitment to truth, humility, and righteousness. These virtues are fundamental to his reign, ensuring that his rule is just and honorable.

Verses 5-7: Military Prowess and Divine Anointing

Verses 5-7: "Your arrows are sharp in the heart of the King's enemies; the peoples fall under You. Your throne, O God, is forever and ever; a scepter of righteousness is the scepter of Your kingdom. You love righteousness and hate wickedness; therefore God, Your God, has anointed You with the oil of gladness more than Your companions."

- "Throne" (כִּסֵּא, kisse) signifies enduring authority.

- "Scepter" (שֵׁבֶט, shevet) symbolizes the king's rule.

- "Anointed" (מָשַׁח, mashach) refers to ceremonial consecration.

The king's sharp arrows and military prowess depict his ability to vanquish enemies and maintain peace. His eternal throne and scepter of righteousness signify a just and enduring reign. The divine anointing with the oil of gladness indicates special favor and joy bestowed upon him by God.

Verses 8-9: Royal Splendor

Verses 8-9: "All Your garments are scented with myrrh and aloes and cassia, out of the ivory palaces, by which they have made You glad. Kings' daughters are among Your honorable women; at Your right hand stands the queen in gold from Ophir."

- "Myrrh" (מֹר, mor), "aloes" (אֲהָלוֹת, ahaloth), and "cassia" (קְצִיעָה, qetsi'ah) are aromatic spices signifying wealth and luxury.

- "Ivory palaces" (שֵׁן הֵיכְלֵי, heykle shen) suggest opulence and grandeur.

The description of the king's royal splendor, including luxurious garments and palatial surroundings, highlights his elevated status and the honor of his court. The presence of queens and daughters of kings signifies his widespread influence and the respect he commands.

Verses 10-12: The Bride's Call to Devotion

Verses 10-12: "Listen, O daughter, consider and incline your ear; forget your own people also, and your father's house; so the King will greatly desire your beauty; because He is your Lord, worship Him. And the daughter of Tyre will come with a gift; the rich among the people will seek your favor."

- "Forget your own people" (עַמֵּךְ שִׁכְחִי, shekhi'chi 'amech) indicates leaving behind past allegiances.

- "Worship Him" (וְהִשְׁתַּחֲוִי־לוֹ, vehishtachavi-lo) signifies reverence and submission.

The psalmist addresses the bride, encouraging her to leave her past behind and fully embrace her new life with the king. Her beauty and submission to the king will earn his desire and favor. The mention of the daughter of Tyre and wealthy people seeking her favor underscores the honor and influence she will gain.

Verses 13-15: The Bride's Glorious Presentation

Verses 13-15: "The royal daughter is all glorious within the palace; her clothing is woven with gold. She shall be brought to the King in robes of many colors; the virgins, her companions who follow her, shall be brought to You. With gladness and rejoicing they shall be brought; they shall enter the King's palace."

- "Glorious" (כָּבוֹד, kavod) indicates beauty and splendor.

- "Robes of many colors" (רִקְמָה, rikmah) suggest rich adornment.

The bride's glorious presentation, adorned in gold and colorful robes, prefigures the church's ultimate glorification. The joyful procession into the king's palace reflects the eschatological hope of the church's union with Christ, celebrated with gladness and rejoicing.

Verses 16-17: The King's Eternal Legacy

Verses 16-17: "Instead of Your fathers shall be Your sons, whom You shall make princes in all the earth. I will make Your name to be remembered in all generations; therefore the people shall praise You forever and ever."

- "Princes" (שָׂרִים, sarim) signify leaders and rulers.

- "Remembered" (זָכַר, zakar) indicates enduring legacy.

The prophecy of the king's sons becoming princes and his name being remembered forever points to the eternal impact of Christ's reign. Believers, as spiritual descendants, are called to leadership and witness, ensuring that Christ's name is praised through all generations.

Theological Significance

Messianic Fulfillment in Jesus

1. Eternal Kingship: The psalmist's depiction of an eternal throne (verses 6-7) finds its ultimate fulfillment in Jesus Christ, whose reign is everlasting. Hebrews 1:8-9 directly applies this passage to Christ, affirming His divine kingship and righteous rule.

2. Divine Anointing: The anointing with the oil of gladness (verse 7) symbolizes Christ's unique role and favor from God. This anointing sets Jesus apart as the Messiah, the anointed one who brings salvation and joy to His people.

3. Righteous Rule: The emphasis on truth, humility, and righteousness (verses 4-5) characterizes Jesus' ministry and mission. Jesus embodies these virtues perfectly, establishing a kingdom founded on righteousness and justice.

The Church as the Bride of Christ

1. Call to Devotion: The bride's call to leave her past and worship the king (verses 10-12) symbolizes the church's

call to total devotion to Christ. Believers are called to forsake former ways and fully commit to following Jesus.

2. Glorious Adornment: The bride's glorious presentation (verses 13-15) reflects the church's future glorification. The church, as the bride of Christ, is adorned with spiritual beauty and destined for eternal union with Christ.

3. Eternal Impact: The prophecy of the king's sons becoming princes and his name being remembered (verses 16-17) underscores the enduring legacy of Christ's reign. Believers are called to be leaders and witnesses, ensuring that Christ's name is exalted for all generations.

Practical Applications

1. Embrace Christ's Righteous Rule: Believers are called to live by the virtues of truth, humility, and righteousness exemplified by Christ. This involves pursuing justice, loving mercy, and walking humbly with God (Micah 6:8).

2. Commit to Total Devotion: The bride's call to worship the king reminds believers of their call to total devotion to Christ. This commitment involves leaving behind former ways and prioritizing their relationship with Jesus (Romans 12:1-2).

3. Anticipate Future Glorification: The imagery of the bride's glorious presentation encourages believers to anticipate their future glorification with Christ. This hope inspires perseverance and faithfulness in the present (Revelation 19:7-9).

4. Ensure an Enduring Legacy: The prophecy of future generations and the eternal remembrance of the king's name calls believers to leave a lasting impact through their faith and witness. This involves discipling others and spreading the Gospel (Matthew 28:19-20).

Comprehensive Commentary

Theological and Messianic Implications

1. Hebrews 1:8-9: The citation of Psalm 45:6-7 in Hebrews directly applies the psalm to Jesus Christ, affirming His divine nature and eternal kingship. This New Testament interpretation solidifies the messianic understanding of the psalm and highlights its prophetic significance.

2. Revelation 19:7-9: The imagery of the royal wedding in Psalm 45 parallels the eschatological wedding feast of the Lamb in Revelation. This connection underscores the ultimate fulfillment of the psalm's prophetic vision in the union between Christ and His church.

3. Ephesians 5:25-27: Paul's description of the church as the bride of Christ echoes the themes of Psalm 45. The church is called to be holy and blameless, reflecting the spiritual beauty and devotion described in the psalm.

Exegetical Insights

1. Psalm 45:1-2: The psalmist's enthusiastic praise and description of the king's beauty and grace highlight the ideal qualities of a righteous ruler. The eternal blessing from God points to the divine favor upon the king, prefiguring Christ's ultimate kingship.

2. Psalm 45:3-5: The imagery of the warrior king emphasizes the king's role in upholding justice and righteousness. This portrayal foreshadows Jesus' mission to confront evil and establish a kingdom of truth and righteousness.

3. Psalm 45:6-7: The declaration of the king's eternal throne and divine anointing explicitly points to Jesus. The New Testament application of this passage to Christ in Hebrews underscores its messianic significance.

4. Psalm 45:8-9: The luxurious description of the king's garments and palace, along with the honorable women in his court, symbolizes the glory and honor of Christ's heavenly reign.

5. Psalm 45:10-12: The bride's call to devotion and worship of the king symbolizes the church's call to commitment and reverence for Christ. Her beauty and worship reflect the church's honored position before Christ.

6. Psalm 45:13-15: The bride's glorious presentation and the joyful celebration of her marriage to the king illustrate the beauty and festivity of the ultimate union between Christ and the church.

7. Psalm 45:16-17: The prophecy of future generations of leaders and the perpetual remembrance of the king's name emphasize the enduring legacy and eternal praise due to Christ's reign.

Conclusion

Psalm 45 presents a vivid portrayal of the Righteous King, whose majesty, righteousness, and eternal reign point to the ultimate fulfillment in Jesus Christ. Through detailed expository study and comprehensive commentary, we have explored the theological significance and practical applications of this psalm. This chapter has provided a thorough examination of the attributes of the Righteous King, enhancing our understanding of Christ's kingship and inspiring believers to live out these principles in their daily lives.

New Testament Revelations

Psalm 45, though originally a royal wedding song celebrating an earthly king, contains profound prophetic elements that find their ultimate fulfillment in Jesus Christ. The New Testament sheds light on these revelations, revealing Jesus as the Righteous King who embodies the virtues and characteristics outlined in the psalm. This chapter explores the New Testament revelations that connect Psalm 45 to the life, mission, and reign of Jesus Christ, providing a comprehensive understanding of its messianic significance.

The Eternal Kingship of Jesus

Hebrews 1:8-9: The Divine Throne

Hebrews 1:8-9: "But to the Son He says: 'Your throne, O God, is forever and ever; a scepter of righteousness is the scepter of Your kingdom. You have loved righteousness and hated lawlessness; therefore God, Your God, has anointed You with the oil of gladness more than Your companions.'"

- "Throne" (θρόνος, thronos) signifies enduring authority and kingship.

- "Scepter" (ῥάβδος, rhabdos) symbolizes royal power and rule.

- "Anointed" (χρίω, chriō) refers to being consecrated or set apart by God.

The author of Hebrews directly quotes Psalm 45:6-7, applying it to Jesus Christ. This passage affirms the eternal nature of Jesus' kingship and His divine authority. Jesus is described as loving righteousness and hating lawlessness, qualities that are essential to His reign. The anointing with the oil of gladness signifies Jesus' unique role and the joy associated with His messianic mission.

Revelation 19:11-16: The Victorious King

Revelation 19:11-16: "Now I saw heaven opened, and behold, a white horse. And He who sat on him was called Faithful and True, and in righteousness He judges and makes war. His eyes were like a flame of fire, and on His head were many crowns. He had a name written that no one knew except Himself. He was clothed with a robe dipped in blood, and His name is called The Word of God. And the armies in heaven, clothed in fine linen, white and clean, followed Him on white horses. Now out of His mouth goes a sharp sword, that with it He should strike the nations. And He Himself will rule them with a rod of iron. He Himself treads the winepress of the fierceness and wrath of Almighty God. And He has on His robe and on His thigh a name written: KING OF KINGS AND LORD OF LORDS."

- "Faithful and True" (πιστὸς καὶ ἀληθινός, pistos kai alēthinos) emphasizes Jesus' reliability and truthfulness.

- "Sharp sword" (ῥομφαία ὀξεῖα, rhomphaia oxeia) symbolizes the power of His word and judgment.

- "King of Kings and Lord of Lords" (βασιλεὺς βασιλέων καὶ κύριος κυρίων, basileus basileōn kai kyrios kyriōn) signifies His supreme authority over all rulers.

In Revelation, Jesus is depicted as the victorious King who judges and makes war in righteousness. His royal attributes, such as faithfulness, truth, and righteousness, align with the virtues described in Psalm 45. The imagery of the sharp sword and the title "King of Kings and Lord of Lords" highlight His ultimate authority and power over all creation.

The Bride of Christ

Ephesians 5:25-27: The Church as the Bride

Ephesians 5:25-27: "Husbands, love your wives, just as Christ also loved the church and gave Himself for her, that He might sanctify and cleanse her with the washing of water by the word, that He might present her to Himself a glorious church, not having spot or wrinkle or any such thing, but that she should be holy and without blemish."

- "Sanctify" (ἁγιάζω, hagiazō) means to make holy or set apart.

- "Cleanse" (καθαρίζω, katharizō) refers to purification.

- "Glorious" (ἔνδοξος, endoxos) indicates honor and beauty.

Paul's analogy of the church as the bride of Christ reflects the imagery in Psalm 45 of the bride being presented to the king. Jesus' sacrificial love and cleansing of the church highlight His role as the bridegroom who prepares His bride for a holy and blameless union. This relationship underscores the spiritual beauty and honor of the church as it awaits its ultimate glorification.

Revelation 19:7-9: The Marriage Supper of the Lamb

Revelation 19:7-9: "Let us be glad and rejoice and give Him glory, for the marriage of the Lamb has come, and His wife has made herself ready. And to her it was granted to be arrayed in fine linen, clean and bright, for the fine linen is the righteous acts of the saints. Then he said to me, 'Write: "Blessed are those who are called to the marriage supper of the Lamb!"' And he said to me, 'These are the true sayings of God.'"

- "Marriage of the Lamb" (γάμος τοῦ Ἀρνίου, gamos tou Arniou) symbolizes the union of Christ and the church.

- "Fine linen" (βύσσινον καθαρὸν, byssinon katharon) represents the righteous deeds of believers.

The eschatological vision of the marriage supper of the Lamb in Revelation parallels the royal wedding imagery in Psalm 45. The church, as the bride of Christ, is adorned in fine linen, symbolizing its righteous deeds. This celebration marks the ultimate union between Christ and His church, fulfilling the prophetic vision of Psalm 45.

The Attributes of Jesus as the Righteous King

Truth, Humility, and Righteousness

Psalm 45:4: "And in Your majesty ride prosperously because of truth, humility, and righteousness; and Your right hand shall teach You awesome things."

- "Truth" (אֱמֶת, emeth), "humility" (עֲנָוָה, anavah), and "righteousness" (צֶדֶק, tsedeq) are virtues epitomized by Christ.

Jesus' life and ministry exemplify truth, humility, and righteousness. He is the embodiment of divine truth (John 14:6), demonstrated humility by His incarnation and sacrificial death (Philippians 2:5-8), and upheld righteousness in all His actions (Matthew 5:17-20). These attributes underscore His qualifications as the Righteous King.

Love for Righteousness and Hatred of Wickedness

Psalm 45:7: "You love righteousness and hate wickedness; therefore God, Your God, has anointed You with the oil of gladness more than Your companions."

- "Love" (אָהַב, ahav) and "hate" (שָׂנֵא, sane) denote deep emotional commitments.

Jesus' commitment to righteousness and His opposition to wickedness are evident throughout the New Testament. His anointing with the oil of gladness signifies His unique role and divine favor. This anointing is a testament to His perfect character and mission (Luke 4:18-19).

Eternal Throne and Divine Authority

Psalm 45:6: "Your throne, O God, is forever and ever; a scepter of righteousness is the scepter of Your kingdom."

- "Throne" (כִּסֵּא, kisse) signifies enduring authority.

- "Scepter" (שֵׁבֶט, shevet) symbolizes royal power.

Jesus' eternal throne and divine authority are affirmed in various New Testament passages. His resurrection and ascension to the right hand of God establish Him as the eternal King (Hebrews 1:3, Acts 2:33). His scepter of righteousness symbolizes His just and righteous rule over all creation.

Practical Applications

1. Embrace the Reign of Christ: Believers are called to recognize and submit to the eternal kingship of Jesus. This involves living under His authority, embracing His truth, and upholding His standards of righteousness (Colossians 3:17).

2. Live Out the Virtues of the King: Followers of Christ are encouraged to embody the virtues of truth, humility, and righteousness in their daily lives. By reflecting these attributes, believers honor their Righteous King and become effective witnesses for His kingdom (Ephesians 4:1-3).

3. Prepare as the Bride of Christ: The church, as the bride of Christ, is called to prepare for the ultimate union with

the Bridegroom. This preparation involves living holy and blameless lives, engaging in righteous deeds, and cultivating a deep relationship with Jesus (2 Corinthians 11:2).

4. Celebrate the Eternal Union: Believers can find joy and hope in the promise of the marriage supper of the Lamb. This eschatological event signifies the culmination of God's redemptive plan and the eternal union between Christ and His church. Celebrating this future reality encourages perseverance and faithfulness (Revelation 21:2-4).

Comprehensive Commentary

Theological and Messianic Implications

1. Hebrews 1:8-9: The direct application of Psalm 45:6-7 to Jesus Christ in Hebrews underscores the psalm's messianic significance. This New

Testament revelation confirms Jesus' divine nature, eternal kingship, and righteous rule.

2. Revelation 19:7-16: The depiction of Jesus as the victorious King and the celebration of the marriage supper of the Lamb provide a comprehensive fulfillment of Psalm 45's prophetic vision. These revelations highlight the ultimate victory and eternal union between Christ and His church.

3. Ephesians 5:25-27: Paul's analogy of the church as the bride of Christ aligns with the themes of Psalm 45. The call to sanctification and the presentation of a glorious church reflect the psalm's emphasis on spiritual beauty and devotion.

Exegetical Insights

1. Psalm 45:4: The virtues of truth, humility, and righteousness are foundational to Jesus' ministry and mission. These attributes define His character and actions, setting Him apart as the Righteous King.

2. Psalm 45:6-7: The eternal throne and divine anointing of the king find their ultimate fulfillment in Jesus Christ. The New Testament application of these verses highlights Jesus' unique role and divine favor.

3. Psalm 45:10-15: The imagery of the bride's preparation and presentation to the king parallels the New Testament depiction of the church's relationship with Christ. This eschatological vision underscores the spiritual beauty and eternal union between the Bridegroom and His bride.

Conclusion

Psalm 45, with its rich imagery and prophetic elements, points to Jesus Christ as the Righteous King and the Bridegroom of the church. Through detailed expository study and comprehensive commentary, we have explored the New Testament revelations that connect this psalm to the life, mission, and reign of Jesus. This chapter has provided a thorough examination of the messianic significance of Psalm 45, enhancing our understanding of Christ's kingship and inspiring believers to live out these principles in their daily lives.

CHAPTER 10

THE ETERNAL REIGN IN PSALM 89

Psalm 89 is a profound reflection on God's covenant with David and the promises of an eternal reign through his lineage. This psalm combines praise for God's faithfulness with a lament over apparent contradictions in the current state of the Davidic dynasty. It ultimately points to the fulfillment of these promises in Jesus Christ, the eternal King. This chapter will provide a detailed analysis of Psalm 89:1-52, exploring its theological significance and messianic implications. Using Bible verses, an expository study, and comprehensive commentary supported by Strong's Exhaustive Concordance, we will delve into the eternal reign promised in this psalm.

Text of Psalm 89 (NKJV)

1. I will sing of the mercies of the LORD forever; with my mouth will I make known Your faithfulness to all generations.

2. For I have said, "Mercy shall be built up forever; Your faithfulness You shall establish in the very heavens."

3. "I have made a covenant with My chosen, I have sworn to My servant David:

4. 'Your seed I will establish forever, and build up your throne to all generations.'" Selah

5. And the heavens will praise Your wonders, O LORD; Your faithfulness also in the assembly of the saints.

6. For who in the heavens can be compared to the LORD? Who among the sons of the mighty can be likened to the LORD?

7. God is greatly to be feared in the assembly of the saints, and to be held in reverence by all those around Him.

8. O LORD God of hosts, who is mighty like You, O LORD? Your faithfulness also surrounds You.

9. You rule the raging of the sea; when its waves rise, You still them.

10. You have broken Rahab in pieces, as one who is slain; You have scattered Your enemies with Your mighty arm.

11. The heavens are Yours, the earth also is Yours; the world and all its fullness, You have founded them.

12. The north and the south, You have created them; Tabor and Hermon rejoice in Your name.

13. You have a mighty arm; strong is Your hand, and high is Your right hand.

14. Righteousness and justice are the foundation of Your throne; mercy and truth go before Your face.

15. Blessed are the people who know the joyful sound! They walk, O LORD, in the light of Your countenance.

16. In Your name they rejoice all day long, and in Your righteousness they are exalted.

17. For You are the glory of their strength, and in Your favor our horn is exalted.

18. For our shield belongs to the LORD, and our king to the Holy One of Israel.

19. Then You spoke in a vision to Your holy one, and said: "I have given help to one who is mighty; I have exalted one chosen from the people.

20. I have found My servant David; with My holy oil I have anointed him,

21. With whom My hand shall be established; also My arm shall strengthen him.

22. The enemy shall not outwit him, nor the son of wickedness afflict him.

23. I will beat down his foes before his face, and plague those who hate him.

24. But My faithfulness and My mercy shall be with him, and in My name his horn shall be exalted.

25. Also I will set his hand over the sea, and his right hand over the rivers.

26. He shall cry to Me, 'You are my Father, my God, and the rock of my salvation.'

27. Also I will make him My firstborn, the highest of the kings of the earth.

28. My mercy I will keep for him forever, and My covenant shall stand firm with him.

29. His seed also I will make to endure forever, and his throne as the days of heaven.

30. If his sons forsake My law and do not walk in My judgments,

31. If they break My statutes and do not keep My commandments,

32. Then I will punish their transgression with the rod, and their iniquity with stripes.

33. Nevertheless My lovingkindness I will not utterly take from him, nor allow My faithfulness to fail.

34. My covenant I will not break, nor alter the word that has gone out of My lips.

35. Once I have sworn by My holiness; I will not lie to David:

36. His seed shall endure forever, and his throne as the sun before Me;

37. It shall be established forever like the moon, even like the faithful witness in the sky." Selah

38. But You have cast off and abhorred, You have been furious with Your anointed.

39. You have renounced the covenant of Your servant; You have profaned his crown by casting it to the ground.

40. You have broken down all his hedges; You have brought his strongholds to ruin.

41. All who pass by the way plunder him; he is a reproach to his neighbors.

42. You have exalted the right hand of his adversaries; You have made all his enemies rejoice.

43. You have also turned back the edge of his sword, and have not sustained him in the battle.

44. You have made his glory cease, and cast his throne down to the ground.

45. The days of his youth You have shortened; You have covered him with shame. Selah

46. How long, LORD? Will You hide Yourself forever? Will Your wrath burn like fire?

47. Remember how short my time is; for what futility have You created all the children of men?

48. What man can live and not see death? Can he deliver his life from the power of the grave? Selah

49. Lord, where are Your former lovingkindnesses, which You swore to David in Your truth?

50. Remember, Lord, the reproach of Your servants; how I bear in my bosom the reproach of all the many peoples,

51. With which Your enemies have reproached, O LORD, with which they have reproached the footsteps of Your anointed.

52. Blessed be the LORD forevermore! Amen and Amen.

Expository Study

Verses 1-4: Declaration of God's Faithfulness

Verses 1-4: "I will sing of the mercies of the LORD forever; with my mouth will I make known Your faithfulness to all generations. For I have said, 'Mercy shall be built up forever; Your faithfulness You shall establish in the very heavens.' 'I have made a covenant with My chosen, I have sworn to My servant David: Your seed I will establish forever, and build up your throne to all generations.'" Selah

- "Mercies" (חֶסֶד, chesed) refers to God's steadfast love and kindness.

- "Faithfulness" (אֱמוּנָה, emunah) signifies reliability and trustworthiness.

- "Covenant" (בְּרִית, berit) indicates a solemn agreement or promise.

The psalmist begins with a declaration of God's enduring mercies and faithfulness. He recalls God's covenant with David, emphasizing the eternal promise to establish David's seed and throne forever. This covenant is a central theme of the psalm, reflecting God's unwavering commitment to His promises.

Verses 5-14: Praise for God's Sovereignty

Verses 5-14: "And the heavens will praise Your wonders, O LORD; Your faithfulness also in the assembly of the saints. For who in the heavens can be compared to the LORD? Who among the sons of the mighty can be likened to the LORD? God is greatly to be feared in the assembly of the saints, and to be held in reverence by all those around Him. O LORD God of hosts, who is mighty like You, O LORD? Your faithfulness also surrounds You. You rule the raging of the sea; when its waves rise, You still them. You have broken Rahab in pieces, as one who is slain; You have scattered Your enemies with Your mighty arm. The heavens are Yours, the earth also is Yours; the world and all its fullness, You have founded them. The north and the south, You have created them; Tabor and Hermon rejoice in Your name. You have a mighty arm; strong is Your hand, and high is Your right hand. Righteousness and justice are the foundation of Your throne; mercy and truth go before Your face."

- "Rahab" (רַהַב, rahav) symbolizes chaos and opposition, often referring to Egypt.

- "Righteousness" (צֶדֶק, tsedeq) and "justice" (מִשְׁפָּט, mishpat) are fundamental attributes of God's rule.

These verses extol God's sovereignty and power over creation and history. His faithfulness, might, and authority are unparalleled. The psalmist praises God's righteous and just rule, highlighting His control over nature and nations. This section underscores the trustworthiness of God's promises, as His authority is absolute and His throne is founded on righteousness and justice.

Verses 15-18: The Blessedness of God's People

Verses 15-18: "Blessed are the people who know the joyful sound! They walk, O LORD, in the light of Your countenance. In Your name they rejoice all day long, and in Your righteousness they are exalted. For You are the glory of their strength, and in Your favor our horn is exalted. For our shield belongs to the LORD, and our king to the Holy One of Israel."

- "Joyful sound" (תְּרוּעָה, teruah) refers to the shout of triumph and worship.

- "Horn" (קֶרֶן, keren) symbolizes strength and honor.

The psalmist describes the blessedness of those who walk in God's presence and experience His favor. These people rejoice in God's name and righteousness, finding strength and exaltation in His glory. The imagery of God as a shield and the Holy One of Israel as their king reinforces the security and honor bestowed upon His people.

Verses 19-29: The Covenant with David

Verses 19-29: "Then You spoke in a vision to Your holy one, and said: 'I have given help to one who is mighty; I have exalted one chosen from the people. I have found My servant David; with My holy oil I have anointed him, with whom My hand shall be established; also My arm shall strengthen him. The enemy shall not outwit him, nor the son of wickedness afflict him. I will beat down his foes before his face, and plague those who hate him. But My faithfulness and My mercy shall be with him, and in My name his horn shall be exalted. Also I will set his hand over the sea, and his right hand over the rivers. He shall cry to Me, "You are my Father, my God, and the rock of my salvation." Also I will make him My firstborn, the highest of the kings of the earth. My mercy I will keep for him forever, and My covenant shall stand firm with him. His seed also I will make to endure forever, and his throne as the days of heaven.'"

- "Anointed" (מָשַׁח, mashach) refers to being consecrated with holy oil.

- "Firstborn" (בְּכוֹר, bekhor) indicates preeminence and special status.

God's covenant with David is reiterated in these verses, emphasizing His divine selection and anointing of

David. The promises include protection from enemies, enduring mercy, and an eternal throne. The covenant assures David's descendants of a perpetual reign, with the Messiah ultimately fulfilling this promise.

Verses 30-37: Conditions and Assurance

Verses 30-37: "If his sons forsake My law and do not walk in My judgments, if they break My statutes and do not keep My commandments, then I will punish their transgression with the rod, and their iniquity with stripes. Nevertheless My lovingkindness I will not utterly take from him, nor allow My faithfulness to fail. My covenant I will not break, nor alter the word that has gone out of My lips. Once I have sworn by My holiness; I will not lie to David: His seed shall endure forever, and his throne as the sun before Me; it shall be established forever like the moon, even like the faithful witness in the sky." Selah

- "Lovingkindness" (חֶסֶד, chesed) emphasizes God's steadfast love.

- "Sworn" (שָׁבַע, shava) signifies a solemn oath.

While the covenant includes conditions for David's descendants, God's commitment to His promises remains unwavering. Even if David's descendants are disobedient, God's lovingkindness and faithfulness will endure. The promise of an eternal throne is assured, likened to the enduring sun and moon.

Verses 38-45: Lament over Broken Promises

Verses 38-45: "But You have cast off and abhorred, You have been furious with Your anointed. You have renounced the covenant of Your servant; You have profaned his crown by casting it to the ground. You have broken down all his hedges; You have brought his strongholds to ruin. All who pass by the way plunder him; he is a reproach to his neighbors. You have exalted the right hand of his adversaries; You have made all his enemies rejoice. You have also turned back the edge of his sword, and have not sustained him in the battle. You have made his glory cease, and cast his throne down to the ground. The days of his youth You have shortened; You have covered him with shame. Selah"

- "Cast off" (נָטַשׁ, natash) and "abhorred" (מָאַס, ma'as) indicate rejection and disdain.

- "Profaned" (חָלַל, chalal) signifies desecration or defilement.

The psalmist laments the apparent contradiction between God's promises and the current state of the Davidic dynasty. The imagery of a broken crown and strongholds, along with the triumph of enemies, reflects a profound sense of abandonment and shame. This section expresses deep sorrow and confusion over the perceived failure of God's covenant.

Verses 46-52: Plea for Restoration

Verses 46-52: "How long, LORD? Will You hide Yourself forever? Will Your wrath burn like fire? Remember how short my time is; for what futility have You created all the children of men? What man can live and not see death? Can he deliver his life from the power of the grave? Selah Lord, where are Your former lovingkindnesses, which You swore to David in Your truth? Remember, Lord, the reproach of Your servants; how I bear in my bosom the reproach of all the many peoples, with which Your enemies have reproached, O LORD, with which they have reproached the footsteps of Your anointed. Blessed be the LORD forevermore! Amen and Amen."

- "Hide Yourself" (סָתַר, sathar) suggests divine absence or concealment.

- "Reproach" (חֶרְפָּה, cherpah) indicates disgrace or scorn.

The psalmist ends with a heartfelt plea for restoration and a return to God's former lovingkindness. He acknowledges human mortality and the futility of life without divine intervention. The psalmist calls on God to remember His covenant with David and to restore the honor of His anointed. Despite the lament, the psalm concludes with a declaration of God's eternal blessedness.

Theological Significance

The Davidic Covenant and Its Fulfillment in Christ

1. Eternal Kingship: The promise of an eternal throne for David's descendants is a central theme in Psalm 89. This promise finds its ultimate fulfillment in Jesus Christ, who reigns forever as the eternal King (Luke 1:32-33).

2. Messianic Hope: The lament over the apparent failure of the Davidic covenant highlights the longing for the Messiah. Jesus, as the descendant of David, fulfills this hope, restoring the throne and establishing an eternal kingdom (Acts 2:30-31).

3. God's Faithfulness: Despite the apparent contradictions, the psalm emphasizes God's unwavering faithfulness. The ultimate fulfillment of God's promises in Christ demonstrates His steadfast love and reliability (2 Corinthians 1:20).

The Attributes of God's Rule

1. Righteousness and Justice: The foundation of God's throne is righteousness and justice, underscoring the moral perfection of His rule. Jesus embodies these attributes, establishing a kingdom characterized by justice and righteousness (Isaiah 9:6-7).

2. Mercy and Truth: God's rule is also marked by mercy and truth, reflecting His compassionate and faithful character. These qualities are evident in Jesus' ministry and His redemptive work (John 1:14).

Human Mortality and Divine Eternity

1. Mortality: The psalmist's reflection on human mortality and the futility of life without God's intervention

highlights the need for divine salvation. Jesus' victory over death and the grave offers hope and assurance of eternal life (1 Corinthians 15:54-57).

2. Eternal Covenant: The everlasting nature of God's covenant with David points to the eternal relationship between God and His people through Christ. This covenant assures believers of God's enduring love and commitment (Hebrews 13:20-21).

Practical Applications

1. Trust in God's Promises: Believers are called to trust in God's faithfulness and the fulfillment of His promises, even in times of apparent contradiction or delay. This trust is grounded in the ultimate fulfillment of God's promises in Christ (Romans 8:28).

2. Live Righteously: Reflecting the attributes of God's rule, believers are encouraged to live righteously, pursuing justice and mercy in their daily lives. This involves imitating Christ and upholding His standards (Micah 6:8).

3. Find Hope in Christ: In times of lament and uncertainty, believers can find hope and assurance in the eternal reign of Christ. His victory over death and the grave offers a secure foundation for faith and perseverance (Romans 5:1-5).

4. Proclaim God's Faithfulness: Like the psalmist, believers are called to proclaim God's faithfulness and steadfast love to all generations. This involves sharing the gospel and bearing witness to God's transformative work in their lives (Psalm 89:1).

Comprehensive Commentary

Theological and Messianic Implications

1. Luke 1:32-33: The promise of an eternal throne for David's descendants is fulfilled in Jesus Christ, affirming His divine kingship and eternal reign. This New Testament revelation confirms the messianic significance of Psalm 89.

2. Acts 2:30-31: Peter's sermon on the day of Pentecost connects Jesus' resurrection and exaltation to the fulfillment of God's covenant with David. This highlights the continuity of God's redemptive plan and the ultimate fulfillment in Christ.

3. 2 Corinthians 1:20: Paul emphasizes that all of God's promises find their

"Yes" in Christ, underscoring His faithfulness and the assurance of His promises. This theological insight reinforces the reliability of God's covenant and the fulfillment in Jesus.

Exegetical Insights

1. Psalm 89:1-4: The psalmist's declaration of God's faithfulness and the eternal covenant with David sets the foundation for the psalm's themes. The focus on God's steadfast love and commitment highlights the enduring nature of His promises.

2. Psalm 89:5-14: The praise for God's sovereignty and attributes underscores His unparalleled authority and trustworthiness. The imagery of God's rule over creation and history emphasizes His control and reliability.

3. Psalm 89:19-29: The reiteration of the covenant with David emphasizes God's divine selection and anointing of David. The promises of protection, enduring mercy, and an eternal throne point to the messianic fulfillment in Christ.

4. Psalm 89:38-45: The lament over the apparent failure of God's promises reflects the psalmist's deep sorrow and confusion. This section highlights the tension between human perception and divine reality, ultimately pointing to the need for faith in God's faithfulness.

5. Psalm 89:46-52: The plea for restoration and the return to God's former lovingkindness express the psalmist's longing for divine intervention. The concluding declaration of God's eternal blessedness reaffirms faith in His ultimate sovereignty and goodness.

Conclusion

Psalm 89 presents a profound reflection on God's covenant with David, combining praise for His faithfulness with a lament over apparent contradictions. Through detailed expository study and comprehensive commentary, we have explored the theological significance and messianic implications of this psalm. This chapter has provided a thorough examination of the eternal reign promised in Psalm 89, enhancing our understanding of God's faithfulness and the ultimate fulfillment of His promises in Jesus Christ. Believers are encouraged to trust in God's faithfulness, live righteously, find hope in Christ, and proclaim His steadfast love to all generations.

The Davidic Covenant and Jesus' Eternal Reign

The Davidic Covenant, a central theme in biblical theology, promises an everlasting dynasty through David's lineage, culminating in the eternal reign of Jesus Christ. Psalm 89 eloquently captures the essence of this covenant, expressing both praise for God's steadfast love and lament over the seeming failures of the Davidic line. This chapter explores the Davidic Covenant as presented in Psalm 89 and its ultimate fulfillment in the eternal reign of Jesus. Through detailed expository study and comprehensive commentary, we will uncover the profound theological significance and messianic implications of this covenant.

Text of Psalm 89 (NKJV)

1. I will sing of the mercies of the LORD forever; with my mouth will I make known Your faithfulness to all generations.

2. For I have said, "Mercy shall be built up forever; Your faithfulness You shall establish in the very heavens."

3. "I have made a covenant with My chosen, I have sworn to My servant David:

4. 'Your seed I will establish forever, and build up your throne to all generations.'" Selah

5. And the heavens will praise Your wonders, O LORD; Your faithfulness also in the assembly of the saints.

6. For who in the heavens can be compared to the LORD? Who among the sons of the mighty can be likened to the LORD?

7. God is greatly to be feared in the assembly of the saints, and to be held in reverence by all those around Him.

8. O LORD God of hosts, who is mighty like You, O LORD? Your faithfulness also surrounds You.

9. You rule the raging of the sea; when its waves rise, You still them.

10. You have broken Rahab in pieces, as one who is slain; You have scattered Your enemies with Your mighty arm.

11. The heavens are Yours, the earth also is Yours; the world and all its fullness, You have founded them.

12. The north and the south, You have created them; Tabor and Hermon rejoice in Your name.

13. You have a mighty arm; strong is Your hand, and high is Your right hand.

14. Righteousness and justice are the foundation of Your throne; mercy and truth go before Your face.

15. Blessed are the people who know the joyful sound! They walk, O LORD, in the light of Your countenance.

16. In Your name they rejoice all day long, and in Your righteousness they are exalted.

17. For You are the glory of their strength, and in Your favor our horn is exalted.

18. For our shield belongs to the LORD, and our king to the Holy One of Israel.

19. Then You spoke in a vision to Your holy one, and said: "I have given help to one who is mighty; I have exalted one chosen from the people.

20. I have found My servant David; with My holy oil I have anointed him,

21. With whom My hand shall be established; also My arm shall strengthen him.

22. The enemy shall not outwit him, nor the son of wickedness afflict him.

23. I will beat down his foes before his face, and plague those who hate him.

24. But My faithfulness and My mercy shall be with him, and in My name his horn shall be exalted.

25. Also I will set his hand over the sea, and his right hand over the rivers.

26. He shall cry to Me, 'You are my Father, my God, and the rock of my salvation.'

27. Also I will make him My firstborn, the highest of the kings of the earth.

28. My mercy I will keep for him forever, and My covenant shall stand firm with him.

29. His seed also I will make to endure forever, and his throne as the days of heaven.

30. If his sons forsake My law and do not walk in My judgments,

31. If they break My statutes and do not keep My commandments,

32. Then I will punish their transgression with the rod, and their iniquity with stripes.

33. Nevertheless My lovingkindness I will not utterly take from him, nor allow My faithfulness to fail.

34. My covenant I will not break, nor alter the word that has gone out of My lips.

35. Once I have sworn by My holiness; I will not lie to David:

36. His seed shall endure forever, and his throne as the sun before Me;

37. It shall be established forever like the moon, even like the faithful witness in the sky." Selah

38. But You have cast off and abhorred, You have been furious with Your anointed.

39. You have renounced the covenant of Your servant; You have profaned his crown by casting it to the ground.

40. You have broken down all his hedges; You have brought his strongholds to ruin.

41. All who pass by the way plunder him; he is a reproach to his neighbors.

42. You have exalted the right hand of his adversaries; You have made all his enemies rejoice.

43. You have also turned back the edge of his sword, and have not sustained him in the battle.

44. You have made his glory cease, and cast his throne down to the ground.

45. The days of his youth You have shortened; You have covered him with shame. Selah

46. How long, LORD? Will You hide Yourself forever? Will Your wrath burn like fire?

47. Remember how short my time is; for what futility have You created all the children of men?

48. What man can live and not see death? Can he deliver his life from the power of the grave? Selah

49. Lord, where are Your former lovingkindnesses, which You swore to David in Your truth?

50. Remember, Lord, the reproach of Your servants; how I bear in my bosom the reproach of all the many peoples,

51. With which Your enemies have reproached, O LORD, with which they have reproached the footsteps of Your anointed.

52. Blessed be the LORD forevermore! Amen and Amen.

Expository Study

Verses 1-4: The Covenant Promise

Verses 1-4: "I will sing of the mercies of the LORD forever; with my mouth will I make known Your faithfulness to all generations. For I have said, 'Mercy shall be built up forever; Your faithfulness You shall establish in the very heavens.' 'I have made a covenant with My chosen, I have sworn to My servant David: Your seed I will establish forever, and build up your throne to all generations.'" Selah

- "Mercies" (חֶסֶד, chesed) emphasizes God's steadfast love and kindness.

- "Covenant" (בְּרִית, berit) signifies a solemn, binding agreement.

The psalmist begins by celebrating God's steadfast love and faithfulness, which are foundational to the covenant with David. This covenant assures that David's lineage and throne will endure forever, establishing an eternal dynasty.

Verses 5-14: God's Sovereign Power

Verses 5-14: "And the heavens will praise Your wonders, O LORD; Your faithfulness also in the assembly of the saints. For who in the heavens can be compared to the LORD? Who among the sons of the mighty can be likened to the LORD? God is greatly to be feared in the assembly of the saints, and to be held in reverence by all those around Him. O LORD God of hosts, who is mighty like You, O LORD? Your faithfulness also surrounds You. You rule the raging of the sea; when its waves rise, You still them. You have broken Rahab in pieces, as one who is slain; You have scattered Your enemies with Your mighty arm. The heavens are Yours, the earth also is Yours; the world and all its fullness, You have founded them. The north and the south, You have created them; Tabor and Hermon rejoice in Your name. You have a mighty arm; strong is Your hand, and high is Your right hand. Righteousness and justice are the foundation of Your throne; mercy and truth go before Your face."

- "Rahab" (רַהַב, rahav) represents chaos and opposition, often referring to Egypt.

- "Righteousness" (צֶדֶק, tsedeq) and "justice" (מִשְׁפָּט, mishpat) are essential attributes of God's rule.

These verses extol God's unrivaled sovereignty, emphasizing His power over creation and history. His rule is characterized by righteousness and justice, and His faithfulness is celebrated in the heavenly realms. This section underscores the trustworthiness of God's covenant promises, as His authority is absolute.

Verses 15-18: The Blessedness of God's People

Verses 15-18: "Blessed are the people who know the joyful sound! They walk, O LORD, in the light of Your countenance. In Your name they rejoice all day long, and in Your righteousness they are exalted. For You are the glory of their strength, and in Your favor our horn is exalted. For our shield belongs to the LORD, and our king to the Holy One of Israel."

- "Joyful sound" (תְּרוּעָה, teruah) refers to the shout of triumph and worship.

- "Horn" (קֶרֶן, keren) symbolizes strength and honor.

The psalmist describes the blessedness of those who experience God's presence and favor. These people walk in the light of His countenance, rejoicing in His righteousness and strength. The imagery of God as a shield and the Holy One of Israel as their king reinforces their security and honor.

Verses 19-29: The Covenant with David

Verses 19-29: "Then You spoke in a vision to Your holy one, and said: 'I have given help to one who is mighty; I have exalted one chosen from the people. I have found My servant David; with My holy oil I have anointed him, with whom My hand shall be established; also My arm shall strengthen him. The enemy shall not outwit him, nor the son of wickedness afflict him. I will beat down his foes before his face, and plague those who hate him. But My faithfulness and My mercy shall be with him, and in My name his horn shall be exalted. Also I will set his hand over the sea, and his right hand over the rivers. He shall cry to Me, "You are my Father, my God, and the rock of my salvation." Also I will make him My firstborn, the highest of the kings of the earth. My mercy I will keep for him forever, and My covenant shall stand firm with him. His seed also I will make to endure forever, and his throne as the days of heaven.'"

- "Anointed" (מָשַׁח, mashach) refers to being consecrated with holy oil.

- "Firstborn" (בְּכוֹר, bekhor) indicates preeminence and special status.

God's covenant with David is reiterated, emphasizing His divine selection and anointing of David. The promises include protection, enduring mercy, and an eternal throne. The covenant assures David's descendants of a perpetual reign, ultimately fulfilled in Jesus Christ.

Verses 30-37: Conditions and Assurance

Verses 30-37: "If his sons forsake My law and do not walk in My judgments, if they break My statutes and do not keep My commandments, then I will punish their transgression with the rod, and their iniquity with stripes. Nevertheless My lovingkindness I will not utterly take from him, nor allow My faithfulness to fail. My covenant I will not break, nor alter the word that has gone out of My lips. Once I have sworn by My holiness; I will not lie to David: His seed shall endure forever, and his throne as the sun before Me; it shall be established forever like the moon, even like the faithful witness in the sky." Selah

- "Lovingkindness" (חֶסֶד, chesed) underscores God's steadfast love.

- "Sworn" (שָׁבַע, shava) signifies a solemn oath.

While the covenant includes conditions for David's descendants, God's commitment to His promises remains unwavering. Even if David's descendants are disobedient, God's lovingkindness and faithfulness will endure. The promise of an eternal throne is assured, likened to the enduring sun and moon.

Verses 38-45: Lament over Broken Promises

Verses 38-45: "But You have cast off and abhorred, You have been furious with Your anointed. You have renounced the covenant of Your servant; You have profaned his crown by casting it to the ground. You have broken down all his hedges; You have brought his strongholds to ruin. All who pass by the way plunder him; he is a reproach to his neighbors. You have exalted the right hand of his adversaries; You have made all his enemies rejoice. You have also turned back the edge of his sword, and have not sustained him in the battle. You have made his glory cease, and cast his throne down to the ground. The days of his youth You have shortened; You have covered him with shame. Selah"

- "Cast off" (נָטַשׁ, natash) and "abhorred" (מָאַס, ma'as) indicate rejection and disdain.

- "Profaned" (חָלַל, chalal) signifies desecration or defilement.

The psalmist laments the apparent contradiction between God's promises and the current state of the Davidic dynasty. The imagery of a broken crown and strongholds, along with the triumph of enemies, reflects a profound sense of abandonment and shame. This section expresses deep sorrow and confusion over the perceived failure of God's covenant.

Verses 46-52: Plea for Restoration

Verses 46-52: "How long, LORD? Will You hide Yourself forever? Will Your wrath burn like fire? Remember how short my time is; for what futility have You created all the children of men? What man can live and not see death? Can he deliver his life from the power of the grave? Selah Lord, where are Your former lovingkindnesses, which You swore to David in Your truth? Remember, Lord, the reproach of Your servants; how I bear in my bosom the reproach of all the many peoples, with which Your enemies have reproached, O LORD, with which they have reproached the footsteps of Your anointed. Blessed be the LORD forevermore! Amen and Amen."

- "Hide Yourself" (סָתַר, sathar) suggests divine absence or concealment.

- "Reproach" (חֶרְפָּה, cherpah) indicates disgrace or scorn.

The psalmist ends with a heartfelt plea for restoration and a return to God's former lovingkindness. He acknowledges human mortality and the futility of life without divine intervention. The psalmist calls on God to remember His covenant with David and to restore the honor of His anointed. Despite the lament, the psalm concludes with a declaration of God's eternal blessedness.

Theological Significance

The Davidic Covenant and Its Fulfillment in Christ

1. Eternal Kingship: The promise of an eternal throne for David's descendants is a central theme in Psalm 89. This promise finds its ultimate fulfillment in Jesus Christ, who reigns forever as the eternal King (Luke 1:32-33).

2. Messianic Hope: The lament over the apparent failure of the Davidic covenant highlights the longing for the

Messiah. Jesus, as the descendant of David, fulfills this hope, restoring the throne and establishing an eternal kingdom (Acts 2:30-31).

3. God's Faithfulness: Despite the apparent contradictions, the psalm emphasizes God's unwavering faithfulness. The ultimate fulfillment of God's promises in Christ demonstrates His steadfast love and reliability (2 Corinthians 1:20).

The Attributes of God's Rule

1. Righteousness and Justice: The foundation of God's throne is righteousness and justice, underscoring the moral perfection of His rule. Jesus embodies these attributes, establishing a kingdom characterized by justice and righteousness (Isaiah 9:6-7).

2. Mercy and Truth: God's rule is also marked by mercy and truth, reflecting His compassionate and faithful character. These qualities are evident in Jesus' ministry and His redemptive work (John 1:14).

Human Mortality and Divine Eternity

1. Mortality: The psalmist's reflection on human mortality and the futility of life without God's intervention highlights the need for divine salvation. Jesus' victory over death and the grave offers hope and assurance of eternal life (1 Corinthians 15:54-57).

2. Eternal Covenant: The everlasting nature of God's covenant with David points to the eternal relationship between God and His people through Christ. This covenant assures believers of God's enduring love and commitment (Hebrews 13:20-21).

Practical Applications

1. Trust in God's Promises: Believers are called to trust in God's faithfulness and the fulfillment of His promises, even in times of apparent contradiction or delay. This trust is

grounded in the ultimate fulfillment of God's promises in Christ (Romans 8:28).

2. Live Righteously: Reflecting the attributes of God's rule, believers are encouraged to live righteously, pursuing justice and mercy in their daily lives. This involves imitating Christ and upholding His standards (Micah 6:8).

3. Find Hope in Christ: In times of lament and uncertainty, believers can find hope and assurance in the eternal reign of Christ. His victory over death and the grave offers a secure foundation for faith and perseverance (Romans 5:1-5).

4. Proclaim God's Faithfulness: Like the psalmist, believers are called to proclaim God's faithfulness and steadfast love to all generations. This involves sharing the gospel and bearing witness to God's transformative work in their lives (Psalm 89:1).

Comprehensive Commentary

Theological and Messianic Implications

1. Luke 1:32-33: The promise of an eternal throne for David's descendants is fulfilled in Jesus Christ, affirming His divine kingship and eternal reign. This New Testament revelation confirms the messianic significance of Psalm 89.

2. Acts 2:30-31: Peter's sermon on the day of Pentecost connects Jesus' resurrection and exaltation to the fulfillment of God's covenant with David. This highlights the continuity of God's redemptive plan and the ultimate fulfillment in Christ.

3. 2 Corinthians 1:20: Paul emphasizes that all of God's promises find their "Yes" in Christ, underscoring His faithfulness and the assurance of His promises. This theological insight reinforces the reliability of God's covenant and the fulfillment in Jesus.

Exegetical Insights

1. Psalm 89:1-4: The psalmist's declaration of God's faithfulness and the eternal covenant with David sets the foundation for the psalm's themes. The focus on God's steadfast love and commitment highlights the enduring nature of His promises.

2. Psalm 89:5-14: The praise for God's sovereignty and attributes underscores His unparalleled authority and trustworthiness. The imagery of God's rule over creation and history emphasizes His control and reliability.

3. Psalm 89:19-29: The reiteration of the covenant with David emphasizes God's divine selection and anointing of David. The promises of protection, enduring mercy, and an eternal throne point to the messianic fulfillment in Christ.

4. Psalm 89:38-45: The lament over the apparent failure of God's promises reflects the psalmist's deep sorrow and confusion. This section highlights the tension between human perception and divine reality, ultimately pointing to the need for faith in God's faithfulness.

5. Psalm 89:46-52: The plea for restoration and the return to God's former lovingkindness express the psalmist's longing for divine intervention. The concluding declaration of God's eternal blessedness reaffirms faith in His ultimate sovereignty and goodness.

Conclusion

Psalm 89 presents a profound reflection on God's covenant with David, combining praise for His faithfulness with a lament over apparent contradictions. Through detailed expository study and comprehensive commentary, we have explored the theological significance and messianic implications of this psalm. This chapter has provided a thorough examination of the Davidic Covenant and its ultimate fulfillment in Jesus' eternal reign. Believers are encouraged to trust in God's faithfulness, live righteously, find hope in Christ, and proclaim His steadfast love to all generations.

Jesus as the Fulfillment of God's Promise

The Bible is a grand narrative of God's redemptive plan, and one of its central themes is the promise of an eternal kingdom through the Davidic Covenant. This covenant, highlighted in Psalm 89, reaches its ultimate fulfillment in Jesus Christ. This chapter explores how Jesus embodies the fulfillment of God's promise, as prophesied in Psalm 89, and examines the New Testament revelations that confirm this fulfillment. Through detailed expository study and comprehensive commentary, we will delve into the theological significance of Jesus as the promised eternal King.

Text of Psalm 89 (NKJV)

1. I will sing of the mercies of the LORD forever; with my mouth will I make known Your faithfulness to all generations.

2. For I have said, "Mercy shall be built up forever; Your faithfulness You shall establish in the very heavens."

3. "I have made a covenant with My chosen, I have sworn to My servant David:

4. 'Your seed I will establish forever, and build up your throne to all generations.'" Selah

5. And the heavens will praise Your wonders, O LORD; Your faithfulness also in the assembly of the saints.

6. For who in the heavens can be compared to the LORD? Who among the sons of the mighty can be likened to the LORD?

7. God is greatly to be feared in the assembly of the saints, and to be held in reverence by all those around Him.

8. O LORD God of hosts, who is mighty like You, O LORD? Your faithfulness also surrounds You.

9. You rule the raging of the sea; when its waves rise, You still them.

10. You have broken Rahab in pieces, as one who is slain; You have scattered Your enemies with Your mighty arm.

11. The heavens are Yours, the earth also is Yours; the world and all its fullness, You have founded them.

12. The north and the south, You have created them; Tabor and Hermon rejoice in Your name.

13. You have a mighty arm; strong is Your hand, and high is Your right hand.

14. Righteousness and justice are the foundation of Your throne; mercy and truth go before Your face.

15. Blessed are the people who know the joyful sound! They walk, O LORD, in the light of Your countenance.

16. In Your name they rejoice all day long, and in Your righteousness they are exalted.

17. For You are the glory of their strength, and in Your favor our horn is exalted.

18. For our shield belongs to the LORD, and our king to the Holy One of Israel.

19. Then You spoke in a vision to Your holy one, and said: "I have given help to one who is mighty; I have exalted one chosen from the people.

20. I have found My servant David; with My holy oil I have anointed him,

21. With whom My hand shall be established; also My arm shall strengthen him.

22. The enemy shall not outwit him, nor the son of wickedness afflict him.

23. I will beat down his foes before his face, and plague those who hate him.

24. But My faithfulness and My mercy shall be with him, and in My name his horn shall be exalted.

25. Also I will set his hand over the sea, and his right hand over the rivers.

26. He shall cry to Me, 'You are my Father, my God, and the rock of my salvation.'

27. Also I will make him My firstborn, the highest of the kings of the earth.

28. My mercy I will keep for him forever, and My covenant shall stand firm with him.

29. His seed also I will make to endure forever, and his throne as the days of heaven.

30. If his sons forsake My law and do not walk in My judgments,

31. If they break My statutes and do not keep My commandments,

32. Then I will punish their transgression with the rod, and their iniquity with stripes.

33. Nevertheless My lovingkindness I will not utterly take from him, nor allow My faithfulness to fail.

34. My covenant I will not break, nor alter the word that has gone out of My lips.

35. Once I have sworn by My holiness; I will not lie to David:

36. His seed shall endure forever, and his throne as the sun before Me;

37. It shall be established forever like the moon, even like the faithful witness in the sky." Selah

38. But You have cast off and abhorred, You have been furious with Your anointed.

39. You have renounced the covenant of Your servant; You have profaned his crown by casting it to the ground.

40. You have broken down all his hedges; You have brought his strongholds to ruin.

41. All who pass by the way plunder him; he is a reproach to his neighbors.

42. You have exalted the right hand of his adversaries; You have made all his enemies rejoice.

43. You have also turned back the edge of his sword, and have not sustained him in the battle.

44. You have made his glory cease, and cast his throne down to the ground.

45. The days of his youth You have shortened; You have covered him with shame. Selah

46. How long, LORD? Will You hide Yourself forever? Will Your wrath burn like fire?

47. Remember how short my time is; for what futility have You created all the children of men?

48. What man can live and not see death? Can he deliver his life from the power of the grave? Selah

49. Lord, where are Your former lovingkindnesses, which You swore to David in Your truth?

50. Remember, Lord, the reproach of Your servants; how I bear in my bosom the reproach of all the many peoples,

51. With which Your enemies have reproached, O LORD, with which they have reproached the footsteps of Your anointed.

52. Blessed be the LORD forevermore! Amen and Amen.

Expository Study

Verses 1-4: The Promise of an Eternal Throne

Verses 1-4: "I will sing of the mercies of the LORD forever; with my mouth will I make known Your faithfulness to all generations. For I have said, 'Mercy shall be built up forever; Your faithfulness You shall establish in the very heavens.' 'I have made a covenant with My chosen, I have sworn to My servant David: Your seed I will establish forever, and build up your throne to all generations.'" Selah

- "Mercies" (חֶסֶד, chesed) emphasizes God's steadfast love.

- "Covenant" (בְּרִית, berit) signifies a solemn, binding agreement.

The psalmist opens with a declaration of God's enduring mercy and faithfulness, foundational to the covenant made with David. This covenant ensures an eternal throne, a promise that points directly to the coming of Jesus Christ, the ultimate fulfillment of David's lineage.

Verses 5-14: Praise for God's Sovereignty

Verses 5-14: "And the heavens will praise Your wonders, O LORD; Your faithfulness also in the assembly of the saints. For who in the heavens can be compared to the LORD? Who among the sons of the mighty can be likened to the LORD? God is greatly to be feared in the assembly of the saints, and to be held in reverence by all those around Him. O LORD God of hosts, who is mighty like You, O LORD? Your faithfulness also surrounds You. You rule the raging of the sea; when its waves rise, You still them. You have broken Rahab in pieces, as one who is slain; You have scattered Your enemies with Your mighty arm. The heavens are Yours, the earth also is Yours; the world and all its fullness, You have founded them. The north and the south, You have created them; Tabor and Hermon rejoice in Your name. You have a mighty arm; strong is Your hand, and high is Your right hand. Righteousness and justice are the foundation of Your throne; mercy and truth go before Your face."

- "Rahab" (רַהַב, rahav) represents chaos and opposition, often referring to Egypt.

- "Righteousness" (צֶדֶק, tsedeq) and "justice" (מִשְׁפָּט, mishpat) are essential attributes of God's rule.

The psalmist praises God's unmatched sovereignty and power over creation and history. His rule is characterized by righteousness and justice, underscoring the reliability of His promises. This section assures that God's covenant with David is grounded in His unchanging nature.

Verses 15-18: The Blessedness of God's People

Verses 15-18: "Blessed are the people who know the joyful sound! They walk, O LORD, in the light of Your countenance. In Your name they rejoice all day long, and in Your righteousness they are exalted. For You are the glory of their strength, and in Your favor our horn is exalted. For our shield belongs to the LORD, and our king to the Holy One of Israel."

- "Joyful sound" (תְּרוּעָה, teruah) refers to the shout of triumph and worship.

- "Horn" (קֶרֶן, keren) symbolizes strength and honor.

The psalmist describes the blessedness of those who experience God's presence and favor. These people walk in the light of His countenance, rejoicing in His righteousness and strength

. The imagery of God as a shield and the Holy One of Israel as their king reinforces their security and honor.

Verses 19-29: The Covenant with David

Verses 19-29: "Then You spoke in a vision to Your holy one, and said: 'I have given help to one who is mighty; I have exalted one chosen from the people. I have found My servant David; with My holy oil I have anointed him, with whom My hand shall be established; also My arm shall strengthen him. The enemy shall not outwit him, nor the son of wickedness afflict him. I will beat down his foes before his face, and plague those who hate him. But My faithfulness and My mercy shall be with him, and in My name his horn shall be exalted. Also I will set his hand over the sea, and his right hand over the rivers. He shall cry to Me, "You are my Father, my God, and the rock of my salvation." Also I will make him My firstborn, the highest of the kings of the earth. My mercy I will keep for him forever, and My covenant shall stand firm with him. His seed also I will make to endure forever, and his throne as the days of heaven.'"

- "Anointed" (מָשַׁח, mashach) refers to being consecrated with holy oil.

- "Firstborn" (בְּכוֹר, bekhor) indicates preeminence and special status.

God's covenant with David is reiterated, emphasizing His divine selection and anointing of David. The promises include protection, enduring mercy, and an eternal throne. These assurances find their ultimate fulfillment in Jesus Christ, who is both the Son of David and the eternal King.

Verses 30-37: Conditions and Assurance

Verses 30-37: "If his sons forsake My law and do not walk in My judgments, if they break My statutes and do not keep My commandments, then I will punish their transgression with the rod, and their iniquity with stripes. Nevertheless My lovingkindness I will not utterly take from him, nor allow My faithfulness to fail. My covenant I will not break, nor alter the word that has gone out of My lips. Once I have sworn by My holiness; I will not lie to David: His seed shall endure forever, and his throne as the sun before Me; it shall be established forever like the moon, even like the faithful witness in the sky." Selah

- "Lovingkindness" (חֶסֶד, chesed) underscores God's steadfast love.

- "Sworn" (שָׁבַע, shava) signifies a solemn oath.

While the covenant includes conditions for David's descendants, God's commitment to His promises remains unwavering. Even if David's descendants are disobedient, God's lovingkindness and faithfulness will endure. The promise of an eternal throne is assured, likened to the enduring sun and moon.

Verses 38-45: Lament Over Broken Promises

Verses 38-45: "But You have cast off and abhorred, You have been furious with Your anointed. You have renounced the covenant of Your servant; You have profaned his crown by casting it to the ground. You have broken down all his hedges; You have brought his strongholds to ruin. All who pass by the way plunder him; he is a reproach to his neighbors. You have exalted the right hand of his adversaries; You have made all his enemies rejoice. You have also turned back the edge of his sword, and have not sustained him in the battle. You have made his glory cease, and cast his throne down to the ground. The days of his youth You have shortened; You have covered him with shame. Selah"

- "Cast off" (נָטַשׁ, natash) and "abhorred" (מָאַס, ma'as) indicate rejection and disdain.

- "Profaned" (חָלַל, chalal) signifies desecration or defilement.

The psalmist laments the apparent contradiction between God's promises and the current state of the Davidic dynasty. The imagery of a broken crown and strongholds, along with the triumph of enemies, reflects a profound sense of abandonment and shame. This section expresses deep sorrow and confusion over the perceived failure of God's covenant.

Verses 46-52: Plea for Restoration

Verses 46-52: "How long, LORD? Will You hide Yourself forever? Will Your wrath burn like fire? Remember how short my time is; for what futility have You created all the children of men? What man can live and not see death? Can he deliver his life from the power of the grave? Selah Lord, where are Your former lovingkindnesses, which You swore to David in Your truth? Remember, Lord, the reproach of Your servants; how I bear in my bosom the reproach of all the many peoples, with which Your enemies have reproached, O LORD, with which they have reproached the footsteps of Your anointed. Blessed be the LORD forevermore! Amen and Amen."

- "Hide Yourself" (סָתַר, sathar) suggests divine absence or concealment.

- "Reproach" (חֶרְפָּה, cherpah) indicates disgrace or scorn.

The psalmist ends with a heartfelt plea for restoration and a return to God's former lovingkindness. He acknowledges human mortality and the futility of life without divine intervention. The psalmist calls on God to remember His covenant with David and to restore the honor of His anointed. Despite the lament, the psalm concludes with a declaration of God's eternal blessedness.

Theological Significance

The Davidic Covenant and Its Fulfillment in Christ

1. Eternal Kingship: The promise of an eternal throne for David's descendants is a central theme in Psalm 89. This promise finds its ultimate fulfillment in Jesus Christ, who reigns forever as the eternal King (Luke 1:32-33).

2. Messianic Hope: The lament over the apparent failure of the Davidic covenant highlights the longing for the Messiah. Jesus, as the descendant of David, fulfills this hope, restoring the throne and establishing an eternal kingdom (Acts 2:30-31).

3. God's Faithfulness: Despite the apparent contradictions, the psalm emphasizes God's unwavering faithfulness. The ultimate fulfillment of God's promises in Christ demonstrates His steadfast love and reliability (2 Corinthians 1:20).

Jesus as the Righteous King

1. Righteousness and Justice: The foundation of God's throne is righteousness and justice, underscoring the moral perfection of His rule. Jesus embodies these attributes, establishing a kingdom characterized by justice and righteousness (Isaiah 9:6-7).

2. Mercy and Truth: God's rule is also marked by mercy and truth, reflecting His compassionate and faithful character. These qualities are evident in Jesus' ministry and His redemptive work (John 1:14).

Jesus and the Human Condition

1. Mortality: The psalmist's reflection on human mortality and the futility of life without God's intervention highlights the need for divine salvation. Jesus' victory over death and the grave offers hope and assurance of eternal life (1 Corinthians 15:54-57).

2. Eternal Covenant: The everlasting nature of God's covenant with David points to the eternal relationship between God and His people through Christ. This covenant assures believers of God's enduring love and commitment (Hebrews 13:20-21).

Practical Applications

1. Trust in God's Promises: Believers are called to trust in God's faithfulness and the fulfillment of His promises, even in times of apparent contradiction or delay. This trust is grounded in the ultimate fulfillment of God's promises in Christ (Romans 8:28).

2. Live Righteously: Reflecting the attributes of God's rule, believers are encouraged to live righteously, pursuing justice and mercy in their daily lives. This involves imitating Christ and upholding His standards (Micah 6:8).

3. Find Hope in Christ: In times of lament and uncertainty, believers can find hope and assurance in the eternal reign of Christ. His victory over death and the grave offers a secure foundation for faith and perseverance (Romans 5:1-5).

4. Proclaim God's Faithfulness: Like the psalmist, believers are called to proclaim God's faithfulness and steadfast love to all generations. This involves sharing the

gospel and bearing witness to God's transformative work in their lives (Psalm 89:1).

Comprehensive Commentary

Theological and Messianic Implications

1. Luke 1:32-33: The promise of an eternal throne for David's descendants is fulfilled in Jesus Christ, affirming His divine kingship and eternal reign. This New Testament revelation confirms the messianic significance of Psalm 89.

2. Acts 2:30-31: Peter's sermon on the day of Pentecost connects Jesus' resurrection and exaltation to the fulfillment of God's covenant with David. This highlights the continuity of God's redemptive plan and the ultimate fulfillment in Christ.

3. 2 Corinthians 1:20: Paul emphasizes that all of God's promises find their "Yes" in Christ, underscoring His faithfulness and the assurance of His promises. This theological insight reinforces the reliability of God's covenant and the fulfillment in Jesus.

Exegetical Insights

1. Psalm 89:1-4: The psalmist's declaration of God's faithfulness and the eternal covenant with David sets the foundation for the psalm's themes. The focus on God's steadfast love and commitment highlights the enduring nature of His promises.

2. Psalm 89:5-14: The praise for God's sovereignty and attributes underscores His unparalleled authority and trustworthiness. The imagery of God's rule over creation and history emphasizes His control and reliability.

3. Psalm 89:19-29: The reiteration of the covenant with David emphasizes God's divine selection and anointing of David. The promises of protection, enduring mercy, and an eternal throne point to the messianic fulfillment in Christ.

4. Psalm 89:38-45: The lament over the apparent failure of God's promises reflects the psalmist's deep sorrow

and confusion. This section highlights the tension between human perception and divine reality, ultimately pointing to the need for faith in God's faithfulness.

5. Psalm 89:46-52: The plea for restoration and the return to God's former lovingkindness express the psalmist's longing for divine intervention. The concluding declaration of God's eternal blessedness reaffirms faith in His ultimate sovereignty and goodness.

Conclusion

Psalm 89 provides a profound reflection on God's covenant with David, blending praise for His faithfulness with lament over apparent contradictions. Through detailed expository study and comprehensive commentary, we have explored the theological significance and messianic implications of this psalm. This chapter has provided a thorough examination of how Jesus fulfills God's promise of an eternal kingdom, reinforcing the reliability and steadfast love of God. Believers are encouraged to trust in God's faithfulness, live righteously, find hope in Christ, and proclaim His steadfast love to all generations.

New Testament Perspectives

The New Testament provides profound insights into the fulfillment of the Old Testament promises, particularly the Davidic Covenant, through Jesus Christ. This chapter explores the New Testament perspectives on Psalm 89 and its messianic implications, illustrating how Jesus embodies the fulfillment of God's promises. By examining key passages and themes, we will uncover the theological depth and significance of Jesus as the eternal King and the realization of God's covenant with David.

Text of Psalm 89 (NKJV)

1. I will sing of the mercies of the LORD forever; with my mouth will I make known Your faithfulness to all generations.

2. For I have said, "Mercy shall be built up forever; Your faithfulness You shall establish in the very heavens."

3. "I have made a covenant with My chosen, I have sworn to My servant David:

4. 'Your seed I will establish forever, and build up your throne to all generations.'" Selah

5. And the heavens will praise Your wonders, O LORD; Your faithfulness also in the assembly of the saints.

6. For who in the heavens can be compared to the LORD? Who among the sons of the mighty can be likened to the LORD?

7. God is greatly to be feared in the assembly of the saints, and to be held in reverence by all those around Him.

8. O LORD God of hosts, who is mighty like You, O LORD? Your faithfulness also surrounds You.

9. You rule the raging of the sea; when its waves rise, You still them.

10. You have broken Rahab in pieces, as one who is slain; You have scattered Your enemies with Your mighty arm.

11. The heavens are Yours, the earth also is Yours; the world and all its fullness, You have founded them.

12. The north and the south, You have created them; Tabor and Hermon rejoice in Your name.

13. You have a mighty arm; strong is Your hand, and high is Your right hand.

14. Righteousness and justice are the foundation of Your throne; mercy and truth go before Your face.

15. Blessed are the people who know the joyful sound! They walk, O LORD, in the light of Your countenance.

16. In Your name they rejoice all day long, and in Your righteousness they are exalted.

17. For You are the glory of their strength, and in Your favor our horn is exalted.

18. For our shield belongs to the LORD, and our king to the Holy One of Israel.

19. Then You spoke in a vision to Your holy one, and said: "I have given help to one who is mighty; I have exalted one chosen from the people.

20. I have found My servant David; with My holy oil I have anointed him,

21. With whom My hand shall be established; also My arm shall strengthen him.

22. The enemy shall not outwit him, nor the son of wickedness afflict him.

23. I will beat down his foes before his face, and plague those who hate him.

24. But My faithfulness and My mercy shall be with him, and in My name his horn shall be exalted.

25. Also I will set his hand over the sea, and his right hand over the rivers.

26. He shall cry to Me, 'You are my Father, my God, and the rock of my salvation.'

27. Also I will make him My firstborn, the highest of the kings of the earth.

28. My mercy I will keep for him forever, and My covenant shall stand firm with him.

29. His seed also I will make to endure forever, and his throne as the days of heaven.

30. If his sons forsake My law and do not walk in My judgments,

31. If they break My statutes and do not keep My commandments,

32. Then I will punish their transgression with the rod, and their iniquity with stripes.

33. Nevertheless My lovingkindness I will not utterly take from him, nor allow My faithfulness to fail.

34. My covenant I will not break, nor alter the word that has gone out of My lips.

35. Once I have sworn by My holiness; I will not lie to David:

36. His seed shall endure forever, and his throne as the sun before Me;

37. It shall be established forever like the moon, even like the faithful witness in the sky." Selah

38. But You have cast off and abhorred, You have been furious with Your anointed.

39. You have renounced the covenant of Your servant; You have profaned his crown by casting it to the ground.

40. You have broken down all his hedges; You have brought his strongholds to ruin.

41. All who pass by the way plunder him; he is a reproach to his neighbors.

42. You have exalted the right hand of his adversaries; You have made all his enemies rejoice.

43. You have also turned back the edge of his sword, and have not sustained him in the battle.

44. You have made his glory cease, and cast his throne down to the ground.

45. The days of his youth You have shortened; You have covered him with shame. Selah

46. How long, LORD? Will You hide Yourself forever? Will Your wrath burn like fire?

47. Remember how short my time is; for what futility have You created all the children of men?

48. What man can live and not see death? Can he deliver his life from the power of the grave? Selah

49. Lord, where are Your former loving kindnesses, which You swore to David in Your truth?

50. Remember, Lord, the reproach of Your servants; how I bear in my bosom the reproach of all the many peoples,

51. With which Your enemies have reproached, O LORD, with which they have reproached the footsteps of Your anointed.

52. Blessed be the LORD forevermore! Amen and Amen.

New Testament Revelations

The Eternal Throne of David Fulfilled in Jesus

Luke 1:32-33: "He will be great, and will be called the Son of the Highest; and the Lord God will give Him the throne of His father David. And He will reign over the house of Jacob forever, and of His kingdom there will be no end."

- The angel Gabriel's announcement to Mary highlights Jesus as the fulfillment of the promise made to David. Jesus is identified as the one who will inherit David's throne and reign eternally.

Acts 2:30-31: "Therefore, being a prophet, and knowing that God had sworn with an oath to him that of the fruit of his body, according to the flesh, He would raise up the Christ to sit on his throne, he, foreseeing this, spoke concerning the resurrection of the Christ, that His soul was not left in Hades, nor did His flesh see corruption."

- Peter's sermon on the day of Pentecost links Jesus' resurrection and exaltation to the fulfillment of God's promise to David. This confirms that Jesus, as the resurrected Messiah, is the eternal King foretold in the covenant.

Revelation 22:16: "I, Jesus, have sent My angel to testify to you these things in the churches. I am the Root and the Offspring of David, the Bright and Morning Star."

- Jesus identifies Himself as both the Root and Offspring of David, emphasizing His fulfillment of the Davidic Covenant and His eternal kingship.

Jesus as the Righteous King

Hebrews 1:8-9: "But to the Son He says: 'Your throne, O God, is forever and ever; a scepter of righteousness is the scepter of Your kingdom. You have loved righteousness and hated lawlessness; therefore God, Your God, has anointed You with the oil of gladness more than Your companions.'"

- This passage, quoting Psalm 45:6-7, applies to Jesus, affirming His eternal throne and righteous reign. Jesus embodies the qualities of righteousness and justice, fulfilling the attributes of the promised King.

Revelation 19:11-16: "Now I saw heaven opened, and behold, a white horse. And He who sat on him was called Faithful and True, and in righteousness He judges and makes war. His eyes were like a flame of fire, and on His head were many crowns. He had a name written that no one knew except Himself. He was clothed with a robe dipped in blood, and His name is called The Word of God. And the armies in heaven, clothed in fine linen, white and clean, followed Him on white horses. Now out of His mouth goes a sharp sword, that with it He should strike the nations. And He Himself will rule them with a rod of iron. He Himself treads the winepress of the fierceness and wrath of Almighty God. And He has on His robe and on His thigh a name written: KING OF KINGS AND LORD OF LORDS."

- This vivid imagery in Revelation portrays Jesus as the triumphant, righteous King who judges and rules the nations. His title "King of Kings and Lord of Lords" underscores His supreme authority and fulfillment of the Davidic Covenant.

Jesus and the Human Condition

1 Corinthians 15:54-57: "So when this corruptible has put on incorruption, and this mortal has put on immortality, then shall be brought to pass the saying that is written: 'Death is swallowed up in victory.' 'O Death, where is your sting? O Hades, where is your victory?' The sting of death is sin, and

the strength of sin is the law. But thanks be to God, who gives us the victory through our Lord Jesus Christ."

- Paul's words highlight Jesus' victory over death, providing eternal life to believers. This victory is a crucial aspect of Jesus' fulfillment of the eternal promises of the Davidic Covenant.

Hebrews 13:20-21: "Now may the God of peace who brought up our Lord Jesus from the dead, that great Shepherd of the sheep, through the blood of the everlasting covenant, make you complete in every good work to do His will, working in you what is well pleasing in His sight, through Jesus Christ, to whom be glory forever and ever. Amen."

- This passage emphasizes the everlasting nature of the covenant fulfilled in Jesus. The resurrection of Jesus confirms the enduring commitment of God's promises and assures believers of their eternal relationship with Him.

Theological Significance

Jesus as the Fulfillment of the Davidic Covenant

1. Eternal Kingship: Jesus' reign as the eternal King is a direct fulfillment of God's promise to David. His kingship is established forever, transcending temporal limitations and embodying divine authority (Luke 1:32-33, Acts 2:30-31).

2. Messianic Hope: The New Testament perspectives emphasize Jesus as the long-awaited Messiah who restores and fulfills the Davidic Covenant. This realization of messianic hope is central to the Christian faith (Revelation 22:16).

3. God's Faithfulness: The fulfillment of the Davidic Covenant in Jesus underscores God's unwavering faithfulness. Despite apparent contradictions and delays, God's promises are ultimately realized in Christ (2 Corinthians 1:20).

The Righteous Reign of Jesus

1. Righteousness and Justice: Jesus' reign is characterized by righteousness and justice, fulfilling the attributes of the promised King. His righteous judgment and rule establish a kingdom founded on divine principles (Hebrews 1:8-9, Revelation 19:11-16).

2. Mercy and Truth: The qualities of mercy and truth are evident in Jesus' ministry and redemptive work. These attributes reflect the compassionate and faithful nature of His rule, aligning with the promises of the Davidic Covenant (John 1:14).

The Impact of Jesus' Fulfillment

1. Victory Over Death: Jesus' victory over death and the grave offers believers assurance of eternal life. This triumph is a significant aspect of the fulfillment of the eternal promises of the Davidic Covenant (1 Corinthians 15:54-57).

2. Eternal Covenant: The everlasting nature of the covenant fulfilled in Jesus assures believers of an eternal relationship with God. This covenant, grounded in Jesus' resurrection, provides a foundation for faith and hope (Hebrews 13:20-21).

Practical Applications

1. Trust in God's Faithfulness: Believers are encouraged to trust in God's faithfulness and the fulfillment of His promises, even in times of uncertainty. The realization of the Davidic Covenant in Jesus demonstrates God's reliability (Romans 8:28).

2. Live Righteously: Reflecting the attributes of Jesus' reign, believers are called to live righteously, pursuing justice and mercy in their daily lives. This involves imitating Christ and upholding His standards (Micah 6:8).

3. Find Hope in Christ: In times of difficulty, believers can find hope in the eternal reign of Jesus. His victory over death and His fulfillment of God's promises provide a secure foundation for faith (Romans 5:1-5).

4. Proclaim God's Faithfulness: Like the psalmist, believers are called to proclaim God's faithfulness and steadfast love to all generations. This involves sharing the gospel and bearing witness to God's transformative work in their lives (Psalm 89:1).

Comprehensive Commentary

Theological and Messianic Implications

1. Luke 1:32-33: The promise of an eternal throne for David's descendants is fulfilled in Jesus Christ, affirming His divine kingship and eternal reign. This New Testament revelation confirms the messianic significance of Psalm 89.

2. Acts 2:30-31: Peter's sermon on the day of Pentecost connects Jesus' resurrection and exaltation to the fulfillment of God's covenant with David. This highlights the continuity of God's redemptive plan and the ultimate fulfillment in Christ.

3. 2 Corinthians 1:20: Paul emphasizes that all of God's promises find their "Yes" in Christ, underscoring His faithfulness and the assurance of His promises. This theological insight reinforces the reliability of God's covenant and the fulfillment in Jesus.

Exegetical Insights

1. Psalm 89:1-4: The psalmist's declaration of God's faithfulness and the eternal covenant with David sets the foundation for the psalm's themes. The focus on God's steadfast love and commitment highlights the enduring nature of His promises.

2. Psalm 89:5-14: The praise for God's sovereignty and attributes underscores His unparalleled authority and trustworthiness. The imagery of God's rule over creation and history emphasizes His control and reliability.

3. Psalm 89:19-29: The reiteration of the covenant with David emphasizes God's divine selection and anointing

of David. The promises of protection, enduring mercy, and an eternal throne point to the messianic fulfillment in Christ.

4. Psalm 89:38-45: The lament over the apparent failure of God's promises reflects the psalmist's deep sorrow and confusion. This section highlights the tension between human perception and divine reality, ultimately pointing to the need for faith in God's faithfulness.

5. Psalm 89:46-52: The plea for restoration and the return to God's former lovingkindness express the psalmist's longing for divine intervention. The concluding declaration of God's eternal blessedness reaffirms faith in His ultimate sovereignty and goodness.

Conclusion

The New Testament perspectives on Psalm 89 provide a rich and profound understanding of how Jesus fulfills the Davidic Covenant. Through detailed expository study and comprehensive commentary, we have explored the theological significance and messianic implications of Jesus as the eternal King. This chapter has provided a thorough examination of the New Testament revelations that confirm Jesus as the fulfillment of God's promises, reinforcing the reliability and steadfast love of God. Believers are encouraged to trust in God's faithfulness, live righteously, find hope in Christ, and proclaim His steadfast love to all generations.

CHAPTER 11

THE LORD'S DELIVERANCE IN PSALM 34

Psalm 34 is a profound expression of praise and thanksgiving for God's deliverance. Written by David, it reflects his personal experience of God's salvation and serves as a testament to the Lord's faithfulness and protection. This chapter will provide a detailed analysis of Psalm 34:1-22, exploring its themes of deliverance, trust, and divine care. Through expository study and comprehensive commentary, we will uncover the theological significance and practical applications of this psalm.

Text of Psalm 34 (NKJV)

1. I will bless the LORD at all times; His praise shall continually be in my mouth.

2. My soul shall make its boast in the LORD; the humble shall hear of it and be glad.

3. Oh, magnify the LORD with me, and let us exalt His name together.

4. I sought the LORD, and He heard me, and delivered me from all my fears.

5. They looked to Him and were radiant, and their faces were not ashamed.

6. This poor man cried out, and the LORD heard him, and saved him out of all his troubles.

7. The angel of the LORD encamps all around those who fear Him, and delivers them.

8. Oh, taste and see that the LORD is good; blessed is the man who trusts in Him!

9. Oh, fear the LORD, you His saints! There is no want to those who fear Him.

10. The young lions lack and suffer hunger; but those who seek the LORD shall not lack any good thing.

11. Come, you children, listen to me; I will teach you the fear of the LORD.

12. Who is the man who desires life, and loves many days, that he may see good?

13. Keep your tongue from evil, and your lips from speaking deceit.

14. Depart from evil and do good; seek peace and pursue it.

15. The eyes of the LORD are on the righteous, and His ears are open to their cry.

16. The face of the LORD is against those who do evil, to cut off the remembrance of them from the earth.

17. The righteous cry out, and the LORD hears, and delivers them out of all their troubles.

18. The LORD is near to those who have a broken heart, and saves such as have a contrite spirit.

19. Many are the afflictions of the righteous, but the LORD delivers him out of them all.

20. He guards all his bones; not one of them is broken.

21. Evil shall slay the wicked, and those who hate the righteous shall be condemned.

22. The LORD redeems the soul of His servants, and none of those who trust in Him shall be condemned.

Expository Study

Verses 1-3: A Call to Praise

Verses 1-3: "I will bless the LORD at all times; His praise shall continually be in my mouth. My soul shall make its boast in the LORD; the humble shall hear of it and be glad. Oh, magnify the LORD with me, and let us exalt His name together."

- "Bless" (בָּרַךְ, barak) means to kneel or to praise.

- "Boast" (הָלַל, halal) signifies rejoicing or celebrating.

David begins the psalm with a declaration of continuous praise to the Lord, inviting others to join him in magnifying God's name. This communal call to worship highlights the importance of collective praise and the joy found in exalting God together.

Verses 4-7: Deliverance from Fear

Verses 4-7: "I sought the LORD, and He heard me, and delivered me from all my fears. They looked to Him and were radiant, and their faces were not ashamed. This poor man cried out, and the LORD heard him, and saved him out of all his troubles. The angel of the LORD encamps all around those who fear Him, and delivers them."

- "Sought" (דָּרַשׁ, darash) implies seeking with care or diligence.

- "Radiant" (נָהַר, nahar) means to shine or beam with joy.

David recounts his personal experience of seeking the Lord and being delivered from fear. He assures that those who look to God are filled with joy and are never put to shame. The angel of the Lord encamping around those who fear Him signifies divine protection and deliverance.

Verses 8-10: Experiencing God's Goodness

Verses 8-10: "Oh, taste and see that the LORD is good; blessed is the man who trusts in Him! Oh, fear the LORD, you His saints! There is no want to those who fear Him. The young lions lack and suffer hunger; but those who seek the LORD shall not lack any good thing."

- "Taste" (טָעַם, taam) means to perceive or experience.

- "Good" (טוֹב, tov) signifies moral goodness and favor.

David invites others to experience the goodness of the Lord firsthand. He emphasizes that those who trust and fear the Lord will be blessed and lack nothing good. This contrasts with the young lions, symbolizing strength and self-reliance, which may still lack, while those who depend on the Lord are fully provided for.

Verses 11-14: Instruction in the Fear of the Lord

Verses 11-14: "Come, you children, listen to me; I will teach you the fear of the LORD. Who is the man who desires life, and loves many days, that he may see good? Keep your tongue from evil, and your lips from speaking deceit. Depart from evil and do good; seek peace and pursue it."

- "Fear" (יִרְאָה, yirah) denotes reverence and awe.

- "Peace" (שָׁלוֹם, shalom) encompasses well-being and completeness.

David shifts to a teaching mode, instructing his listeners in the fear of the Lord. He provides practical advice: refrain from evil speech, turn away from wickedness, and actively pursue peace. These actions are the pathway to a fulfilling life marked by God's favor.

Verses 15-18: God's Attention to the Righteous

Verses 15-18: "The eyes of the LORD are on the righteous, and His ears are open to their cry. The face of the LORD is against those who do evil, to cut off the remembrance of them from the earth. The righteous cry out, and the LORD hears, and delivers them out of all their troubles. The LORD is near to those who have a broken heart, and saves such as have a contrite spirit."

- "Righteous" (צַדִּיק, tsaddiq) means just or in right standing with God.

- "Contrite" (דַּכָּא, dakka) refers to being crushed or deeply humbled.

David highlights God's attentiveness to the righteous and His responsiveness to their cries for help. In contrast, God opposes evildoers, ensuring their eventual eradication. He assures that the Lord is especially close to the brokenhearted and the contrite, offering salvation and comfort.

Verses 19-22: Assurance of Deliverance

Verses 19-22: "Many are the afflictions of the righteous, but the LORD delivers him out of them all. He guards all his bones; not one of them is broken. Evil shall slay the wicked, and those who hate the righteous shall be condemned. The LORD redeems the soul of His servants, and none of those who trust in Him shall be condemned."

- "Afflictions" (רָעוֹת, raot) refers to adversities or troubles.

- "Redeems" (פָּדָה, padah) means to rescue or deliver.

David concludes the psalm by acknowledging the numerous afflictions faced by the righteous, yet he reassures that the Lord delivers from them all. He emphasizes God's protective care and the ultimate triumph of good over evil. The Lord's redemption guarantees that His servants will not face condemnation.

Theological Significance

The Lord's Deliverance

1. Personal Testimony: David's personal experience of deliverance forms the basis of his testimony. This highlights the importance of personal encounters with God as a foundation for faith and testimony (Psalm 34:4-7).

2. Divine Protection: The imagery of the angel of the Lord encamping around those who fear Him signifies God's active and ongoing protection over His people (Psalm 34:7).

3. Experiencing God's Goodness: The call to "taste and see" emphasizes an experiential knowledge of God's goodness, encouraging believers to trust in the Lord and experience His blessings (Psalm 34:8).

Instruction in Righteous Living

1. Fear of the Lord: Reverence for God is foundational to righteous living. David's instruction to fear the Lord and to pursue peace and righteousness outlines a practical path to experiencing God's favor (Psalm 34:11-14).

2. Divine Attention: God's attentiveness to the cries of the righteous assures believers of His nearness and willingness to intervene in their lives. This fosters trust and reliance on God (Psalm 34:15-18).

Assurance of Deliverance and Protection

1. Deliverance from Afflictions: David acknowledges that the righteous will face many afflictions, but he reassures that the Lord will deliver them from all troubles. This promise provides hope and perseverance (Psalm 34:19).

2. Ultimate Redemption: The Lord's redemption of His servants and the promise that they will not face condemnation underscores the ultimate victory of God's people over evil (Psalm 34:22).

Practical Applications

1. Continuous Praise: Believers are encouraged to maintain an attitude of continuous praise and thanksgiving,

acknowledging God's faithfulness and deliverance in their lives (Psalm 34:1-3).

2. Trust and Fear the Lord: Trusting in the Lord and living in reverence before Him are key to experiencing His goodness and provision. Believers are called to seek the Lord diligently and rely on His protection (Psalm 34:8-10).

3. Pursue Righteousness: Living a righteous life involves controlling one's speech, avoiding evil, and actively pursuing peace. These actions align believers with God's will and attract His favor (Psalm 34:11-14).

4. Rely on God's Nearness: In times of trouble, believers can find comfort in knowing that God is near to the brokenhearted and contrite. This assurance fosters a deeper reliance on God's presence and help (Psalm 34:15-18).

5. Hold on to God's Promises: Despite facing numerous challenges, believers are encouraged to hold on to God's promises of deliverance and protection. Trusting in God's ultimate redemption provides hope and endurance (Psalm 34:19-22).

Comprehensive Commentary

Theological and Practical Insights

1. Psalm 34:1-3: The psalmist's commitment to continuous praise and communal worship highlights the importance of collective expressions of faith and thanksgiving. This fosters a community of believers who support and encourage one another in their walk with God.

2. Psalm 34:4-7: David's testimony of deliverance and the assurance of divine protection emphasize the importance of personal experiences with God. These encounters strengthen faith and provide a foundation for sharing God's goodness with others.

3. Psalm 34:8-10: The invitation to "taste and see" underscores the experiential nature of faith. Believers are

encouraged to actively engage with God, trusting in His goodness and provision.

4. Psalm 34:11-14: The practical instructions for righteous living provide a clear pathway for experiencing God's favor. Emphasizing the fear of the Lord and the pursuit of peace and righteousness aligns believers with God's will.

5. Psalm 34:15-18: God's attentiveness to the righteous and His nearness to the brokenhearted offer comfort and assurance. This reinforces the importance of maintaining a close relationship with God, especially during difficult times.

6. Psalm 34:19-22: The acknowledgment of afflictions and the promise of deliverance highlight the reality of life's challenges and the hope found in God's intervention. Believers are encouraged to persevere, trusting in God's ultimate redemption and protection.

Conclusion

Psalm 34 provides a rich tapestry of praise, thanksgiving, and practical instruction for living a life of faith and reliance on God. Through detailed expository study and comprehensive commentary, we have explored the themes of deliverance, trust, and divine care. This chapter has provided a thorough examination of how the Lord's deliverance in Psalm 34 underscores God's faithfulness and the assurance of His protection and provision for His people. Believers are encouraged to continuously praise God, trust in His goodness, pursue righteousness, rely on His nearness, and hold on to His promises of deliverance and redemption.

Jesus as the Deliverer from All Fears and Troubles

Psalm 34 is a beautiful and profound testament to God's faithfulness in delivering His people from their fears and troubles. This psalm, written by David, captures the essence of divine deliverance and provides a powerful foreshadowing of Jesus Christ, who is the ultimate Deliverer.

This chapter explores how Jesus fulfills the promises of deliverance in Psalm 34, offering a comprehensive analysis that includes theological insights and practical applications for believers.

Text of Psalm 34 (NKJV)

1. I will bless the LORD at all times; His praise shall continually be in my mouth.

2. My soul shall make its boast in the LORD; the humble shall hear of it and be glad.

3. Oh, magnify the LORD with me, and let us exalt His name together.

4. I sought the LORD, and He heard me, and delivered me from all my fears.

5. They looked to Him and were radiant, and their faces were not ashamed.

6. This poor man cried out, and the LORD heard him, and saved him out of all his troubles.

7. The angel of the LORD encamps all around those who fear Him, and delivers them.

8. Oh, taste and see that the LORD is good; blessed is the man who trusts in Him!

9. Oh, fear the LORD, you His saints! There is no want to those who fear Him.

10. The young lions lack and suffer hunger; but those who seek the LORD shall not lack any good thing.

11. Come, you children, listen to me; I will teach you the fear of the LORD.

12. Who is the man who desires life, and loves many days, that he may see good?

13. Keep your tongue from evil, and your lips from speaking deceit.

14. Depart from evil and do good; seek peace and pursue it.

15. The eyes of the LORD are on the righteous, and His ears are open to their cry.

16. The face of the LORD is against those who do evil, to cut off the remembrance of them from the earth.

17. The righteous cry out, and the LORD hears, and delivers them out of all their troubles.

18. The LORD is near to those who have a broken heart, and saves such as have a contrite spirit.

19. Many are the afflictions of the righteous, but the LORD delivers him out of them all.

20. He guards all his bones; not one of them is broken.

21. Evil shall slay the wicked, and those who hate the righteous shall be condemned.

22. The LORD redeems the soul of His servants, and none of those who trust in Him shall be condemned.

Expository Study

Verses 1-3: Continuous Praise and Exaltation

Verses 1-3: "I will bless the LORD at all times; His praise shall continually be in my mouth. My soul shall make its boast in the LORD; the humble shall hear of it and be glad. Oh, magnify the LORD with me, and let us exalt His name together."

- "Bless" (בָּרַךְ, barak) means to kneel or praise.
- "Boast" (הָלַל, halal) signifies rejoicing or celebrating.

David's commitment to continuous praise reflects the believer's response to God's deliverance. This call to collective worship and exaltation of the Lord's name emphasizes the importance of communal praise, which strengthens faith and fosters unity among believers.

Verses 4-7: Deliverance from Fear and Troubles

Verses 4-7: "I sought the LORD, and He heard me, and delivered me from all my fears. They looked to Him and were radiant, and their faces were not ashamed. This poor man cried out, and the LORD heard him, and saved him out of all his troubles. The angel of the LORD encamps all around those who fear Him, and delivers them."

- "Sought" (דָּרַשׁ, darash) implies seeking with care or diligence.

- "Radiant" (נָהַר, nahar) means to shine or beam with joy.

David testifies to the Lord's deliverance from fear and troubles. The deliverance provided by Jesus encompasses both physical and spiritual salvation, transforming lives and bringing joy and confidence to those who trust in Him.

Verses 8-10: Experiencing God's Goodness

Verses 8-10: "Oh, taste and see that the LORD is good; blessed is the man who trusts in Him! Oh, fear the LORD, you His saints! There is no want to those who fear Him. The young lions lack and suffer hunger; but those who seek the LORD shall not lack any good thing."

- "Taste" (טָעַם, taam) means to perceive or experience.

- "Good" (טוֹב, tov) signifies moral goodness and favor.

David's invitation to experience the Lord's goodness is fulfilled in Jesus, who reveals God's character and love. Trusting in Jesus ensures believers will not lack any good thing, as He provides abundantly for those who seek Him.

Verses 11-14: Instruction in the Fear of the Lord

Verses 11-14: "Come, you children, listen to me; I will teach you the fear of the LORD. Who is the man who desires life, and loves many days, that he may see good? Keep your tongue from evil, and your lips from speaking deceit. Depart from evil and do good; seek peace and pursue it."

- "Fear" (יִרְאָה, yirah) denotes reverence and awe.

- "Peace" (שָׁלוֹם, shalom) encompasses well-being and completeness.

David's teachings on fearing the Lord align with Jesus' instructions on living righteously. Jesus emphasizes the importance of truth, integrity, and pursuing peace, guiding believers to live in a way that pleases God.

Verses 15-18: God's Attention to the Righteous

Verses 15-18: "The eyes of the LORD are on the righteous, and His ears are open to their cry. The face of the LORD is against those who do evil, to cut off the remembrance of them from the earth. The righteous cry out, and the LORD hears, and delivers them out of all their troubles. The LORD is near to those who have a broken heart, and saves such as have a contrite spirit."

- "Righteous" (צַדִּיק, tsaddiq) means just or in right standing with God.

- "Contrite" (דַּכָּא, dakka) refers to being crushed or deeply humbled.

Jesus fulfills the promise of God's attentive care for the righteous. He hears their cries and delivers them, embodying the nearness of God to the brokenhearted and the salvation offered to the contrite.

Verses 19-22: Assurance of Deliverance

Verses 19-22: "Many are the afflictions of the righteous, but the LORD delivers him out of them all. He guards all his bones; not one of them is broken. Evil shall slay the wicked, and those who hate the righteous shall be condemned. The LORD redeems the soul of His servants, and none of those who trust in Him shall be condemned."

- "Afflictions" (רָעוֹת, raot) refers to adversities or troubles.

- "Redeems" (פָּדָה, padah) means to rescue or deliver.

David acknowledges the reality of suffering but reassures that the Lord delivers the righteous from all afflictions. Jesus, as the Redeemer, ensures the ultimate deliverance and protection of His followers, who will not face condemnation.

Theological Significance

Jesus as the Deliverer

1. Personal Deliverance: Jesus provides personal deliverance from fears and troubles, just as David experienced. His presence and intervention transform lives, offering peace and confidence (John 14:27, 2 Timothy 1:7).

2. Divine Protection: Jesus, the embodiment of the angel of the Lord, offers continual protection to those who fear Him. His deliverance is comprehensive, encompassing both physical and spiritual safety (Hebrews 1:14).

3. Experiencing Jesus' Goodness: Trusting in Jesus allows believers to experience God's goodness. Jesus reveals the Father's love and provision, ensuring that His followers lack nothing good (John 10:10).

Instruction and Righteous Living

1. Fear of the Lord: Reverence for Jesus is foundational to righteous living. His teachings guide believers in truth, integrity, and peace, reflecting a life that pleases God (Matthew 5:9, John 14:15).

2. Divine Attention: Jesus assures that God's eyes are on the righteous and His ears are open to their cries. He is near to the brokenhearted, offering comfort and salvation (Matthew 11:28-30).

Assurance of Deliverance and Protection

1. Deliverance from Afflictions: Jesus acknowledges the reality of suffering but promises deliverance for the righteous. His resurrection assures believers of victory over all troubles (John 16:33, 1 Peter 5:10).

2. Ultimate Redemption: Jesus' redemption ensures that His followers will not face condemnation. His sacrifice provides eternal security and the assurance of God's unfailing love (Romans 8:1, 8:38-39).

Practical Applications

1. Maintain Continuous Praise: Believers are encouraged to continually praise Jesus, acknowledging His

deliverance and faith fulness in their lives. This fosters a heart of gratitude and strengthens faith (1 Thessalonians 5:18).

2. Trust in Jesus' Deliverance: Trusting in Jesus for deliverance from fears and troubles brings peace and confidence. Believers are called to seek Him diligently and rely on His protection (Philippians 4:6-7).

3. Live Righteously: Following Jesus' teachings on truth, integrity, and peace aligns believers with God's will. Living righteously attracts God's favor and reflects His character (Colossians 3:12-15).

4. Rely on Jesus' Nearness: In times of trouble, believers can find comfort in knowing that Jesus is near to the brokenhearted. His presence offers peace and reassurance (Hebrews 13:5).

5. Hold on to Jesus' Promises: Despite facing challenges, believers are encouraged to hold on to Jesus' promises of deliverance and protection. Trusting in His ultimate redemption provides hope and perseverance (Hebrews 10:23).

Comprehensive Commentary

Theological and Messianic Implications

1. John 14:27: Jesus offers peace that transcends all fears and troubles, fulfilling the promise of deliverance found in Psalm 34. His peace is a source of comfort and assurance for believers.

2. Hebrews 1:14: The role of angels in protecting and delivering believers is ultimately fulfilled in Jesus, who commands divine protection over His followers. This reinforces the promise of divine encampment around those who fear God.

3. John 10:10: Jesus promises abundant life to those who trust in Him, fulfilling the invitation to "taste and see that the LORD is good." His provision ensures believers will not lack any good thing.

Exegetical Insights

1. Psalm 34:1-3: The psalmist's commitment to continuous praise and communal worship underscores the importance of collective expressions of faith and thanksgiving. This fosters a community of believers who support and encourage one another in their walk with God.

2. Psalm 34:4-7: David's testimony of deliverance and the assurance of divine protection emphasize the importance of personal experiences with God. These encounters strengthen faith and provide a foundation for sharing God's goodness with others.

3. Psalm 34:8-10: The invitation to "taste and see" underscores the experiential nature of faith. Believers are encouraged to actively engage with God, trusting in His goodness and provision.

4. Psalm 34:11-14: The practical instructions for righteous living provide a clear pathway for experiencing God's favor. Emphasizing the fear of the Lord and the pursuit of peace and righteousness aligns believers with God's will.

5. Psalm 34:15-18: God's attentiveness to the righteous and His nearness to the brokenhearted offer comfort and assurance. This reinforces the importance of maintaining a close relationship with God, especially during difficult times.

6. Psalm 34:19-22: The acknowledgment of afflictions and the promise of deliverance highlight the reality of life's challenges and the hope found in God's intervention. Believers are encouraged to persevere, trusting in God's ultimate redemption and protection.

Conclusion

Psalm 34 provides a rich tapestry of praise, thanksgiving, and practical instruction for living a life of faith and reliance on God. Through detailed expository study and comprehensive commentary, we have explored the themes of deliverance, trust, and divine care as fulfilled in Jesus Christ. This chapter has provided a thorough examination of how Jesus, as the ultimate Deliverer, embodies the promises of Psalm 34, offering believers assurance of His faithfulness, protection, and provision. Believers are encouraged to maintain continuous praise, trust in Jesus' deliverance, live righteously, rely on His nearness, and hold on to His promises of deliverance and redemption.

The Promise of Protection and Salvation

Psalm 34 offers profound insights into God's promises of protection and salvation for His people. David's personal testimony of deliverance, coupled with his teachings, provide a rich understanding of God's faithfulness. This chapter explores these promises in depth, highlighting their fulfillment in Jesus Christ. Through an expository study and comprehensive commentary, we will uncover the theological significance and practical applications of God's promises of protection and salvation.

Text of Psalm 34 (NKJV)

1. I will bless the LORD at all times; His praise shall continually be in my mouth.

2. My soul shall make its boast in the LORD; the humble shall hear of it and be glad.

3. Oh, magnify the LORD with me, and let us exalt His name together.

4. I sought the LORD, and He heard me, and delivered me from all my fears.

5. They looked to Him and were radiant, and their faces were not ashamed.

6. This poor man cried out, and the LORD heard him, and saved him out of all his troubles.

7. The angel of the LORD encamps all around those who fear Him, and delivers them.

8. Oh, taste and see that the LORD is good; blessed is the man who trusts in Him!

9. Oh, fear the LORD, you His saints! There is no want to those who fear Him.

10. The young lions lack and suffer hunger; but those who seek the LORD shall not lack any good thing.

11. Come, you children, listen to me; I will teach you the fear of the LORD.

12. Who is the man who desires life, and loves many days, that he may see good?

13. Keep your tongue from evil, and your lips from speaking deceit.

14. Depart from evil and do good; seek peace and pursue it.

15. The eyes of the LORD are on the righteous, and His ears are open to their cry.

16. The face of the LORD is against those who do evil, to cut off the remembrance of them from the earth.

17. The righteous cry out, and the LORD hears, and delivers them out of all their troubles.

18. The LORD is near to those who have a broken heart, and saves such as have a contrite spirit.

19. Many are the afflictions of the righteous, but the LORD delivers him out of them all.

20. He guards all his bones; not one of them is broken.

21. Evil shall slay the wicked, and those who hate the righteous shall be condemned.

22. The LORD redeems the soul of His servants, and none of those who trust in Him shall be condemned.

Expository Study

Verses 1-3: Continuous Praise for God's Faithfulness

Verses 1-3: "I will bless the LORD at all times; His praise shall continually be in my mouth. My soul shall make its boast in the LORD; the humble shall hear of it and be glad.

Oh, magnify the LORD with me, and let us exalt His name together."

    - "Bless" (בָּרַךְ, barak) means to kneel or to praise.

    - "Boast" (הָלַל, halal) signifies rejoicing or celebrating.

David begins by committing to continuous praise, emphasizing God's faithfulness and encouraging others to join in exalting the Lord. This communal call to worship highlights the importance of recognizing and celebrating God's protection and salvation together.

Verses 4-7: Deliverance from Fear and Troubles

Verses 4-7: "I sought the LORD, and He heard me, and delivered me from all my fears. They looked to Him and were radiant, and their faces were not ashamed. This poor man cried out, and the LORD heard him, and saved him out of all his troubles. The angel of the LORD encamps all around those who fear Him, and delivers them."

    - "Sought" (דָּרַשׁ, darash) implies seeking with care or diligence.

    - "Radiant" (נָהַר, nahar) means to shine or beam with joy.

David's testimony of deliverance from fear and troubles underscores God's responsiveness to those who seek Him. The imagery of the angel of the Lord encamping around those who fear Him signifies God's protective presence.

Verses 8-10: Experiencing God's Goodness

Verses 8-10: "Oh, taste and see that the LORD is good; blessed is the man who trusts in Him! Oh, fear the LORD, you His saints! There is no want to those who fear Him. The young lions lack and suffer hunger; but those who seek the LORD shall not lack any good thing."

    - "Taste" (טָעַם, taam) means to perceive or experience.

- "Good" (טוֹב, tov) signifies moral goodness and favor.

David invites others to experience God's goodness firsthand, assuring that those who trust in the Lord will not lack any good thing. This promise contrasts with the self-reliant, symbolized by young lions, who may still lack despite their strength.

Verses 11-14: Instruction in the Fear of the Lord

Verses 11-14: "Come, you children, listen to me; I will teach you the fear of the LORD. Who is the man who desires life, and loves many days, that he may see good? Keep your tongue from evil, and your lips from speaking deceit. Depart from evil and do good; seek peace and pursue it."

- "Fear" (יִרְאָה, yirah) denotes reverence and awe.

- "Peace" (שָׁלוֹם, shalom) encompasses well-being and completeness.

David provides practical instruction on fearing the Lord, which includes controlling one's speech, avoiding evil, and pursuing peace. These actions align believers with God's will and attract His favor.

Verses 15-18: God's Attention to the Righteous

Verses 15-18: "The eyes of the LORD are on the righteous, and His ears are open to their cry. The face of the LORD is against those who do evil, to cut off the remembrance of them from the earth. The righteous cry out, and the LORD hears, and delivers them out of all their troubles. The LORD is near to those who have a broken heart, and saves such as have a contrite spirit."

- "Righteous" (צַדִּיק, tsaddiq) means just or in right standing with God.

- "Contrite" (דַּכָּא, dakka) refers to being crushed or deeply humbled.

David emphasizes God's attentiveness to the righteous and His responsiveness to their cries for help. In contrast, God opposes evildoers, ensuring their eventual eradication. The Lord is especially close to the brokenhearted and the contrite, offering salvation and comfort.

Verses 19-22: Assurance of Deliverance

Verses 19-22: "Many are the afflictions of the righteous, but the LORD delivers him out of them all. He guards all his bones; not one of them is broken. Evil shall slay the wicked, and those who hate the righteous shall be condemned. The LORD redeems the soul of His servants, and none of those who trust in Him shall be condemned."

- "Afflictions" (רָעוֹת, raot) refers to adversities or troubles.

- "Redeems" (פָּדָה, padah) means to rescue or deliver.

David acknowledges the numerous afflictions faced by the righteous but reassures that the Lord delivers them from all troubles. He emphasizes God's protective care and the ultimate triumph of good over evil. The Lord's redemption guarantees that His servants will not face condemnation.

Theological Significance

Jesus as the Fulfillment of God's Promises

1. Divine Protection: Jesus embodies the divine protection promised in Psalm 34. His presence ensures continuous protection for those who trust in Him, mirroring the angel of the Lord encamping around the faithful (Matthew 28:20, John 10:28-29).

2. Experiencing God's Goodness: Through Jesus, believers can taste and see God's goodness. His life, death, and resurrection reveal the depth of God's love and favor, providing abundant life to those who trust in Him (John 10:10, 1 Peter 2:3).

3. Instruction in Righteous Living: Jesus' teachings provide a comprehensive guide to living righteously. He emphasizes the importance of truth, integrity, and peace,

reflecting the instructions given in Psalm 34 (Matthew 5:9, John 14:15).

Assurance of Salvation

1. Deliverance from Afflictions: Jesus assures believers of deliverance from afflictions. His resurrection demonstrates victory over suffering and death, providing hope and assurance to those who trust in Him (John 16:33, 1 Peter 5:10).

2. Ultimate Redemption: Jesus' redemptive work on the cross ensures that believers are saved from condemnation. His sacrifice provides eternal security and the promise of God's unfailing love (Romans 8:1, Ephesians 1:7).

Practical Applications

1. Maintain Continuous Praise: Believers are encouraged to continuously praise Jesus, acknowledging His faithfulness and protection. This fosters a heart of gratitude and strengthens faith (1 Thessalonians 5:18).

2. Trust in Jesus' Protection: Trusting in Jesus for protection from fears and troubles brings peace and confidence. Believers are called to seek Him diligently and rely on His protective presence (Philippians 4:6-7).

3. Live Righteously: Following Jesus' teachings on truth, integrity, and peace aligns believers with God's will. Living righteously attracts God's favor and reflects His character (Colossians 3:12-15).

4. Rely on Jesus' Nearness: In times of trouble, believers can find comfort in knowing that Jesus is near to the brokenhearted. His presence offers peace and reassurance (Hebrews 13:5).

5. Hold on to Jesus' Promises: Despite facing challenges, believers are encouraged to hold on to Jesus' promises of protection and salvation. Trusting in His ultimate redemption provides hope and perseverance (Hebrews 10:23).

Comprehensive Commentary

Theological and Messianic Implications

1. Matthew 28:20: Jesus' promise to be with His disciples always fulfills the assurance of divine protection in Psalm 34. His presence ensures believers are never alone, providing continuous comfort and security.

2. John 10:10: Jesus' promise of abundant life underscores the invitation to experience God's goodness. His provision ensures that believers will not lack any good thing, fulfilling David's assurance in Psalm 34.

3. John 16:33: Jesus' assurance of peace and victory over the world's troubles reinforces the promise of deliverance from afflictions. His victory provides hope and encouragement to persevere through challenges.

Exegetical Insights

1. Psalm 34:1-3: The psalmist's commitment to continuous praise and communal worship underscores the importance of collective expressions of faith and thanksgiving. This fosters a community of believers who support and encourage one another in their walk with God.

2. Psalm 34:4-7: David's testimony of deliverance and the assurance of divine protection emphasize the importance of personal experiences with God. These encounters strengthen faith and provide a foundation for sharing God's goodness with others.

3. Psalm 34:8-10: The invitation to "taste and see" underscores the experiential nature of faith. Believers are encouraged to actively engage with God, trusting in His goodness and provision.

4. Psalm 34:11-14: The practical instructions for righteous living provide a clear pathway for experiencing God's favor. Emphasizing the fear of the Lord and the pursuit of peace and righteousness aligns believers with God's will.

5. Psalm 34:15-18: God's attentiveness to the righteous and His nearness to the brokenhearted offer comfort and assurance. This reinforces the importance of maintaining a close relationship with God, especially during difficult times.

6. Psalm 34:19-22: The acknowledgment of afflictions and the promise of deliverance highlight the reality of life's challenges and the hope found in God's intervention. Believers are encouraged to persevere, trusting in God's ultimate redemption and protection.

Conclusion

Psalm 34 provides a rich tapestry of praise, thanksgiving, and practical instruction for living a life of faith and reliance on God. Through detailed expository study and comprehensive commentary, we have explored the themes of protection and salvation as fulfilled in Jesus Christ. This chapter has provided a thorough examination of how Jesus embodies the promises of Psalm 34, offering believers assurance of His faithfulness, protection, and provision. Believers are encouraged to maintain continuous praise, trust in Jesus' protection, live righteously, rely on His nearness, and hold on to His promises of protection and salvation.

New Testament Applications

Introduction

Psalm 34 is a profound expression of God's promises of protection and salvation. These promises find their ultimate fulfillment in Jesus Christ. This chapter explores the New Testament applications of Psalm 34, illustrating how the teachings and life of Jesus embody the psalm's themes. By examining key passages and principles, we will uncover the practical significance of living out these truths as believers.

Text of Psalm 34 (NKJV)

1. I will bless the LORD at all times; His praise shall continually be in my mouth.

2. My soul shall make its boast in the LORD; the humble shall hear of it and be glad.

3. Oh, magnify the LORD with me, and let us exalt His name together.

4. I sought the LORD, and He heard me, and delivered me from all my fears.

5. They looked to Him and were radiant, and their faces were not ashamed.

6. This poor man cried out, and the LORD heard him, and saved him out of all his troubles.

7. The angel of the LORD encamps all around those who fear Him, and delivers them.

8. Oh, taste and see that the LORD is good; blessed is the man who trusts in Him!

9. Oh, fear the LORD, you His saints! There is no want to those who fear Him.

10. The young lions lack and suffer hunger; but those who seek the LORD shall not lack any good thing.

11. Come, you children, listen to me; I will teach you the fear of the LORD.

12. Who is the man who desires life, and loves many days, that he may see good?

13. Keep your tongue from evil, and your lips from speaking deceit.

14. Depart from evil and do good; seek peace and pursue it.

15. The eyes of the LORD are on the righteous, and His ears are open to their cry.

16. The face of the LORD is against those who do evil, to cut off the remembrance of them from the earth.

17. The righteous cry out, and the LORD hears, and delivers them out of all their troubles.

18. The LORD is near to those who have a broken heart, and saves such as have a contrite spirit.

19. Many are the afflictions of the righteous, but the LORD delivers him out of them all.

20. He guards all his bones; not one of them is broken.

21. Evil shall slay the wicked, and those who hate the righteous shall be condemned.

22. The LORD redeems the soul of His servants, and none of those who trust in Him shall be condemned.

Expository Study

Verses 1-3: Continuous Praise in the New Testament Context

Verses 1-3: "I will bless the LORD at all times; His praise shall continually be in my mouth. My soul shall make its boast in the LORD; the humble shall hear of it and be glad. Oh, magnify the LORD with me, and let us exalt His name together."

- New Testament Application: Believers are called to a life of continuous praise and gratitude. Paul echoes this in 1 Thessalonians 5:18, where he writes, "In everything give thanks; for this is the will of God in Christ Jesus for you." The communal aspect of praise is emphasized in Hebrews 10:24-25, encouraging believers to gather and uplift each other.

Verses 4-7: Deliverance from Fear through Christ

Verses 4-7: "I sought the LORD, and He heard me, and delivered me from all my fears. They looked to Him and were radiant, and their faces were not ashamed. This poor man cried out, and the LORD heard him, and saved him out of all his troubles. The angel of the LORD encamps all around those who fear Him, and delivers them."

- New Testament Application: Jesus delivers believers from fear. In John 14:27, Jesus says, "Peace I leave with you; My peace I give to you; not as the world gives do I give to you. Let not your heart be troubled, neither let it be afraid." Believers are encouraged to cast their anxieties on Him (1 Peter 5:7), knowing He cares for them.

Verses 8-10: Experiencing Christ's Goodness

Verses 8-10: "Oh, taste and see that the LORD is good; blessed is the man who trusts in Him! Oh, fear the LORD, you His saints! There is no want to those who fear Him. The young lions lack and suffer hunger; but those who seek the LORD shall not lack any good thing."

- New Testament Application: Experiencing the goodness of Christ is a recurring theme. Jesus invites us to come to Him and find rest (Matthew 11:28-30). Trusting in Him ensures we will not lack any good thing, as Paul assures in Philippians 4:19, "And my God shall supply all your need according to His riches in glory by Christ Jesus."

Verses 11-14: Living Righteously through Christ

Verses 11-14: "Come, you children, listen to me; I will teach you the fear of the LORD. Who is the man who desires life, and loves many days, that he may see good? Keep your tongue from evil, and your lips from speaking deceit. Depart from evil and do good; seek peace and pursue it."

- New Testament Application: Jesus teaches us how to live righteously. The Sermon on the Mount (Matthew 5-7) provides comprehensive guidance on living in a way that pleases God. James 1:19-27 emphasizes controlling our speech and living out our faith through good works and purity.

Verses 15-18: Assurance of God's Attention

Verses 15-18: "The eyes of the LORD are on the righteous, and His ears are open to their cry. The face of the LORD is against those who do evil, to cut off the remembrance of them from the earth. The righteous cry out, and the LORD hears, and delivers them out of all their troubles. The LORD is near to those who have a broken heart, and saves such as have a contrite spirit."

- New Testament Application: God's attentiveness to the righteous is affirmed by Jesus. He promises that whatever we ask in His name, believing, we will receive (John 14:13-14). Jesus also comforts the brokenhearted, as seen in His interactions with the marginalized and suffering (Luke 4:18-19).

Verses 19-22: Assurance of Deliverance and Redemption

Verses 19-22: "Many are the afflictions of the righteous, but the LORD delivers him out of them all. He guards all his bones; not one of them is broken. Evil shall slay the wicked, and those who hate the righteous shall be condemned. The LORD redeems the soul of His servants, and none of those who trust in Him shall be condemned."

- New Testament Application: Jesus assures believers of deliverance and redemption. In John 16:33, He says, "These things I have spoken to you, that in Me you may have peace. In the world you will have tribulation; but be of good cheer, I have overcome the world." Paul reaffirms in Romans 8:1, "There is therefore now no condemnation to those who are in Christ Jesus."

Theological Significance

Jesus as the Fulfillment of God's Promises

1. Divine Protection: Jesus ensures the divine protection promised in Psalm 34. His presence guarantees continuous security for those who trust in Him, similar to the angel of the Lord encamping around the faithful (John 10:28-29).

2. Experiencing God's Goodness: Through Jesus, believers can fully experience God's goodness. His life and sacrifice reveal the depth of God's love, ensuring that those who trust in Him lack no good thing (John 10:10, Ephesians 1:3).

3. Instruction in Righteous Living: Jesus' teachings provide a comprehensive guide to righteous living. His commands align with the instructions given in Psalm 34,

emphasizing the importance of integrity, peace, and truth (Matthew 5-7).

Assurance of Salvation

1. Deliverance from Afflictions: Jesus assures believers of deliverance from afflictions. His resurrection exemplifies victory over suffering and death, providing hope and assurance to those who trust in Him (John 16:33, 1 Peter 5:10).

2. Ultimate Redemption: Jesus' redemptive work on the cross ensures that believers are saved from condemnation. His sacrifice secures eternal security and the promise of God's unfailing love (Romans 8:1, Ephesians 1:7).

Practical Applications

1. Maintain Continuous Praise: Believers are encouraged to continuously praise Jesus, acknowledging His faithfulness and protection in their lives. This fosters a heart of gratitude and strengthens faith (1 Thessalonians 5:18).

2. Trust in Jesus' Deliverance: Trusting in Jesus for deliverance from fears and troubles brings peace and confidence. Believers are called to seek Him diligently and rely on His protective presence (Philippians 4:6-7).

3. Live Righteously: Following Jesus' teachings on truth, integrity, and peace aligns believers with God's will. Living righteously attracts God's favor and reflects His character (Colossians 3:12-15).

4. Rely on Jesus' Nearness: In times of trouble, believers can find comfort in knowing that Jesus is near to the brokenhearted.

His presence offers peace and reassurance (Hebrews 13:5).

5. Hold on to Jesus' Promises: Despite facing challenges, believers are encouraged to hold on to Jesus' promises of deliverance and redemption. Trusting in His

ultimate victory provides hope and perseverance (Hebrews 10:23).

Comprehensive Commentary

Theological and Messianic Implications

1. John 10:28-29: Jesus' promise of eternal security for His followers fulfills the assurance of divine protection in Psalm 34. Believers can rest in the certainty of His care and safeguarding.

2. Ephesians 1:3: The blessings in Christ ensure believers lack no good thing, fulfilling the invitation to "taste and see that the LORD is good." Through Jesus, we experience the fullness of God's goodness and provision.

3. Romans 8:1: Paul's assurance of no condemnation for those in Christ confirms the promise of ultimate redemption. Jesus' sacrifice provides eternal security and the affirmation of God's steadfast love.

Exegetical Insights

1. Psalm 34:1-3: The call to continuous praise and communal worship underscores the importance of collective expressions of faith and thanksgiving. This fosters a supportive community of believers who encourage one another in their walk with God.

2. Psalm 34:4-7: David's testimony of deliverance and the assurance of divine protection emphasize the significance of personal experiences with God. These encounters strengthen faith and provide a foundation for sharing God's goodness with others.

3. Psalm 34:8-10: The invitation to "taste and see" underscores the experiential nature of faith. Believers are encouraged to actively engage with God, trusting in His goodness and provision.

4. Psalm 34:11-14: The practical instructions for righteous living provide a clear pathway for experiencing

God's favor. Emphasizing the fear of the Lord and the pursuit of peace and righteousness aligns believers with God's will.

5. Psalm 34:15-18: God's attentiveness to the righteous and His nearness to the brokenhearted offer comfort and assurance. This reinforces the importance of maintaining a close relationship with God, especially during difficult times.

6. Psalm 34:19-22: The acknowledgment of afflictions and the promise of deliverance highlight the reality of life's challenges and the hope found in God's intervention. Believers are encouraged to persevere, trusting in God's ultimate redemption and protection.

Conclusion

Psalm 34 provides a rich tapestry of praise, thanksgiving, and practical instruction for living a life of faith and reliance on God. Through detailed expository study and comprehensive commentary, we have explored the themes of protection and salvation as fulfilled in Jesus Christ. This chapter has provided a thorough examination of how the teachings and life of Jesus embody the promises of Psalm 34, offering believers assurance of His faithfulness, protection, and provision. Believers are encouraged to maintain continuous praise, trust in Jesus' deliverance, live righteously, rely on His nearness, and hold on to His promises of protection and redemption.

CHAPTER 12

THE HEART OF WORSHIP IN PSALM 40

Psalm 40 is a profound expression of worship and thanksgiving, capturing the essence of a heart fully devoted to God. Written by David, this psalm encompasses themes of deliverance, trust, and a commitment to God's will. This chapter provides a detailed analysis of Psalm 40:1-17, exploring its theological significance and practical applications for believers today.

Text of Psalm 40 (NKJV)

1. I waited patiently for the LORD; and He inclined to me, and heard my cry.

2. He also brought me up out of a horrible pit, out of the miry clay, and set my feet upon a rock, and established my steps.

3. He has put a new song in my mouth—praise to our God; many will see it and fear, and will trust in the LORD.

4. Blessed is that man who makes the LORD his trust, and does not respect the proud, nor such as turn aside to lies.

5. Many, O LORD my God, are Your wonderful works which You have done; and Your thoughts toward us cannot be recounted to You in order; if I would declare and speak of them, they are more than can be numbered.

6. Sacrifice and offering You did not desire; my ears You have opened. Burnt offering and sin offering You did not require.

7. Then I said, "Behold, I come; in the scroll of the book it is written of me.

8. I delight to do Your will, O my God, and Your law is within my heart."

9. I have proclaimed the good news of righteousness in the great assembly; indeed, I do not restrain my lips, O LORD, You Yourself know.

10. I have not hidden Your righteousness within my heart; I have declared Your faithfulness and Your salvation; I have not concealed Your lovingkindness and Your truth from the great assembly.

11. Do not withhold Your tender mercies from me, O LORD; let Your lovingkindness and Your truth continually preserve me.

12. For innumerable evils have surrounded me; my iniquities have overtaken me, so that I am not able to look up; they are more than the hairs of my head; therefore my heart fails me.

13. Be pleased, O LORD, to deliver me; O LORD, make haste to help me!

14. Let them be ashamed and brought to mutual confusion who seek to destroy my life; let them be driven backward and brought to dishonor who wish me evil.

15. Let them be confounded because of their shame, who say to me, "Aha, aha!"

16. Let all those who seek You rejoice and be glad in You; let such as love Your salvation say continually, "The LORD be magnified!"

17. But I am poor and needy; yet the LORD thinks upon me. You are my help and my deliverer; do not delay, O my God.

Expository Study

Verses 1-3: Patient Waiting and Deliverance

Verses 1-3: "I waited patiently for the LORD; and He inclined to me, and heard my cry. He also brought me up out of a horrible pit, out of the miry clay, and set my feet upon a rock, and established my steps. He has put a new song in my mouth—praise to our God; many will see it and fear, and will trust in the LORD."

- "Waited patiently" (קָוָה, qavah) implies a hopeful and expectant waiting.

- "New song" (שִׁיר חָדָשׁ, shir chadash) signifies a fresh expression of praise.

David begins by recounting his experience of waiting on the Lord and being delivered. This deliverance leads to a transformation, resulting in a new song of praise. The testimony of God's intervention inspires others to trust in Him.

Verses 4-5: Trust in the LORD

Verses 4-5: "Blessed is that man who makes the LORD his trust, and does not respect the proud, nor such as turn aside to lies. Many, O LORD my God, are Your wonderful works which You have done; and Your thoughts toward us cannot be recounted to You in order; if I would declare and speak of them, they are more than can be numbered."

- "Blessed" (אַשְׁרֵי, ashrei) denotes happiness and fulfillment.

- "Wonderful works" (נִפְלָאוֹת, niflaot) refers to extraordinary deeds.

David extols the virtues of trusting in the Lord and avoiding the ways of the proud and deceitful. He reflects on God's countless wonderful works and thoughts towards His people, highlighting the overwhelming nature of God's goodness and care.

Verses 6-8: Delight in God's Will

Verses 6-8: "Sacrifice and offering You did not desire; my ears You have opened. Burnt offering and sin offering You did not require. Then I said, 'Behold, I come; in the scroll of the book it is written of me. I delight to do Your will, O my God, and Your law is within my heart.'"

- "Sacrifice and offering" (וּמִנְחָה זֶבַח, zevach uminchah) indicate ritualistic sacrifices.

- "Delight" (חָפֵץ, chaphetz) expresses deep pleasure and willingness.

David recognizes that God desires obedience and a willing heart more than ritualistic sacrifices. He expresses his commitment to doing God's will, internalizing God's law and finding joy in obedience.

Verses 9-10: Proclamation of God's Righteousness

Verses 9-10: "I have proclaimed the good news of righteousness in the great assembly; indeed, I do not restrain my lips, O LORD, You Yourself know. I have not hidden Your righteousness within my heart; I have declared Your faithfulness and Your salvation; I have not concealed Your lovingkindness and Your truth from the great assembly."

- "Proclaimed" (בִּשֵּׂר, bisher) means to announce or publish.

- "Righteousness" (צֶדֶק, tsedeq) signifies justice and moral uprightness.

David commits to openly proclaiming God's righteousness and faithfulness. He is eager to share the good news of God's salvation and lovingkindness with the congregation, ensuring that others hear and know of God's deeds.

Verses 11-12: Prayer for Continued Mercy

Verses 11-12: "Do not withhold Your tender mercies from me, O LORD; let Your lovingkindness and Your truth continually preserve me. For innumerable evils have surrounded me; my iniquities have overtaken me, so that I am not able to look up; they are more than the hairs of my head; therefore my heart fails me."

- "Tender mercies" (רַחֲמִים, rachamim) denotes compassion and pity.

- "Iniquities" (עֲוֹנוֹת, avonot) refers to sins and moral failings.

David petitions God for ongoing mercy and preservation. He acknowledges his own sinfulness and the overwhelming presence of evil, seeking God's compassion and truth to sustain him.

Verses 13-15: Plea for Deliverance from Enemies

Verses 13-15: "Be pleased, O LORD, to deliver me; O LORD, make haste to help me! Let them be ashamed and brought to mutual confusion who seek to destroy my life; let them be driven backward and brought to dishonor who wish me evil. Let them be confounded because of their shame, who say to me, 'Aha, aha!'"

- "Deliver" (הוֹשִׁיעָה, hoshi'ah) means to save or rescue.

- "Confounded" (בֹּשׁוּ, boshvu) signifies being put to shame or embarrassed.

David cries out for swift deliverance from his enemies. He asks for his adversaries to be put to shame and dishonor, highlighting the urgency and intensity of his plea for divine intervention.

Verses 16-17: Rejoicing and Dependence on God

Verses 16-17: "Let all those who seek You rejoice and be glad in You; let such as love Your salvation say continually, 'The LORD be magnified!' But I am poor and needy; yet the LORD thinks upon me. You are my help and my deliverer; do not delay, O my God."

- "Rejoice" (שָׂמַח, samach) means to be joyful or glad.

- "Magnified" (גָּדַל, gadal) signifies to make great or exalt.

David concludes with a call for all who seek God to rejoice and magnify the Lord. He acknowledges his own neediness and dependence on God, reaffirming his trust in God's help and deliverance.

Theological Significance

Waiting on the Lord

1. Patient Waiting: David's patient waiting for the Lord reflects a deep trust and confidence in God's timing. This theme is echoed in the New Testament, where believers are encouraged to wait on the Lord with patience and faith (Romans 8:25, James 5:7-8).

2. Divine Response: God's inclination towards David's cry underscores His responsiveness to those who earnestly seek Him. Jesus assures believers of God's attentiveness and readiness to answer prayers (Matthew 7:7-8).

Trust and Obedience

1. Trust in God: David's trust in God over human pride and deceit sets a model for believers. Trusting in the Lord brings blessings and fulfillment, as emphasized by Jesus (John 14:1).

2. Obedience Over Sacrifice: David's recognition that God desires obedience more than sacrifice aligns with Jesus' teaching that love and obedience are greater than ritualistic practices (Matthew 9:13, John 14:15).

Proclamation and Praise

1.   Proclaiming   God's   Righteousness: David's commitment to proclaim God's righteousness serves as a call for believers to openly share the gospel and testify of God's goodness (Matthew 28:19-20, Acts 1:8).

2. Continuous Praise: David's continuous praise and proclamation of God's deeds encourage believers to maintain an attitude of gratitude and worship, as Paul exhorts (1 Thessalonians 5:18).

Dependence on God's Mercy

1. Seeking Mercy: David's plea for God's mercy highlights the importance of seeking God's compassion and forgiveness. Jesus' parables often emphasize the necessity of God's mercy in our lives (Luke 18:13-14).

2. Acknowledging Sin: David's acknowledgment of his iniquities and reliance on God's mercy is mirrored in the New Testament call to repentance and confession (1 John 1:9).

Deliverance and Rejoicing

1. Divine Deliverance: David's cry for deliverance from enemies underscores the belief in God's power to save. Jesus embodies this deliverance, offering salvation from sin and eternal security (John 3:16, John 10:28).

2. Rejoicing in God: David's call for rejoicing and magnifying the Lord encourages believers to find joy in God's salvation and continually exalt His name (Philippians 4:4).

Practical Applications

1. Practice Patient Waiting: Believers are encouraged to wait patiently for God's intervention, trusting in His perfect timing and faithfulness (Psalm 37:7, Romans 12:12).

2. Trust in God Over Human Wisdom: Trusting in God rather than human pride or deceit leads to blessings and fulfillment. Believers should seek God's guidance and wisdom in all aspects of life (Proverbs 3:5-6).

3. Prioritize Obedience: God desires a heart of obedience more than ritualistic practices. Believers are called

to internalize God's law and delight in doing His will (Micah 6:8, John 14:21).

4. Proclaim God's Goodness: Like David, believers should be eager to share their testimonies and proclaim God's righteousness, faithfulness, and salvation to others (1 Peter 2:9, Psalm 96:2-3).

5. Seek God's Mercy Daily: Acknowledging our need for God's mercy and forgiveness is crucial. Believers should regularly seek God's compassion and rely on His grace (Lamentations 3:22-23, Hebrews 4:16).

6. Rejoice and Magnify the Lord: Finding joy in God's salvation and continuously praising Him fosters a heart of worship and gratitude (Psalm 34:1, Colossians 3:16).

Comprehensive Commentary

Theological and Messianic Implications

1. Romans 8:25: Paul's exhortation to wait with patience aligns with David's patient waiting for the Lord. Believers are encouraged to trust in God's timing and remain hopeful.

2. John 14:1: Jesus' call to trust in God echoes David's emphasis on trusting the Lord. This trust brings peace and assurance in the midst of challenges.

3. John 14:15: Jesus' teaching that love and obedience are greater than sacrifice mirrors David's understanding of God's desire for a willing heart over ritualistic practices.

Exegetical Insights

1. Psalm 40:1-3: David's patient waiting and subsequent deliverance highlight the importance of trusting in God's timing. His transformation leads to a new song of praise, inspiring others to trust in the Lord.

2. Psalm 40:4-5: Trusting in God over human wisdom leads to blessings. David's reflection on God's wonderful works and thoughts emphasizes the overwhelming nature of God's goodness and care.

3. Psalm 40:6-8: God desires a heart of obedience more than ritualistic sacrifices. David's commitment to doing God's will and internalizing His law reflects a deep relationship with God.

4. Psalm 40:9-10: Proclaiming God's righteousness and faithfulness is crucial. David's eagerness to share the good news with the assembly encourages believers to openly testify of God's deeds.

5. Psalm 40:11-12: Seeking God's mercy and acknowledging our sins is essential. David's plea for ongoing compassion and truth underscores the importance of relying on God's grace.

6. Psalm 40:13-15: David's urgent plea for deliverance from enemies reflects the reality of opposition and the need for divine intervention. His call for his adversaries to be put to shame highlights the intensity of his plea.

7. Psalm 40:16-17: Rejoicing in God's salvation and continuously magnifying the Lord fosters a heart of worship. David's acknowledgment of his neediness and dependence on God reinforces the importance of trusting in God's help and deliverance.

Conclusion

Psalm 40 provides a profound expression of worship, trust, and commitment to God's will. Through detailed expository study and comprehensive commentary, we have explored the themes of patient waiting, divine deliverance, trust, obedience, proclamation, and dependence on God's mercy as reflected in the life and teachings of David. These themes find their ultimate fulfillment in Jesus Christ, who embodies the promises and principles outlined in Psalm 40. Believers are encouraged to practice patient waiting, trust in God, prioritize obedience, proclaim God's goodness, seek His mercy, and rejoice in His salvation. By living out these truths, we cultivate a heart of worship and deepen our relationship with God.

Jesus' Example of Obedience and Worship

Psalm 40 beautifully captures the essence of a heart fully devoted to God through obedience and worship. In the New Testament, Jesus Christ exemplifies these attributes, providing the ultimate model for believers. This chapter explores how Jesus' life and teachings align with the themes of obedience and worship in Psalm 40, offering a detailed analysis of His example and its implications for our faith.

Text of Psalm 40 (NKJV)

1. I waited patiently for the LORD; and He inclined to me, and heard my cry.

2. He also brought me up out of a horrible pit, out of the miry clay, and set my feet upon a rock, and established my steps.

3. He has put a new song in my mouth—praise to our God; many will see it and fear, and will trust in the LORD.

4. Blessed is that man who makes the LORD his trust, and does not respect the proud, nor such as turn aside to lies.

5. Many, O LORD my God, are Your wonderful works which You have done; and Your thoughts toward us cannot be recounted to You in order; if I would declare and speak of them, they are more than can be numbered.

6. Sacrifice and offering You did not desire; my ears You have opened. Burnt offering and sin offering You did not require.

7. Then I said, "Behold, I come; in the scroll of the book it is written of me.

8. I delight to do Your will, O my God, and Your law is within my heart."

9. I have proclaimed the good news of righteousness in the great assembly; indeed, I do not restrain my lips, O LORD, You Yourself know.

10. I have not hidden Your righteousness within my heart; I have declared Your faithfulness and Your salvation; I have not concealed Your lovingkindness and Your truth from the great assembly.

11. Do not withhold Your tender mercies from me, O LORD; let Your lovingkindness and Your truth continually preserve me.

12. For innumerable evils have surrounded me; my iniquities have overtaken me, so that I am not able to look up; they are more than the hairs of my head; therefore my heart fails me.

13. Be pleased, O LORD, to deliver me; O LORD, make haste to help me!

14. Let them be ashamed and brought to mutual confusion who seek to destroy my life; let them be driven backward and brought to dishonor who wish me evil.

15. Let them be confounded because of their shame, who say to me, "Aha, aha!"

16. Let all those who seek You rejoice and be glad in You; let such as love Your salvation say continually, "The LORD be magnified!"

17. But I am poor and needy; yet the LORD thinks upon me. You are my help and my deliverer; do not delay, O my God.

Expository Study

Verses 6-8: Jesus' Obedience and Delight in God's Will

Verses 6-8: "Sacrifice and offering You did not desire; my ears You have opened. Burnt offering and sin offering You did not require. Then I said, 'Behold, I come; in the scroll of the book it is written of me. I delight to do Your will, O my God, and Your law is within my heart.'"

- "Sacrifice and offering" (וּמִנְחָה זֶבַח, zevach uminchah) indicate ritualistic sacrifices.

- "Delight" (חָפֵץ, chaphetz) expresses deep pleasure and willingness.

David acknowledges that God desires obedience over ritualistic sacrifices. This theme is echoed in Jesus' life, who perfectly embodied obedience to God's will. Jesus' declaration in the Garden of Gethsemane, "Not My will, but Yours be done" (Luke 22:42), exemplifies His submission to the Father's plan.

Jesus' Fulfillment of Psalm 40

Hebrews 10:5-7: "Therefore, when He came into the world, He said: 'Sacrifice and offering You did not desire, but a body You have prepared for Me. In burnt offerings and sacrifices for sin You had no pleasure. Then I said, "Behold, I have come—In the volume of the book it is written of Me—To do Your will, O God."'"

- The author of Hebrews directly connects Psalm 40 to Jesus, illustrating that Jesus' mission was to fulfill God's will, transcending the need for traditional sacrifices through His ultimate sacrifice on the cross.

Jesus' Example of Obedience

1. Submission to God's Will: Jesus consistently demonstrated submission to the Father's will. His entire life was marked by obedience, even to the point of death on the cross (Philippians 2:8). This obedience is central to the redemption narrative, highlighting the importance of aligning our wills with God's purpose.

2. Teaching and Living God's Law: Jesus internalized God's law, embodying it in His teachings and actions. In Matthew 5:17, Jesus states, "Do not think that I came to destroy the Law or the Prophets. I did not come to destroy but to fulfill." His life was a perfect reflection of God's commandments, demonstrating love, compassion, and righteousness.

Verses 9-10: Proclamation of God's Righteousness

Verses 9-10: "I have proclaimed the good news of righteousness in the great assembly; indeed, I do not restrain my lips, O LORD, You Yourself know. I have not hidden Your righteousness within my heart; I have declared Your faithfulness and Your salvation; I have not concealed Your lovingkindness and Your truth from the great assembly."

- "Proclaimed" (בִּשֵּׂר, bisher) means to announce or publish.

- "Righteousness" (צֶדֶק, tsedeq) signifies justice and moral uprightness.

Jesus' ministry was characterized by the proclamation of God's kingdom and righteousness. He openly taught in synagogues, on mountainsides, and in cities, declaring the good news of salvation and the nature of God's kingdom (Mark 1:14-15).

Jesus' Proclamation and Teaching

1. Preaching the Kingdom of God: Jesus' primary message was the arrival of God's kingdom. He invited people to repent and believe in the gospel, making known God's righteousness and calling for a transformation of heart and mind (Matthew 4:17, Luke 4:43).

2. Teaching with Authority: Jesus taught with authority, revealing the depth of God's law and emphasizing its fulfillment through love and obedience. His teachings on the Sermon on the Mount (Matthew 5-7) exemplify His commitment to proclaiming God's truth and righteousness.

Verses 11-13: Seeking God's Mercy

Verses 11-13: "Do not withhold Your tender mercies from me, O LORD; let Your lovingkindness and Your truth continually preserve me. For innumerable evils have surrounded me; my iniquities have overtaken me, so that I am not able to look up; they are more than the hairs of my head; therefore my heart fails me. Be pleased, O LORD, to deliver me; O LORD, make haste to help me!"

- "Tender mercies" (רַחֲמִים, rachamim) denotes compassion and pity.

- "Iniquities" (עֲוֹנוֹת, avonot) refers to sins and moral failings.

Jesus, though sinless, understood human frailty and the need for God's mercy. He often prayed, seeking the Father's guidance and strength, especially during moments of trial and temptation (Matthew 26:36-46, Luke 6:12).

Jesus' Example in Prayer

1. Dependence on the Father: Jesus' life of prayer demonstrates His dependence on the Father. He regularly withdrew to solitary places to pray, emphasizing the importance of communion with God (Mark 1:35, Luke 5:16).

2. Intercession for Others: Jesus' prayers often included intercession for His disciples and all believers. In John 17, He prays for their protection, unity, and sanctification, showcasing His love and concern for their spiritual well-being.

Verses 14-17: Confidence in God's Deliverance

Verses 14-17: "Let them be ashamed and brought to mutual confusion who seek to destroy my life; let them be driven backward and brought to dishonor who wish me evil. Let them be confounded because of their shame, who say to me, 'Aha, aha!' Let all those who seek You rejoice and be glad in You; let such as love Your salvation say continually, 'The LORD be magnified!' But I am poor and needy; yet the LORD thinks upon me. You are my help and my deliverer; do not delay, O my God."

- "Rejoice" (שָׂמַח, samach) means to be joyful or glad.

- "Magnified" (גָּדַל, gadal) signifies to make great or exalt.

Jesus faced opposition and betrayal but remained confident in the Father's deliverance. His ultimate trust in God's plan was evident in His submission to the crucifixion, knowing that it would lead to the redemption of humanity and His own resurrection (John 10:17-18, Hebrews 12:2).

Jesus' Trust in God's Plan

1. Facing Betrayal and Suffering: Jesus endured betrayal by Judas and the subsequent suffering of the cross with unwavering faith in the Father's plan. His confidence in God's deliverance was evident as He prayed, "Father, into Your hands I commit My spirit" (Luke 23:46).

2. Encouraging Rejoicing and Faith: Jesus encouraged His followers to rejoice in God's salvation and magnify the Lord. He assured them of God's love and faithfulness, even in the face of persecution and trials (John 16:33).

Theological Significance

Jesus as the Model of Obedience and Worship

1. Perfect Obedience: Jesus exemplified perfect obedience to the Father, fulfilling the law and the prophets. His life was a testament to the importance of aligning one's will with God's purpose (Matthew 5:17-18, John 4:34).

2. Heart of Worship: Jesus demonstrated a heart of worship through His constant communion with the Father, His teachings, and His sacrificial love. He embodied true worship, which is rooted in spirit and truth (John 4:23-24).

Implications for Believers

1. Emulating Jesus' Obedience: Believers are called to follow Jesus' example of obedience, seeking to do God's will in all aspects of life. This involves surrendering personal desires and aligning with God's purpose (Romans 12:1-2).

2. Cultivating a Heart of Worship: Worship goes beyond rituals; it is a lifestyle of devotion and praise. Believers are encouraged to cultivate a heart of worship through prayer, praise, and proclaiming God's goodness (Colossians 3:16-17).

3. Trusting in God's Plan: Jesus' confidence in the Father's plan, even in the face of suffering, inspires believers to trust God's timing and purposes. This trust brings peace

and assurance, knowing that God works all things for good (Romans 8:28).

Practical Applications

1. Commit to Obedience: Believers should commit to obeying God's will, seeking to align their lives with His commands and purposes. This involves daily surrender and a willingness to follow wherever He leads (John 14:21).

2. Engage in Continuous Worship: Worship should be a continuous expression of gratitude and devotion. Believers are encouraged to praise God in all circumstances, fostering a heart of worship that glorifies Him (1 Thessalonians 5:16-18).

3. Proclaim God's Righteousness: Like Jesus, believers should proclaim the good news of God's kingdom and righteousness. Sharing testimonies and witnessing to others are vital aspects of living out our faith (Matthew 28:19-20).

4. Seek God's Mercy and Guidance: Regular prayer and seeking God's mercy are essential for spiritual growth. Believers should depend on God's grace and guidance, especially during challenging times (Hebrews 4:16).

5. Rejoice in God's Salvation: Believers are called to rejoice in God's salvation and magnify His name. This joy and gratitude should be evident in our lives, reflecting our trust in God's deliverance and love (Philippians 4:4).

Comprehensive Commentary

Theological and Messianic Implications

1. Luke 22:42: Jesus' submission to the Father's will in Gethsemane exemplifies the obedience and delight in doing God's will described in Psalm 40. His willingness to endure suffering for the sake of God's plan is the ultimate act of obedience.

2. John 4:34: Jesus' declaration that His food is to do the will of the Father and finish His work underscores the importance of obedience. Believers are called to find their sustenance and purpose in fulfilling God's will.

3. Hebrews 12:2: Jesus, the author and finisher of our faith, endured the cross for the joy set before Him. His confidence in God's plan and His ultimate victory through the resurrection inspire believers to trust and rejoice in God's deliverance.

Exegetical Insights

1. Psalm 40:6-8: David's acknowledgment of God's desire for obedience over sacrifice aligns with Jesus' life and mission. Jesus fulfilled the law through His perfect obedience, offering Himself as the ultimate sacrifice.

2. Psalm 40:9-10: Jesus' ministry of proclaiming God's righteousness and salvation mirrors David's commitment to declaring God's deeds. Jesus' teachings and miracles were testimonies of God's kingdom and love.

3. Psalm 40:11-13: Jesus' dependence on the Father's mercy and guidance highlights the importance of prayer and seeking God's help. His example encourages believers to rely on God's grace in all circumstances.

4. Psalm 40:14-17: Jesus' trust in God's plan, even in the face of opposition and suffering, demonstrates unwavering faith. His assurance of God's deliverance and His call for believers to rejoice in God's salvation provide a model for enduring trials with hope and confidence.

Conclusion

Psalm 40 provides a profound reflection on obedience and worship, themes that find their ultimate fulfillment in the life and teachings of Jesus Christ. Through detailed expository study and comprehensive commentary, we have explored how Jesus exemplifies these principles, offering believers a perfect model to follow. By committing to obedience, engaging in continuous worship, proclaiming God's righteousness, seeking God's mercy, and rejoicing in His salvation, we cultivate a heart of worship that glorifies God and deepens our relationship with Him. Jesus' example inspires us to trust in God's plan and live a life that reflects His love and faithfulness.

The Call to a Sacrificial Life

Psalm 40 not only highlights themes of obedience and worship but also emphasizes the importance of living a sacrificial life. In the New Testament, Jesus Christ exemplifies the ultimate sacrificial life, demonstrating what it means to live wholly dedicated to God's will. This chapter explores how Jesus' life and teachings call believers to embrace a life of sacrifice, offering a detailed analysis of Psalm 40:1-17 and its New Testament fulfillment.

Text of Psalm 40 (NKJV)

1. I waited patiently for the LORD; and He inclined to me, and heard my cry.

2. He also brought me up out of a horrible pit, out of the miry clay, and set my feet upon a rock, and established my steps.

3. He has put a new song in my mouth—praise to our God; many will see it and fear, and will trust in the LORD.

4. Blessed is that man who makes the LORD his trust, and does not respect the proud, nor such as turn aside to lies.

5. Many, O LORD my God, are Your wonderful works which You have done; and Your thoughts toward us cannot be recounted to You in order; if I would declare and speak of them, they are more than can be numbered.

6. Sacrifice and offering You did not desire; my ears You have opened. Burnt offering and sin offering You did not require.

7. Then I said, "Behold, I come; in the scroll of the book it is written of me.

8. I delight to do Your will, O my God, and Your law is within my heart."

9. I have proclaimed the good news of righteousness in the great assembly; indeed, I do not restrain my lips, O LORD, You Yourself know.

10. I have not hidden Your righteousness within my heart; I have declared Your faithfulness and Your salvation; I have not concealed Your lovingkindness and Your truth from the great assembly.

11. Do not withhold Your tender mercies from me, O LORD; let Your lovingkindness and Your truth continually preserve me.

12. For innumerable evils have surrounded me; my iniquities have overtaken me, so that I am not able to look up; they are more than the hairs of my head; therefore my heart fails me.

13. Be pleased, O LORD, to deliver me; O LORD, make haste to help me!

14. Let them be ashamed and brought to mutual confusion who seek to destroy my life; let them be driven backward and brought to dishonor who wish me evil.

15. Let them be confounded because of their shame, who say to me, "Aha, aha!"

16. Let all those who seek You rejoice and be glad in You; let such as love Your salvation say continually, "The LORD be magnified!"

17. But I am poor and needy; yet the LORD thinks upon me. You are my help and my deliverer; do not delay, O my God.

Expository Study

Verses 6-8: The Heart of Sacrifice

Verses 6-8: "Sacrifice and offering You did not desire; my ears You have opened. Burnt offering and sin offering You did not require. Then I said, 'Behold, I come; in the scroll of the book it is written of me. I delight to do Your will, O my God, and Your law is within my heart.'"

- "Sacrifice and offering" (וּמִנְחָה זֶבַח, zevach uminchah) indicate ritualistic sacrifices.

- "Delight" (חָפֵץ, chaphetz) expresses deep pleasure and willingness.

David acknowledges that God desires obedience and a willing heart more than ritualistic sacrifices. This theme is profoundly echoed in the life of Jesus, who perfectly embodied the ultimate sacrifice through His death on the cross, fulfilling God's will and demonstrating true devotion.

Jesus' Fulfillment of Psalm 40

Hebrews 10:5-7: "Therefore, when He came into the world, He said: 'Sacrifice and offering You did not desire, but a body You have prepared for Me. In burnt offerings and sacrifices for sin You had no pleasure. Then I said, "Behold, I have come—In the volume of the book it is written of Me—To do Your will, O God."'"

- The author of Hebrews directly connects Psalm 40 to Jesus, illustrating that Jesus' mission was to fulfill God's will, transcending traditional sacrifices through His ultimate sacrifice on the cross.

Jesus' Example of Sacrificial Living

1. The Ultimate Sacrifice: Jesus' entire life was characterized by self-sacrifice. His willingness to leave His divine throne and become human, ultimately dying on the cross, represents the epitome of sacrificial love (Philippians 2:5-8).

2. Daily Sacrifices: Beyond His ultimate sacrifice, Jesus lived a life of daily sacrifices, constantly serving others, healing the sick, and teaching about God's kingdom. His life exemplified the principle of putting others' needs before His own (Mark 10:45).

Verses 1-3: Patient Waiting and Deliverance

Verses 1-3: "I waited patiently for the LORD; and He inclined to me, and heard my cry. He also brought me up out of a horrible pit, out of the miry clay, and set my feet upon a rock, and established my steps. He has put a new song in my mouth—praise to our God; many will see it and fear, and will trust in the LORD."

- "Waited patiently" (קָוָה, qavah) implies a hopeful and expectant waiting.

- "New song" (שִׁיר חָדָשׁ, shir chadash) signifies a fresh expression of praise.

David's patient waiting and subsequent deliverance reflect a deep trust in God. Jesus embodied this trust, often retreating to pray and wait upon the Father, demonstrating patience and reliance on God's timing (Luke 5:16).

Jesus' Example of Patience and Trust

1. Waiting on God: Jesus frequently sought solitude to pray and wait on God, showing dependence on the Father's guidance and strength (Mark 1:35). His patience and trust in God's plan were evident throughout His ministry.

2. Expressing Praise: After deliverance or significant moments, Jesus expressed gratitude and praise to the Father, setting an example for believers to continually acknowledge God's goodness (John 11:41).

Verses 9-10: Proclamation of God's Righteousness

Verses 9-10: "I have proclaimed the good news of righteousness in the great assembly; indeed, I do not restrain my lips, O LORD, You Yourself know. I have not hidden Your righteousness within my heart; I have declared Your faithfulness and Your salvation; I have not concealed Your lovingkindness and Your truth from the great assembly."

- "Proclaimed" (בִּשֵּׂר, bisher) means to announce or publish.

- "Righteousness" (צֶדֶק, tsedeq) signifies justice and moral uprightness.

Jesus' ministry was marked by the proclamation of God's righteousness and salvation. He openly taught about

God's kingdom, performing miracles and sharing the good news, inviting all to experience God's love and mercy (Luke 4:18-19).

Jesus' Commitment to Proclamation

1. Teaching with Authority: Jesus taught with authority and clarity, making known the righteousness and kingdom of God. His teachings were transformative, revealing deep truths about God's character and His expectations for humanity (Matthew 7:28-29).

2. Demonstrating God's Love: Through His actions, Jesus demonstrated God's love and compassion, healing the sick, feeding the hungry, and forgiving sins. His life was a living proclamation of God's righteousness (Matthew 9:35-36).

Verses 11-13: Seeking God's Mercy

Verses 11-13: "Do not withhold Your tender mercies from me, O LORD; let Your lovingkindness and Your truth continually preserve me. For innumerable evils have surrounded me; my iniquities have overtaken me, so that I am not able to look up; they are more than the hairs of my head; therefore my heart fails me. Be pleased, O LORD, to deliver me; O LORD, make haste to help me!"

- "Tender mercies" (רַחֲמִים, rachamim) denotes compassion and pity.

- "Iniquities" (עֲוֹנוֹת, avonot) refers to sins and moral failings.

Jesus, though sinless, understood the human need for God's mercy and modeled a life of seeking God's grace through prayer. He empathized with human weaknesses and interceded on behalf of others (Hebrews 4:15-16).

Jesus' Life of Prayer and Intercession

1. Dependence on the Father: Jesus' frequent prayers demonstrate His dependence on the Father's mercy and

guidance. He sought strength and direction through communion with God (Luke 6:12).

2. Interceding for Others: Jesus often prayed for His disciples and all believers, asking for their protection, unity, and sanctification. His prayers reflect His deep compassion and commitment to others' spiritual well-being (John 17).

Verses 14-17: Confidence in God's Deliverance

Verses 14-17: "Let them be ashamed and brought to mutual confusion who seek to destroy my life; let them be driven backward and brought to dishonor who wish me evil. Let them be confounded because of their shame, who say to me, 'Aha, aha!' Let all those who seek You rejoice and be glad in You; let such as love Your salvation say continually, 'The LORD be magnified!' But I am poor and needy; yet the LORD thinks upon me. You are my help and my deliverer; do not delay, O my God."

- "Rejoice" (שָׂמַח, samach) means to be joyful or glad.

- "Magnified" (גָּדַל, gadal) signifies to make great or exalt.

Jesus faced betrayal, suffering, and death with unwavering confidence in the Father's deliverance. His ultimate sacrifice on the cross was a testament to His trust in God's redemptive plan, resulting in victory over sin and death (John 19:30, Hebrews 12:2).

Jesus' Trust and Victory

1. Enduring Suffering: Jesus endured immense suffering, trusting in God's plan for redemption. His sacrificial death was the ultimate expression of His confidence in the Father's deliverance (Matthew 26:39, Philippians 2:8).

2. Encouraging Rejoicing: Jesus encouraged His followers to rejoice in God's salvation, even in the face of trials and persecution. He assured them of God's love and ultimate victory (John 16:33).

Theological Significance

Jesus as the Model of Sacrificial Living

1. Ultimate Sacrifice: Jesus' sacrificial death on the cross is the foundation of Christian faith. His willingness to suffer and die for humanity's sins exemplifies the ultimate act of love and obedience (John 15:13, Romans 5:8).

2. Daily Sacrifices: Jesus' daily life of service, compassion, and teaching provides a model for believers to emulate. Living a sacrificial life involves putting others' needs above our own and following Jesus' example of selfless love (Matthew 20:28, Ephesians 5:2).

Implications for Believers

1. Embracing Sacrifice: Believers are called to embrace a life of sacrifice, following Jesus' example of selflessness and devotion to God's will. This involves daily acts of service, compassion, and obedience (Romans 12:1-2).

2. Living with Purpose: A sacrificial life is purposeful, seeking to glorify God and advance His kingdom. Believers are encouraged to live intentionally, using their gifts and resources for God's glory (Colossians 3:17).

3. Trusting in God's Deliverance: Jesus' confidence in the Father's deliverance inspires believers to trust in God's plan, even in difficult circumstances. This trust brings peace and assurance, knowing that God is faithful (Romans 8:28).

Practical Applications

1. Commit to Sacrificial Living: Believers should commit to living sacrificially, following Jesus' example of selfless love and service. This involves daily choices to put others' needs before our own and seeking to glorify God in all we do (Philippians 2:3-4).

2. Engage in Continuous Worship: Worship should be a continuous expression of gratitude and devotion. Believers are encouraged to praise God in all circumstances, fostering a heart of worship that glorifies Him (1 Thessalonians 5:16-18).

3. Proclaim God's Righteousness: Like Jesus, believers should proclaim the good news of God's kingdom and righteousness. Sharing testimonies and witnessing to others are vital aspects of living out our faith (Matthew 28:19-20).

4. Seek God's Mercy and Guidance: Regular prayer and seeking God's mercy are essential for spiritual growth. Believers should depend on God's grace and guidance, especially during challenging times (Hebrews 4:16).

5. Rejoice in God's Salvation: Believers are called to rejoice in God's salvation and magnify His name. This joy and gratitude should be evident in our lives, reflecting our trust in God's deliverance and love (Philippians 4:4).

Comprehensive Commentary

Theological and Messianic Implications

1. Philippians 2:5-8: Jesus' willingness to humble Himself and become obedient to death on the cross exemplifies the ultimate sacrificial life. Believers are called to adopt the same mindset of humility and obedience.

2. John 17: Jesus' intercessory prayer for His disciples and all believers underscores His role as our mediator and advocate. His prayers reflect His deep love and commitment to our spiritual well-being.

3. Romans 12:1-2: Paul's exhortation to offer our bodies as living sacrifices aligns with the call to a sacrificial life. Believers are encouraged to live holy and pleasing lives, dedicated to God's service.

Exegetical Insights

1. Psalm 40:6-8: David's acknowledgment of God's desire for obedience over sacrifice aligns with Jesus' life and mission. Jesus fulfilled the law through His perfect obedience, offering Himself as the ultimate sacrifice.

2. Psalm 40:9-10: Jesus' ministry of proclaiming God's righteousness and salvation mirrors David's commitment to

declaring God's deeds. Jesus' teachings and miracles were testimonies of God's kingdom and love.

3. Psalm 40:11-13: Seeking God's mercy and acknowledging our sins is essential. David's plea for ongoing compassion and truth underscores the importance of relying on God's grace.

4. Psalm 40:14-17: Jesus' trust in God's plan, even in the face of opposition and suffering, demonstrates unwavering faith. His assurance of God's deliverance and His call for believers to rejoice in God's salvation provide a model for enduring trials with hope and confidence.

Conclusion

Psalm 40 provides a profound reflection on obedience, worship, and the call to a sacrificial life, themes that find their ultimate fulfillment in the life and teachings of Jesus Christ. Through detailed expository study and comprehensive commentary, we have explored how Jesus exemplifies these principles, offering believers a perfect model to follow. By committing to sacrificial living, engaging in continuous worship, proclaiming God's righteousness, seeking God's mercy, and rejoicing in His salvation, we cultivate a heart of worship that glorifies God and deepens our relationship with Him. Jesus' example inspires us to trust in God's plan and live a life that reflects His love and faithfulness, embodying the call to a sacrificial life.

Fulfillment in Jesus' Ministry

Psalm 40 encapsulates themes of patience, deliverance, proclamation, and a heart devoted to God's will. These themes find their ultimate fulfillment in the ministry of Jesus Christ. This chapter explores how Jesus' life and teachings embody the essence of Psalm 40, highlighting His perfect obedience, sacrificial love, and the proclamation of God's kingdom. Through detailed analysis, we will uncover the theological significance and practical applications of Jesus' ministry as the fulfillment of Psalm 40.

Text of Psalm 40 (NKJV)

1. I waited patiently for the LORD; and He inclined to me, and heard my cry.

2. He also brought me up out of a horrible pit, out of the miry clay, and set my feet upon a rock, and established my steps.

3. He has put a new song in my mouth—praise to our God; many will see it and fear, and will trust in the LORD.

4. Blessed is that man who makes the LORD his trust, and does not respect the proud, nor such as turn aside to lies.

5. Many, O LORD my God, are Your wonderful works which You have done; and Your thoughts toward us cannot be recounted to You in order; if I would declare and speak of them, they are more than can be numbered.

6. Sacrifice and offering You did not desire; my ears You have opened. Burnt offering and sin offering You did not require.

7. Then I said, "Behold, I come; in the scroll of the book it is written of me.

8. I delight to do Your will, O my God, and Your law is within my heart."

9. I have proclaimed the good news of righteousness in the great assembly; indeed, I do not restrain my lips, O LORD, You Yourself know.

10. I have not hidden Your righteousness within my heart; I have declared Your faithfulness and Your salvation; I have not concealed Your lovingkindness and Your truth from the great assembly.

11. Do not withhold Your tender mercies from me, O LORD; let Your lovingkindness and Your truth continually preserve me.

12. For innumerable evils have surrounded me; my iniquities have overtaken me, so that I am not able to look up; they are more than the hairs of my head; therefore my heart fails me.

13. Be pleased, O LORD, to deliver me; O LORD, make haste to help me!

14. Let them be ashamed and brought to mutual confusion who seek to destroy my life; let them be driven backward and brought to dishonor who wish me evil.

15. Let them be confounded because of their shame, who say to me, "Aha, aha!"

16. Let all those who seek You rejoice and be glad in You; let such as love Your salvation say continually, "The LORD be magnified!"

17. But I am poor and needy; yet the LORD thinks upon me. You are my help and my deliverer; do not delay, O my God.

Expository Study

Verses 1-3: Patient Waiting and Deliverance

Verses 1-3: "I waited patiently for the LORD; and He inclined to me, and heard my cry. He also brought me up out of a horrible pit, out of the miry clay, and set my feet upon a rock, and established my steps. He has put a new song in my mouth—praise to our God; many will see it and fear, and will trust in the LORD."

- "Waited patiently" (קָוָה, qavah) implies a hopeful and expectant waiting.

- "New song" (חָדָשׁ שִׁיר, shir chadash) signifies a fresh expression of praise.

David's patient waiting and subsequent deliverance are vividly reflected in Jesus' ministry. Jesus often withdrew to pray and wait upon God, demonstrating deep trust in the Father's timing and plans (Luke 5:16). His life and resurrection inspire a new song of praise and hope for all believers.

Jesus' Example of Patience and Trust

1. Waiting on God: Jesus frequently sought solitude to pray and wait on God, showing dependence on the Father's guidance and strength (Mark 1:35). His patience and trust in God's plan were evident throughout His ministry, even in the face of suffering and death.

2. Expressing Praise: After significant moments, Jesus expressed gratitude and praise to the Father, setting an example for believers to continually acknowledge God's goodness (John 11:41).

Verses 6-8: Obedience Over Sacrifice

Verses 6-8: "Sacrifice and offering You did not desire; my ears You have opened. Burnt offering and sin offering You did not require. Then I said, 'Behold, I come; in the scroll of the book it is written of me. I delight to do Your will, O my God, and Your law is within my heart.'"

- "Sacrifice and offering" (וּמִנְחָה זֶבַח, zevach uminchah) indicate ritualistic sacrifices.

- "Delight" (חָפֵץ, chaphetz) expresses deep pleasure and willingness.

David acknowledges that God desires obedience over ritualistic sacrifices, a theme profoundly echoed in Jesus' life. Jesus perfectly embodied obedience to God's will, culminating in His sacrificial death on the cross, fulfilling God's redemptive plan (Philippians 2:8).

Jesus' Fulfillment of Psalm 40

Hebrews 10:5-7: "Therefore, when He came into the world, He said: 'Sacrifice and offering You did not desire, but a body You have prepared for Me. In burnt offerings and sacrifices for sin You had no pleasure. Then I said, "Behold, I have come—In the volume of the book it is written of Me— To do Your will, O God."'"

- The author of Hebrews directly connects Psalm 40 to Jesus, illustrating that Jesus' mission was to fulfill God's will, transcending traditional sacrifices through His ultimate sacrifice on the cross.

Jesus' Example of Obedience

1. Submission to God's Will: Jesus consistently demonstrated submission to the Father's will. His entire life was marked by obedience, even to the point of death on the cross (Luke 22:42). This obedience is central to the redemption narrative, highlighting the importance of aligning our wills with God's purpose.

2. Teaching and Living God's Law: Jesus internalized God's law, embodying it in His teachings and actions. In Matthew 5:17, Jesus states, "Do not think that I came to destroy the Law or the Prophets. I did not come to destroy but to fulfill." His life was a perfect reflection of God's commandments, demonstrating love, compassion, and righteousness.

Verses 9-10: Proclamation of God's Righteousness

Verses 9-10: "I have proclaimed the good news of righteousness in the great assembly; indeed, I do not restrain my lips, O LORD, You Yourself know. I have not hidden Your righteousness within my heart; I have declared Your faithfulness and Your salvation; I have not concealed Your lovingkindness and Your truth from the great assembly."

- "Proclaimed" (בִּשֵּׂר, bisher) means to announce or publish.

- "Righteousness" (צֶדֶק, tsedeq) signifies justice and moral uprightness.

Jesus' ministry was characterized by the proclamation of God's kingdom and righteousness. He openly taught in synagogues, on mountainsides, and in cities, declaring the good news of salvation and the nature of God's kingdom (Mark 1:14-15).

Jesus' Proclamation and Teaching

1. Preaching the Kingdom of God: Jesus' primary message was the arrival of God's kingdom. He invited people to repent and believe in the gospel, making known God's righteousness and calling for a transformation of heart and mind (Matthew 4:17, Luke 4:43).

2. Teaching with Authority: Jesus taught with authority, revealing the depth of God's law and emphasizing its fulfillment through love and obedience. His teachings on the Sermon on the Mount (Matthew 5-7) exemplify His commitment to proclaiming God's truth and righteousness.

Verses 11-13: Seeking God's Mercy

Verses 11-13: "Do not withhold Your tender mercies from me, O LORD; let Your lovingkindness and Your truth continually preserve me. For innumerable evils have surrounded me; my iniquities have overtaken me, so that I am not able to look up; they are more than the hairs of my head; therefore my heart fails me. Be pleased, O LORD, to deliver me; O LORD, make haste to help me!"

- "Tender mercies" (רַחֲמִים, rachamim) denotes compassion and pity.

- "Iniquities" (עֲוֹנוֹת, avonot) refers to sins and moral failings.

Jesus, though sinless, understood human frailty and the need for God's mercy. He often prayed, seeking the Father's guidance and strength, especially during moments of trial and temptation (Hebrews 4:15-16).

Jesus' Life of Prayer and Intercession

1. Dependence on the Father: Jesus' life of prayer demonstrates His dependence on the Father. He regularly withdrew to solitary places to pray, emphasizing the importance of communion with God (Luke 5:16).

2. Intercession for Others: Jesus' prayers often included intercession for His disciples and all believers. In

John 17, He prays for their protection, unity, and sanctification, showcasing His love and concern for their spiritual well-being.

Verses 14-17: Confidence in God's Deliverance

Verses 14-17: "Let them be ashamed and brought to mutual confusion who seek to destroy my life; let them be driven backward and brought to dishonor who wish me evil. Let them be confounded because of their shame, who say to me, 'Aha, aha!' Let all those who seek You rejoice and be glad in You; let such as love Your salvation say continually, 'The LORD be magnified!' But I am poor and needy; yet the LORD thinks upon me. You are my help and my deliverer; do not delay, O my God."

- "Rejoice" (שָׂמַח, samach) means to be joyful or glad.

- "Magnified" (גָּדַל, gadal) signifies to make great or exalt.

Jesus faced opposition and betrayal but remained confident in the Father's deliverance. His ultimate trust in God's plan was evident in His submission to the crucifixion, knowing that it would lead to the redemption of humanity and His own resurrection (John 10:17-18, Hebrews 12:2).

Jesus' Trust in God's Plan

1. Facing Betrayal and Suffering: Jesus endured betrayal by Judas and the subsequent suffering of the cross with unwavering faith in the Father's plan. His confidence in God's deliverance was evident as He prayed, "Father, into Your hands I commit My spirit" (Luke 23:46).

2. Encouraging Rejoicing and Faith: Jesus encouraged His followers to rejoice in God's salvation and magnify the Lord. He assured them of God's love and faithfulness, even in the face of persecution and trials (John 16:33).

Theological Significance

Jesus as the Fulfillment of God's Promises

1. Perfect Obedience: Jesus exemplified perfect obedience to the Father, fulfilling the law and the prophets. His life was a testament to the importance of aligning one's will with God's purpose (Matthew 5:17-18, John 4:34).

2. Heart of Worship: Jesus demonstrated a heart of worship through His constant communion with the Father, His teachings, and His sacrificial love. He embodied true worship, which is rooted in spirit and truth (John 4:23-24).

Implications for Believers

1. Emulating Jesus' Obedience: Believers are called to follow Jesus' example of obedience, seeking to do God's will in all aspects of life. This involves surrendering personal desires and aligning with God's purpose (Romans 12:1-2).

2. Cultivating a Heart of Worship: Worship goes beyond rituals; it is a lifestyle of devotion and praise. Believers are encouraged to cultivate a heart of worship through prayer, praise, and proclaiming God's goodness (Colossians 3:16-17).

3. Trusting in God's Plan: Jesus' confidence in the Father's plan, even in the face of suffering, inspires believers to trust God's timing and purposes. This trust brings peace and assurance, knowing that God works all things for good (Romans 8:28).

Practical Applications

1. Commit to Obedience: Believers should commit to obeying God's will, seeking to align their lives with His commands and purposes. This involves daily surrender and a willingness to follow wherever He leads (John 14:21).

2. Engage in Continuous Worship: Worship should be a continuous expression of gratitude and devotion. Believers are encouraged to praise God in all circumstances, fostering a heart of worship that glorifies Him (1 Thessalonians 5:16-18).

3. Proclaim God's Goodness: Like Jesus, believers should proclaim the good news of God's kingdom and

righteousness. Sharing testimonies and witnessing to others are vital aspects of living out our faith (Matthew 28:19-20).

4. Seek God's Mercy and Guidance: Regular prayer and seeking God's mercy are essential for spiritual growth. Believers should depend on God's grace and guidance, especially during challenging times (Hebrews 4:16).

5. Rejoice in God's Salvation: Believers are called to rejoice in God's salvation and magnify His name. This joy and gratitude should be evident in our lives, reflecting our trust in God's deliverance and love (Philippians 4:4).

Comprehensive Commentary

Theological and Messianic Implications

1. Luke 22:42: Jesus' submission to the Father's will in Gethsemane exemplifies the obedience and delight in doing God's will described in Psalm 40. His willingness to endure suffering for the sake of God's plan is the ultimate act of obedience.

2. John 4:34: Jesus' declaration that His food is to do the will of the Father and finish His work underscores the importance of obedience. Believers are called to find their sustenance and purpose in fulfilling God's will.

3. Hebrews 12:2: Jesus, the author and finisher of our faith, endured the cross for the joy set before Him. His confidence in God's plan and His ultimate victory through the resurrection inspire believers to trust and rejoice in God's deliverance.

Exegetical Insights

1. Psalm 40:1-3: David's patient waiting and subsequent deliverance highlight the importance of trusting in God's timing. His transformation leads to a new song of praise, inspiring others to trust in the Lord.

2. Psalm 40:6-8: David's acknowledgment of God's desire for obedience over sacrifice aligns with Jesus' life and

mission. Jesus fulfilled the law through His perfect obedience, offering Himself as the ultimate sacrifice.

3. Psalm 40:9-10: Jesus' ministry of proclaiming God's righteousness and salvation mirrors David's commitment to declaring God's deeds. Jesus' teachings and miracles were testimonies of God's kingdom and love.

4. Psalm 40:11-13: Seeking God's mercy and acknowledging our sins is essential. David's plea for ongoing compassion and truth underscores the importance of relying on God's grace.

5. Psalm 40:14-17: Jesus' trust in God's plan, even in the face of opposition and suffering, demonstrates unwavering faith. His assurance of God's deliverance and His call for believers to rejoice in God's salvation provides a model for enduring trials with hope and confidence.

Conclusion

Psalm 40 provides a profound reflection on obedience, worship, and the call to a sacrificial life, themes that find their ultimate fulfillment in the life and teachings of Jesus Christ. Through detailed expository study and comprehensive commentary, we have explored how Jesus exemplifies these principles, offering believers a perfect model to follow. By committing to obedience, engaging in continuous worship, proclaiming God's righteousness, seeking God's mercy, and rejoicing in His salvation, we cultivate a heart of worship that glorifies God and deepens our relationship with Him. Jesus' example inspires us to trust in God's plan and live a life that reflects His love and faithfulness, embodying the call to a sacrificial life.

CHAPTER 13

THE ETERNAL WORD IN PSALM 119

Psalm 119 is the longest chapter in the Bible and is a profound meditation on the greatness and eternal nature of God's Word. Each verse reflects the psalmist's deep love and reverence for God's law, commandments, and statutes. This chapter will provide an analysis of selected verses from Psalm 119, exploring their theological significance and practical applications. Through this study, we will uncover how these verses highlight the eternal truth of God's Word and its fulfillment in the life and ministry of Jesus Christ.

Text of Psalm 119 (Selected Verses, NKJV)

1. Blessed are the undefiled in the way, who walk in the law of the LORD!

2. Blessed are those who keep His testimonies, who seek Him with the whole heart!

11. Your word I have hidden in my heart, that I might not sin against You.

18. Open my eyes, that I may see wondrous things from Your law.

89. Forever, O LORD, Your word is settled in heaven.

105. Your word is a lamp to my feet and a light to my path.

160. The entirety of Your word is truth, and every one of Your righteous judgments endures forever.

Expository Study

Verses 1-2: The Blessing of Walking in God's Law

Verses 1-2: "Blessed are the undefiled in the way, who walk in the law of the LORD! Blessed are those who keep His testimonies, who seek Him with the whole heart!"

- "Blessed" (אַשְׁרֵי, ashrei) denotes happiness and fulfillment.

- "Undefiled" (תָּמִים, tamim) means blameless or perfect.

These verses introduce the psalm by declaring the blessedness of those who live according to God's law. Walking in God's ways and seeking Him wholeheartedly leads to a life of integrity and joy. This theme resonates throughout Psalm 119, emphasizing the importance of adhering to God's commandments.

Jesus' Fulfillment of Walking in God's Law

1. Perfect Obedience: Jesus exemplified perfect obedience to God's law, fulfilling all righteousness (Matthew 3:15). His sinless life embodies the blessedness described in these verses, setting a model for believers to follow.

2. Wholehearted Devotion: Jesus' devotion to the Father was complete, as seen in His dedication to prayer, teaching, and fulfilling the Father's will (John 5:30). His example encourages believers to seek God with their whole heart.

Verse 11: Hiding God's Word in the Heart

Verse 11: "Your word I have hidden in my heart, that I might not sin against You."

- "Hidden" (צָפַן, tzafan) means to treasure or store up.

This verse emphasizes the importance of internalizing God's Word to resist sin. By treasuring God's commandments in our hearts, we fortify ourselves against temptation and wrongdoing.

Jesus' Example of Treasuring God's Word

1. Resisting Temptation: Jesus used Scripture to resist Satan's temptations in the wilderness (Matthew 4:1-11). His knowledge and application of God's Word exemplify the power of internalizing Scripture to combat sin.

2. Teaching and Living the Word: Jesus consistently taught and lived out the truths of Scripture, demonstrating its authority and relevance. His teachings often referenced the Old Testament, showing the continuity and fulfillment of God's Word in His life (Luke 4:16-21).

Verse 18: The Wondrous Things of God's Law

Verse 18: "Open my eyes, that I may see wondrous things from Your law."

- "Open" (גָּלָה, galah) means to uncover or reveal.

- "Wondrous things" (נִפְלָאוֹת, niflaot) refers to extraordinary or marvelous aspects.

The psalmist prays for spiritual insight to understand the depths of God's law. This verse highlights the need for divine illumination to fully grasp the wonders contained in Scripture.

Jesus' Revelation of God's Word

1. Revealing Truth: Jesus revealed the deeper meanings of God's Word through His teachings and parables. He opened the eyes of His followers to the spiritual truths embedded in the Scriptures (Matthew 13:10-17).

2. The Living Word: As the incarnate Word of God, Jesus embodied the fullness of God's revelation. He is the ultimate expression of God's law and truth (John 1:14).

Verse 89: The Eternal Nature of God's Word

Verse 89: "Forever, O LORD, Your word is settled in heaven."

- "Forever" (עוֹלָם, olam) indicates eternity.

- "Settled" (נָצַב, natzav) means firmly established or fixed.

This verse declares the eternal and unchanging nature of God's Word. It is firmly established in heaven, reflecting God's immutable character and sovereign will.

Jesus as the Eternal Word

1. The Word Made Flesh: Jesus is the eternal Word who became flesh and dwelt among us (John 1:1, 14). His life and ministry fulfill the eternal truths of God's Word, demonstrating its timeless relevance and power.

2. Unchanging Truth: Jesus affirmed the enduring nature of God's Word, stating that not a jot or tittle would pass from the law until all is fulfilled (Matthew 5:18). His teachings reinforce the permanence and authority of Scripture.

Verse 105: God's Word as Light and Guidance

Verse 105: "Your word is a lamp to my feet and a light to my path."

- "Lamp" (נֵר, ner) symbolizes guidance and illumination.

- "Light" (אוֹר, or) signifies clarity and direction.

God's Word provides guidance and direction for our lives, illuminating our path and helping us navigate through the darkness of this world. This metaphor underscores the practical and essential role of Scripture in guiding our daily decisions and actions.

Jesus as the Light of the World

1. Guiding Light: Jesus declared Himself the light of the world, providing spiritual illumination and guidance to those who follow Him (John 8:12). His teachings and example serve as a beacon for believers, leading them in the way of truth and righteousness.

2. Path of Righteousness: Jesus' life and ministry demonstrate the path of righteousness that God's Word illuminates. He is the perfect example of living in the light of God's truth, showing believers how to walk according to God's will (1 John 1:7).

Verse 160: The Truth and Endurance of God's Word

Verse 160: "The entirety of Your word is truth, and every one of Your righteous judgments endures forever."

- "Truth" (אֱמֶת, emet) indicates faithfulness and reliability.

- "Endures forever" (עוֹלָם, olam) reflects perpetuity and eternal existence.

This verse affirms the comprehensive truth and eternal endurance of God's Word. Every aspect of Scripture is reliable and will stand the test of time, highlighting its divine origin and authority.

Jesus as the Embodiment of Truth

1. The Way, the Truth, and the Life: Jesus identified Himself as the way, the truth, and the life (John 14:6). He embodies the fullness of God's truth, providing the ultimate revelation of God's character and will.

2. Eternal Word: Jesus' teachings and actions confirm the enduring truth of God's Word. His resurrection and eternal reign underscore the timeless and unchanging nature of the Scriptures (Hebrews 13:8).

Theological Significance

The Eternal Word

1. God's Unchanging Nature: The eternal nature of God's Word reflects His unchanging character. As God is

eternal and immutable, so is His Word, providing a stable foundation for faith and practice (Isaiah 40:8).

2. Fulfillment in Christ: Jesus Christ, the eternal Word made flesh, embodies the truths of Scripture. His life and ministry fulfill the prophecies and promises of the Old Testament, demonstrating the continuity and consistency of God's Word (Luke 24:44).

Practical Guidance

1. Daily Living: God's Word provides practical guidance for daily living. It illuminates our path, helping us make wise decisions and live in a manner that honors God (Psalm 119:105).

2. Spiritual Insight: Praying for understanding and insight into God's Word is essential for spiritual growth. The Holy Spirit illuminates the Scriptures, revealing their depth and application to our lives (John 16:13).

Commitment to Scripture

1. Internalizing God's Word: Believers are called to internalize God's Word, hiding it in their hearts to guard against sin and live righteously (Psalm 119:11). This involves regular reading, meditation, and memorization of Scripture.

2. Proclaiming God's Truth: Like the psalmist and Jesus, believers are called to proclaim God's righteousness and truth. Sharing the gospel and living out its principles demonstrate the transformative power of God's Word (Matthew 28:19-20).

Practical Applications

1. Engage with Scripture Daily: Believers are encouraged to read and meditate on God's Word daily, allowing its truths to guide their thoughts and actions. Regular engagement with Scripture fosters spiritual growth and maturity (Joshua 1:8).

2. Seek Spiritual Insight: Pray for understanding and insight as you study God's Word. Ask the Holy Spirit to reveal

the wondrous things contained in Scripture and to help you apply them to your life (Ephesians 1:17-18).

3. Internalize Scripture: Memorize key verses that speak to your heart and life situations. Internalizing Scripture helps you draw on God's Word in times of need, providing strength and guidance (Colossians 3:16).

4. Live Out God's Word: Apply the teachings of Scripture to your daily life. Strive to walk in obedience to God's commands, reflecting His truth and righteousness in your actions and relationships (James 1:22).

5. Proclaim the Gospel: Share the good news of God's kingdom with others. Testify to the transformative power of God's Word in your life, encouraging others to seek and follow Him (1 Peter 3:15).

Comprehensive Commentary

Theological and Messianic Implications

1. Isaiah 40:8: "The grass withers, the flower fades, but the word of our God stands forever." This verse underscores the eternal nature of God's Word, aligning with the themes of Psalm 119 and its fulfillment in Jesus Christ.

2. John 1:1, 14: "In the beginning was the Word, and the Word was with God, and the Word was God... And the Word became flesh and dwelt among us." Jesus, as the incarnate Word, embodies the eternal truths of Scripture, fulfilling its promises and prophecies.

3. Hebrews 13:8: "Jesus Christ is the same yesterday, today, and forever." This verse affirms the unchanging nature of Jesus, reflecting the eternal and immutable character of God's Word.

Exegetical Insights

1. Psalm 119:1-2: The blessing of walking in God's law emphasizes the importance of obedience and wholehearted devotion. Jesus' perfect obedience and devotion to the Father set a model for believers to follow.

2. Psalm 119:11: Hiding God's Word in the heart is a defense against sin. Jesus' use of Scripture to resist temptation highlights the power of internalizing God's Word.

3. Psalm 119:18: Praying for spiritual insight reveals the depth and wonder of God's law. Jesus' teachings and parables uncover the deeper meanings of Scripture, providing spiritual illumination.

4. Psalm 119:89: The eternal nature of God's Word is reflected in Jesus, the Word made flesh. His life and ministry confirm the unchanging truth of Scripture.

5. Psalm 119:105: God's Word as a lamp and light guides believers in their daily walk. Jesus, the light of the world, provides spiritual guidance and direction.

6. Psalm 119:160: The entirety of God's Word is truth and endures forever. Jesus, as the embodiment of truth, affirms the reliability and eternal nature of Scripture.

Conclusion

Psalm 119 is a profound meditation on the greatness and eternal nature of God's Word. Through detailed expository study and comprehensive commentary, we have explored selected verses, highlighting their theological significance and practical applications. These verses emphasize the importance of internalizing, understanding, and living out God's Word, reflecting its timeless relevance and authority. Jesus Christ, the eternal Word made flesh, embodies the truths of Scripture, fulfilling its promises and prophecies. By following His example, believers are called to engage with Scripture daily, seek spiritual insight, internalize God's Word, live out its teachings, and proclaim the gospel. Through these practices, we cultivate a deep and abiding relationship with God, grounded in the eternal truth of His Word.

Jesus as the Living Word of God

The concept of Jesus as the living Word of God is foundational to Christian theology. This idea is deeply rooted in both the Old and New Testaments, particularly in the Gospel of John and various epistles. Psalm 119, with its profound meditation on the greatness and eternal nature of God's Word, sets the stage for understanding Jesus as the fulfillment and embodiment of God's Word. This chapter explores how Jesus fulfills this role, highlighting His life, ministry, and the theological significance of Him being the living Word of God.

Text of Psalm 119 (Selected Verses, NKJV)

1. Blessed are the undefiled in the way, who walk in the law of the LORD!

2. Blessed are those who keep His testimonies, who seek Him with the whole heart!

11. Your word I have hidden in my heart, that I might not sin against You.

18. Open my eyes, that I may see wondrous things from Your law.

89. Forever, O LORD, Your word is settled in heaven.

105. Your word is a lamp to my feet and a light to my path.

160. The entirety of Your word is truth, and every one of Your righteous judgments endures forever.

Expository Study

The Word Made Flesh

John 1:1, 14: "In the beginning was the Word, and the Word was with God, and the Word was God... And the Word became flesh and dwelt among us, and we beheld His glory, the glory as of the only begotten of the Father, full of grace and truth."

- "Word" (λόγος, logos) signifies divine reason, order, and communication.

John's Gospel begins with a profound declaration of Jesus' divine nature as the Word. This foundational truth establishes that Jesus is not only the messenger of God's Word but the Word itself incarnate. He embodies the eternal truths of Scripture, fulfilling the promises and prophecies contained within.

Jesus as the Eternal Word

Psalm 119:89: "Forever, O LORD, Your word is settled in heaven."

- "Forever" (עוֹלָם, olam) indicates eternity.

- "Settled" (נִצָּב, natzav) means firmly established or fixed.

This verse highlights the eternal and unchanging nature of God's Word, a concept fully realized in Jesus. As the eternal Word, Jesus embodies the immutable and timeless truths of God. His life and teachings are the perfect fulfillment of the Scriptures, providing a stable foundation for faith.

Jesus' Role in Creation and Revelation

Colossians 1:16-17: "For by Him all things were created that are in heaven and that are on earth, visible and invisible... And He is before all things, and in Him all things consist."

- "Created" (κτίζω, ktizo) means to make or form.

- "Consist" (συνίστημι, sunistemi) indicates being held together or sustained.

Jesus, as the Word, is the agent of creation and the sustainer of all things. This role underscores His divine nature and authority. He is not only the revealer of God's truth but also the Creator and Sustainer of the universe, holding all things together by His powerful word.

The Revelation of God's Truth

Psalm 119:160: "The entirety of Your word is truth, and every one of Your righteous judgments endures forever."

- "Truth" (אֱמֶת, emet) indicates faithfulness and reliability.

- "Endures forever" (עוֹלָם, olam) reflects perpetuity and eternal existence.

Jesus identified Himself as the truth, embodying the reliability and faithfulness of God's Word. His teachings, miracles, and redemptive work reveal the fullness of God's truth. Every word and action of Jesus reflects the enduring righteousness and faithfulness of God.

Jesus as the Light

Psalm 119:105: "Your word is a lamp to my feet and a light to my path."

- "Lamp" (נֵר, ner) symbolizes guidance and illumination.

- "Light" (אוֹר, or) signifies clarity and direction.

John 8:12: "Then Jesus spoke to them again, saying, 'I am the light of the world. He who follows Me shall not walk in darkness, but have the light of life.'"

- "Light" (φῶς, phos) represents revelation and purity.

Jesus declared Himself the light of the world, providing spiritual illumination and guidance. His life and teachings serve as a beacon, directing believers in the way of righteousness. As the living Word, Jesus embodies the clarity and direction offered by God's Word, dispelling darkness and leading to life.

Hiding God's Word in the Heart

Psalm 119:11: "Your word I have hidden in my heart, that I might not sin against You."

- "Hidden" (צָפַן, tzafan) means to treasure or store up.

Jesus exemplified hiding God's Word in the heart through His knowledge and application of Scripture. He used the Word to resist temptation, teach others, and reveal God's will. His example demonstrates the importance of internalizing Scripture to live a life pleasing to God.

Jesus' Use of Scripture

1. Resisting Temptation: In the wilderness, Jesus used Scripture to counter Satan's temptations (Matthew 4:1-11). His reliance on God's Word as a defense against sin highlights its power and necessity in spiritual warfare.

2. Teaching with Authority: Jesus taught with authority, often quoting and interpreting Scripture to reveal deeper truths (Matthew 5:21-22). His teachings brought new understanding and fulfillment to the Old Testament laws and prophecies.

The Word as Life and Sustenance

Matthew 4:4: "But He answered and said, 'It is written, "Man shall not live by bread alone, but by every word that proceeds from the mouth of God."'"

- "Word" (ῥῆμα, rhema) indicates a spoken word or utterance.

Jesus emphasized the sustaining power of God's Word, comparing it to essential nourishment. Just as physical food sustains the body, the Word of God sustains the soul. Jesus, as the living Word, offers the spiritual sustenance necessary for eternal life.

The Word as Judge and Redeemer

Hebrews 4:12: "For the word of God is living and powerful, and sharper than any two-edged sword, piercing even to the division of soul and spirit, and of joints and marrow, and is a discerner of the thoughts and intents of the heart."

- "Living" (ζῶν, zon) means alive or active.

- "Powerful" (ἐνεργής, energes) signifies effective or active.

Jesus, the living Word, is also the ultimate judge and redeemer. His teachings and presence reveal the true condition of the heart, discerning thoughts and intentions.

His sacrificial death and resurrection provide redemption, fulfilling the righteous judgments of God's Word.

Theological Significance

Jesus as the Fulfillment of God's Word

1. Incarnation: The incarnation of Jesus as the Word made flesh signifies God's ultimate communication and revelation to humanity. Through Jesus, God's eternal truths are made manifest in a tangible, relatable way (John 1:14).

2. Redemption: Jesus' life, death, and resurrection fulfill the redemptive plan outlined in Scripture. He is the promised Messiah who brings salvation and reconciliation between God and humanity (Luke 24:44-47).

3. Revelation: Jesus reveals the character and will of God. His teachings, miracles, and compassionate acts provide a complete picture of God's love, justice, and mercy (John 14:9).

Practical Guidance for Believers

1. Follow Jesus' Example: Believers are called to follow Jesus' example of obedience, reliance on Scripture, and devotion to God. Emulating His life leads to spiritual growth and maturity (1 Peter 2:21).

2. Engage with the Word: Regular engagement with Scripture is essential for spiritual health. Reading, studying, and meditating on God's Word helps believers understand and apply its truths (Joshua 1:8).

3. Live by the Word: Believers are encouraged to live according to the principles of God's Word. This involves applying its teachings in daily life, making decisions that align with God's will, and reflecting His character in interactions with others (James 1:22).

4. Proclaim the Word: Like Jesus, believers are called to proclaim the good news of God's kingdom. Sharing the gospel and teaching others about God's Word are vital aspects of fulfilling the Great Commission (Matthew 28:19-20).

Practical Applications

1. Daily Devotion: Commit to daily reading and meditation on God's Word. Allow its truths to guide your thoughts, actions, and decisions, fostering a deeper relationship with God (Psalm 1:2-3).

2. Prayer for Understanding: Pray for spiritual insight and understanding as you study Scripture. Ask the Holy Spirit to reveal the deeper meanings and applications of God's Word (Ephesians 1:17-18).

3. Memorization and Meditation: Memorize key verses that speak to your heart and life situations. Meditating on Scripture helps internalize its truths, providing strength and guidance in times of need (Psalm 119:11).

4. Application in Daily Life: Strive to live out the teachings of Scripture in your daily life. Make conscious efforts to apply biblical principles in your relationships, work, and personal conduct (Colossians 3:16-17).

5. Sharing the Word: Take opportunities to share the gospel and God's Word with others. Testify to the transformative power of Scripture in your life, encouraging others to seek and follow God (1 Peter 3:15).

Comprehensive Commentary

Theological and Messianic Implications

1. John 1:1, 14: The eternal nature of the Word, who is God, becoming flesh in Jesus, signifies the ultimate revelation and fulfillment of God's promises. Jesus' incarnation is the bridge between the Old Testament prophecies and their New Testament fulfillment.

2. Colossians 1:16-17: Jesus' role in creation and sustenance highlights His divine authority and preeminence. As the living Word, He is central to God's plan, from creation to redemption.

3. Hebrews 4:12: The living and active nature of God's Word, embodied in Jesus, emphasizes its power to transform,

judge, and redeem. Jesus' life and ministry demonstrate the penetrating and discerning power of God's truth.

Exegetical Insights

1. Psalm 119:1-2: The blessing of walking in God's law is exemplified in Jesus' perfect obedience and devotion to the Father. His life models the blessedness of living according to God's commands.

2. Psalm 119:11: Hiding God's Word in the heart is a defense against sin. Jesus' use of Scripture to resist temptation underscores its importance and power.

3. Psalm 119:18: Praying for spiritual insight reveals the depth and wonder of God's law. Jesus' teachings and parables uncover the deeper meanings of Scripture, providing spiritual illumination.

4. Psalm 119:89: The eternal nature of God's Word is reflected in Jesus, the Word made flesh. His life and ministry confirm the unchanging truth of Scripture.

5. Psalm 119:105: God's Word as a lamp and light guides believers in their daily walk. Jesus, the light of the world, provides spiritual guidance and direction.

6. Psalm 119:160: The entirety of God's Word is truth and endures forever. Jesus, as the embodiment of truth, affirms the reliability and eternal nature of Scripture.

Conclusion

Psalm 119 provides a profound meditation on the greatness and eternal nature of God's Word. Through detailed expository study and comprehensive commentary, we have explored selected verses, highlighting their theological significance and practical applications. These verses emphasize the importance of internalizing, understanding, and living out God's Word, reflecting its timeless relevance and authority. Jesus Christ, the eternal Word made flesh, embodies the truths of Scripture, fulfilling its promises and prophecies. By following His example, believers are called to engage with Scripture daily, seek spiritual insight, internalize God's Word, live out its teachings, and proclaim the gospel. Through these practices, we cultivate a deep and abiding relationship with God, grounded in the eternal truth of His Word.

The Importance of Scripture in Jesus' Teachings

The teachings of Jesus Christ are foundational to Christian faith and practice. Throughout His ministry, Jesus consistently emphasized the importance of Scripture, using it to teach, correct, and reveal God's truth. This chapter explores how Jesus utilized Scripture in His teachings, demonstrating its central role in His ministry and its significance for believers. By examining key instances and passages, we will uncover the theological and practical implications of Jesus' use of Scripture.

Text of Psalm 119 (Selected Verses, NKJV)

1. Blessed are the undefiled in the way, who walk in the law of the LORD!

2. Blessed are those who keep His testimonies, who seek Him with the whole heart!

11. Your word I have hidden in my heart, that I might not sin against You.

18. Open my eyes, that I may see wondrous things from Your law.

89. Forever, O LORD, Your word is settled in heaven.

105. Your word is a lamp to my feet and a light to my path.

160. The entirety of Your word is truth, and every one of Your righteous judgments endures forever.

Expository Study

Verses 1-2: Walking in the Law of the LORD

Verses 1-2: "Blessed are the undefiled in the way, who walk in the law of the LORD! Blessed are those who keep His testimonies, who seek Him with the whole heart!"

- "Blessed" (אַשְׁרֵי, ashrei) denotes happiness and fulfillment.

- "Undefiled" (תָּמִים, tamim) means blameless or perfect.

These verses emphasize the blessedness of living according to God's law. Jesus perfectly exemplified this by walking blamelessly in the ways of the LORD, seeking God with His whole heart, and teaching others to do the same.

Jesus' Example of Obedience to Scripture

1. Perfect Obedience: Jesus' life was marked by perfect obedience to God's law. He affirmed the importance of the law and the prophets, stating that He came not to abolish them but to fulfill them (Matthew 5:17).

2. Teaching the Law: Jesus taught the law with authority, interpreting it in its fullest and most profound sense. His Sermon on the Mount (Matthew 5-7) is a prime example of how He deepened the understanding of God's commandments.

Verse 11: Hiding God's Word in the Heart

Verse 11: "Your word I have hidden in my heart, that I might not sin against You."

- "Hidden" (צָפַן, tzafan) means to treasure or store up.

This verse highlights the importance of internalizing God's Word to guard against sin. Jesus exemplified this principle, using Scripture as a defense against temptation and teaching His followers to internalize God's commandments.

Jesus' Use of Scripture to Resist Temptation

1. The Temptation in the Wilderness: When Jesus was tempted by Satan in the wilderness, He responded by quoting Scripture, demonstrating its power and relevance (Matthew 4:1-11). Each response began with "It is written," underscoring the authority and importance of God's Word.

2. Teaching the Disciples: Jesus taught His disciples to rely on Scripture for guidance and strength. He encouraged

them to remain in His Word, promising that it would lead to true discipleship and freedom (John 8:31-32).

Verse 18: The Wondrous Things of God's Law

Verse 18: "Open my eyes, that I may see wondrous things from Your law."

- "Open" (גָּלָה, galah) means to uncover or reveal.

- "Wondrous things" (נִפְלָאוֹת, niflaot) refers to extraordinary or marvelous aspects.

The psalmist's prayer for spiritual insight to understand the depths of God's law is echoed in Jesus' teachings. Jesus revealed the deeper meanings of Scripture, uncovering the marvelous truths within.

Jesus as the Revealer of God's Word

1. Parables and Teachings: Jesus often used parables to reveal the deeper truths of God's kingdom. These stories, while simple on the surface, contained profound spiritual insights for those willing to listen and understand (Matthew 13:10-17).

2. Opening the Scriptures: After His resurrection, Jesus opened the Scriptures to His disciples, explaining how the prophecies and writings pointed to Him. This revelation helped them understand the full scope of God's redemptive plan (Luke 24:27, 44-45).

Verse 89: The Eternal Nature of God's Word

Verse 89: "Forever, O LORD, Your word is settled in heaven."

- "Forever" (עוֹלָם, olam) indicates eternity.

- "Settled" (נָצַב, natzav) means firmly established or fixed.

This verse declares the eternal and unchanging nature of God's Word. Jesus affirmed this truth, teaching that God's Word is enduring and reliable.

Jesus Affirming the Permanence of Scripture

1. Enduring Word: Jesus taught that heaven and earth would pass away, but His words would never pass away (Matthew 24:35). This emphasizes the permanence and reliability of Scripture.

2. Fulfillment of Prophecy: Throughout His ministry, Jesus highlighted how His life and actions fulfilled Old Testament prophecies. This fulfillment underscored the continuity and eternal relevance of God's Word (Matthew 5:18).

Verse 105: God's Word as Light and Guidance

Verse 105: "Your word is a lamp to my feet and a light to my path."

- "Lamp" (נֵר, ner) symbolizes guidance and illumination.

- "Light" (אוֹר, or) signifies clarity and direction.

God's Word provides guidance and direction for life. Jesus, as the living Word, embodies this guidance, leading His followers in the way of righteousness.

Jesus as the Light of the World

1. Guiding Light: Jesus declared Himself the light of the world, providing spiritual illumination and direction (John 8:12). His teachings and example guide believers in their daily walk.

2. Path of Righteousness: Jesus' life and ministry demonstrate the path of righteousness illuminated by God's Word. He perfectly exemplifies living according to God's truth, offering believers a model to follow (John 14:6).

Verse 160: The Truth and Endurance of God's Word

Verse 160: "The entirety of Your word is truth, and every one of Your righteous judgments endures forever."

- "Truth" (אֱמֶת, emet) indicates faithfulness and reliability.

- "Endures forever" (עוֹלָם, olam) reflects perpetuity and eternal existence.

This verse affirms the comprehensive truth and eternal endurance of God's Word. Jesus, as the embodiment of truth, affirmed the reliability and everlasting nature of Scripture.

Jesus as the Embodiment of Truth

1. The Way, the Truth, and the Life: Jesus identified Himself as the way, the truth, and the life (John 14:6). He embodies the fullness of God's truth, providing the ultimate revelation of God's character and will.

2. Eternal Word: Jesus' teachings and actions confirm the enduring truth of God's Word. His resurrection and eternal reign underscore the timeless and unchanging nature of the Scriptures (Hebrews 13:8).

Theological Significance

Jesus as the Fulfillment of God's Word

1. Incarnation: The incarnation of Jesus as the Word made flesh signifies God's ultimate communication and revelation to humanity. Through Jesus, God's eternal truths are made manifest in a tangible, relatable way (John 1:14).

2. Redemption: Jesus' life, death, and resurrection fulfill the redemptive plan outlined in Scripture. He is the promised Messiah who brings salvation and reconciliation between God and humanity (Luke 24:44-47).

3. Revelation: Jesus reveals the character and will of God. His teachings, miracles, and compassionate acts provide a complete picture of God's love, justice, and mercy (John 14:9).

Practical Guidance for Believers

1. Follow Jesus' Example: Believers are called to follow Jesus' example of obedience, reliance on Scripture, and devotion to God. Emulating His life leads to spiritual growth and maturity (1 Peter 2:21).

2. Engage with the Word: Regular engagement with Scripture is essential for spiritual health. Reading, studying,

and meditating on God's Word helps believers understand and apply its truths (Joshua 1:8).

3. Live by the Word: Believers are encouraged to live according to the principles of God's Word. This involves applying its teachings in daily life, making decisions that align with God's will, and reflecting His character in interactions with others (James 1:22).

4. Proclaim the Word: Like Jesus, believers are called to proclaim the good news of God's kingdom. Sharing the gospel and teaching others about God's Word are vital aspects of fulfilling the Great Commission (Matthew 28:19-20).

Practical Applications

1. Daily Devotion: Commit to daily reading and meditation on God's Word. Allow its truths to guide your thoughts, actions, and decisions, fostering a deeper relationship with God (Psalm 1:2-3).

2. Prayer for Understanding: Pray for spiritual insight and understanding as you study Scripture. Ask the Holy Spirit to reveal the deeper meanings and applications of God's Word (Ephesians 1:17-18).

3. Memorization and Meditation: Memorize key verses that speak to your heart and life situations. Meditating on Scripture helps internalize its truths, providing strength and guidance in times of need (Psalm 119:11).

4. Application in Daily Life: Strive to live out the teachings of Scripture in your daily life. Make conscious efforts to apply biblical principles in your relationships, work, and personal conduct (Colossians 3:16-17).

5. Sharing the Word: Take opportunities to share the gospel and God's Word with others. Testify to the transformative power of Scripture in your life, encouraging others to seek and follow God (1 Peter 3:15).

Comprehensive Commentary

Theological and Messianic Implications

1. Matthew 4:1-11: Jesus' use of Scripture to resist temptation underscores the authority and importance of God's Word. His example demonstrates that Scripture is a powerful tool for spiritual warfare and personal holiness.

2. Matthew 5:17: Jesus' statement that He came to fulfill the law and the prophets emphasizes the continuity and fulfillment of Scripture in His life and ministry. This fulfillment underscores the reliability and eternal relevance of God's Word.

3. John 14:6: Jesus' identification as the way, the truth, and the life highlights His role as the ultimate revelation of God's truth. His life and teachings provide the clearest and fullest expression of God's will and character.

Exegetical Insights

1. Psalm 119:1-2: The blessing of walking in God's law is exemplified in Jesus' perfect obedience and devotion to the Father. His life models the blessedness of living according to God's commands.

2. Psalm 119:11: Hiding God's Word in the heart is a defense against sin. Jesus' use of Scripture to resist temptation underscores its importance and power.

3. Psalm 119:18: Praying for spiritual insight reveals the depth and wonder of God's law. Jesus' teachings and parables uncover the deeper meanings of Scripture, providing spiritual illumination.

4. Psalm 119:89: The eternal nature of God's Word is reflected in Jesus, the Word made flesh. His life and ministry confirm the unchanging truth of Scripture.

5. Psalm 119:105: God's Word as a lamp and light guides believers in their daily walk. Jesus, the light of the world, provides spiritual guidance and direction.

6. Psalm 119:160: The entirety of God's Word is truth and endures forever. Jesus, as the embodiment of truth, affirms the reliability and eternal nature of Scripture.

Conclusion

Psalm 119 provides a profound meditation on the greatness and eternal nature of God's Word. Through detailed expository study and comprehensive commentary, we have explored selected verses, highlighting their theological significance and practical applications. These verses emphasize the importance of internalizing, understanding, and living out God's Word, reflecting its timeless relevance and authority. Jesus Christ, the eternal Word made flesh, embodies the truths of Scripture, fulfilling its promises and prophecies. By following His example, believers are called to engage with Scripture daily, seek spiritual insight, internalize God's Word, live out its teachings, and proclaim the gospel. Through these practices, we cultivate a deep and abiding relationship with God, grounded in the eternal truth of His Word.

New Testament Affirmations

The New Testament is filled with affirmations of the importance, authority, and fulfillment of Scripture. Jesus Christ and the apostles consistently referenced and affirmed the Old Testament, demonstrating its enduring relevance and divine inspiration. This chapter explores key New Testament passages that affirm the significance of Scripture, highlighting how Jesus and His followers upheld and fulfilled the Word of God. By examining these affirmations, we will uncover the theological and practical implications for believers today.

Text of Psalm 119 (Selected Verses, NKJV)

1. Blessed are the undefiled in the way, who walk in the law of the LORD!

2. Blessed are those who keep His testimonies, who seek Him with the whole heart!

11. Your word I have hidden in my heart, that I might not sin against You.

18. Open my eyes, that I may see wondrous things from Your law.

89. Forever, O LORD, Your word is settled in heaven.

105. Your word is a lamp to my feet and a light to my path.

160. The entirety of Your word is truth, and every one of Your righteous judgments endures forever.

Expository Study

Jesus' Affirmation of Scripture

Matthew 5:17-18: "Do not think that I came to destroy the Law or the Prophets. I did not come to destroy but to fulfill. For assuredly, I say to you, till heaven and earth pass away, one jot or one tittle will by no means pass from the law till all is fulfilled."

- "Fulfill" (πληρόω, plēroō) means to complete or bring to its intended meaning.

Jesus' statement in the Sermon on the Mount underscores His commitment to fulfilling the Old Testament Scriptures. He affirms the enduring validity of the Law and the Prophets, emphasizing that not even the smallest detail will disappear until everything is accomplished.

Jesus' Use of Scripture in Teaching

1. Teaching with Authority: Jesus frequently referenced Scripture in His teachings, interpreting and applying it with divine authority. His use of Scripture in the Sermon on the Mount (Matthew 5-7) and other teachings demonstrated its relevance and authority.

2. Clarifying the Law: Jesus often clarified and expanded the understanding of the law, revealing its deeper moral and spiritual implications. For example, in Matthew

5:21-22, He explains that the commandment against murder also condemns unjust anger.

Jesus' Fulfillment of Prophecy

Luke 24:44-45: "Then He said to them, 'These are the words which I spoke to you while I was still with you, that all things must be fulfilled which were written in the Law of Moses and the Prophets and the Psalms concerning Me.' And He opened their understanding, that they might comprehend the Scriptures."

- "Fulfilled" (πληρόω, plēroō) again emphasizes completion or bringing to fruition.

After His resurrection, Jesus explained to His disciples how His life, death, and resurrection fulfilled the Old Testament prophecies. This affirmation reinforces the interconnectedness of the Old and New Testaments and the fulfillment of God's redemptive plan in Christ.

The Apostolic Affirmation of Scripture

2 Timothy 3:16-17: "All Scripture is given by inspiration of God, and is profitable for doctrine, for reproof, for correction, for instruction in righteousness, that the man of God may be complete, thoroughly equipped for every good work."

- "Inspiration" (θεόπνευστος, theopneustos) means God-breathed.

Paul's affirmation of Scripture's divine inspiration underscores its authority and usefulness for teaching, reproof, correction, and training in righteousness. This passage highlights the comprehensive nature of Scripture, providing all that is necessary for a godly life.

The Role of Scripture in the Early Church

1. Teaching and Doctrine: The early church relied heavily on Scripture for teaching and establishing doctrine. The apostles frequently referenced the Old Testament to explain and validate their teachings about Jesus (Acts 17:2-3).

2. Correction and Reproof: Scripture was used to address errors and guide believers back to the truth. Paul's letters often corrected doctrinal misunderstandings and ethical missteps, using Scripture as the foundation for his arguments (Galatians 3:10-14).

The Permanence and Authority of Scripture

Matthew 24:35: "Heaven and earth will pass away, but My words will by no means pass away."

- "Pass away" (παρέρχομαι, parerchomai) means to disappear or perish.

Jesus affirmed the eternal nature of His words, equating them with the enduring truth of Scripture. This statement underscores the unchanging and authoritative nature of Jesus' teachings, reinforcing their divine origin.

The Power of Scripture

Hebrews 4:12: "For the word of God is living and powerful, and sharper than any two-edged sword, piercing even to the division of soul and spirit, and of joints and marrow, and is a discerner of the thoughts and intents of the heart."

- "Living" (ζῶν, zōn) means alive or active.

- "Powerful" (ἐνεργής, energēs) signifies effective or active.

This passage highlights the dynamic and penetrating power of God's Word. Scripture is described as living and active, capable of discerning the deepest thoughts and intentions of the heart. This underscores the transformative impact of Scripture on believers.

Theological Significance

The Unity of Scripture

1. Old and New Testament Continuity: The New Testament frequently affirms and fulfills the Old Testament, demonstrating the unity and continuity of God's Word. Jesus and the apostles viewed the Old Testament as authoritative

and foundational for understanding God's redemptive plan (Luke 24:27).

2. Fulfillment in Christ: Jesus' life and ministry fulfill the promises and prophecies of the Old Testament. This fulfillment validates the truth and reliability of Scripture, showing that God's Word is consistent and trustworthy (Matthew 5:17).

The Authority of Scripture

1. Divine Inspiration: Scripture's divine inspiration means that it is authoritative and trustworthy. Believers can rely on Scripture for doctrine, correction, and guidance in righteousness (2 Timothy 3:16-17).

2. Jesus' Affirmation: Jesus' frequent use and affirmation of Scripture underscore its authority. He consistently upheld the Old Testament as the Word of God, interpreting and applying it with divine insight (Matthew 4:4).

The Practical Application of Scripture

1. Guidance and Instruction: Scripture provides guidance and instruction for living a godly life. Believers are called to engage with God's Word regularly, allowing it to shape their thoughts, actions, and decisions (Psalm 119:105).

2. Spiritual Growth and Maturity: Engaging with Scripture leads to spiritual growth and maturity. It equips believers for every good work, helping them become more like Christ (2 Timothy 3:17).

Practical Applications

1. Daily Engagement with Scripture: Commit to daily reading and meditation on God's Word. Allow its truths to guide your thoughts, actions, and decisions, fostering a deeper relationship with God (Psalm 1:2-3).

2. Study and Understand Scripture: Invest time in studying and understanding Scripture. Use resources such as commentaries, study guides, and biblical dictionaries to

deepen your knowledge and application of God's Word (2 Timothy 2:15).

3. Memorization and Meditation: Memorize key verses that speak to your heart and life situations. Meditating on Scripture helps internalize its truths, providing strength and guidance in times of need (Psalm 119:11).

4. Application in Daily Life: Strive to live out the teachings of Scripture in your daily life. Make conscious efforts to apply biblical principles in your relationships, work, and personal conduct (James 1:22).

5. Sharing the Word: Take opportunities to share the gospel and God's Word with others. Testify to the transformative power of Scripture in your life, encouraging others to seek and follow God (1 Peter 3:15).

Comprehensive Commentary

Theological and Messianic Implications

1. Matthew 5:17-18: Jesus' affirmation that He came to fulfill the law and the prophets emphasizes the continuity and fulfillment of Scripture in His life and ministry. This fulfillment underscores the reliability and eternal relevance of God's Word.

2. Luke 24:44-45: Jesus' explanation of how the Scriptures point to Him reinforces the interconnectedness of the Old and New Testaments. This affirmation highlights the coherence and divine inspiration of the entire Bible.

3. 2 Timothy 3:16-17: Paul's declaration of the divine inspiration and usefulness of Scripture underscores its authority and comprehensive nature. Scripture is essential for teaching, correcting, and training in righteousness.

Exegetical Insights

1. Psalm 119:1-2: The blessing of walking in God's law is exemplified in Jesus' perfect obedience and devotion to the Father. His life models the blessedness of living according to God's commands.

2. Psalm 119:11: Hiding God's Word in the heart is a defense against sin. Jesus' use of Scripture to resist temptation underscores its importance and power.

3. Psalm 119:18: Praying for spiritual insight reveals the depth and wonder of God's law. Jesus' teachings and parables uncover the deeper meanings of Scripture, providing spiritual illumination.

4. Psalm 119:89: The eternal nature of God's Word is reflected in Jesus, the Word made flesh. His life and ministry confirm the unchanging truth of Scripture.

5. Psalm 119:105: God's Word as a lamp and light guides believers in their daily walk. Jesus, the light of the world, provides spiritual guidance and direction.

6. Psalm 119:160: The entirety of God's Word is truth and endures forever. Jesus, as the embodiment of truth, affirms the reliability and eternal nature of Scripture.

Conclusion

Psalm 119 provides a profound meditation on the greatness and eternal nature of God's Word. Through detailed expository study and comprehensive commentary, we have explored selected verses, highlighting their theological significance and practical applications. These verses emphasize the importance of internalizing, understanding, and living out God's Word, reflecting its timeless relevance and authority. The New Testament consistently affirms the significance of Scripture, demonstrating its fulfillment in the life and ministry of Jesus Christ. By following His example and engaging with Scripture daily, believers can grow in their faith, live according to God's will, and proclaim the transformative power of His Word. Through these practices, we cultivate a deep and abiding relationship with God, grounded in the eternal truth of His Word.

CHAPTER 14

RECAPITULATION OF JESUS' LESSON IN THE PSALMS

The Psalms, a collection of poetic writings, are rich with prophetic insights and divine revelations that point to Jesus Christ. Throughout this study, we have explored various Psalms that illustrate the life, ministry, and teachings of Jesus. This concluding chapter recapitulates the lessons of Jesus as revealed in the Psalms, highlighting the theological significance and practical applications for believers today.

Recapitulation of Key Psalms

Psalm 2: The Anointed One

Psalm 2 presents a vivid image of the Messiah, the Anointed One, who is appointed by God to rule the nations. This Psalm underscores the divine authority and kingship of Jesus, emphasizing His role as God's chosen ruler.

Key Lessons:

1. Jesus as King: Jesus is the sovereign King appointed by God, possessing all authority in heaven and on earth (Matthew 28:18).

2. Call to Worship: The Psalm calls nations and rulers to serve the Lord with reverence and to submit to His Son, highlighting the importance of recognizing Jesus' lordship (Philippians 2:10-11).

Psalm 22: The Suffering Servant

Psalm 22 provides a prophetic glimpse into the suffering of Jesus on the cross. This Psalm poignantly describes the anguish and abandonment that Jesus experienced, fulfilling the Messianic prophecies.

Key Lessons:

1. Suffering and Redemption: Jesus' suffering was part of God's redemptive plan, demonstrating His deep love and sacrifice for humanity (Isaiah 53:4-5).

2. Trust in God: Despite His suffering, Jesus trusted in God's deliverance, setting an example for believers to trust God in their own trials (Hebrews 5:7-9).

Psalm 23: The Good Shepherd

Psalm 23 is a beloved Psalm that portrays God as the Shepherd who guides, provides, and protects His flock. Jesus identifies Himself as the Good Shepherd, fulfilling the role depicted in this Psalm.

Key Lessons:

1. Guidance and Provision: Jesus, as the Good Shepherd, provides spiritual nourishment and guidance, leading believers on paths of righteousness (John 10:11-14).

2. Protection and Comfort: Jesus offers protection and comfort, reassuring believers of His presence even in the darkest times (John 10:27-28).

Psalm 110: The Priestly King

Psalm 110 speaks of a royal priesthood, portraying the Messiah as both King and Priest. This dual role is fulfilled in Jesus, who is both our eternal King and High Priest.

Key Lessons:

1. Eternal Priesthood: Jesus' priesthood is eternal, offering a once-for-all sacrifice for sins and continually interceding for believers (Hebrews 7:24-25).

2. Divine Kingship: Jesus reigns as the divine King, executing justice and righteousness, and establishing God's kingdom on earth (1 Corinthians 15:25).

Psalm 118: The Cornerstone

Psalm 118 celebrates God's deliverance and proclaims the Messiah as the cornerstone. Jesus identifies Himself as this cornerstone, the foundation of God's spiritual house.

Key Lessons:

1. Foundation of Faith: Jesus is the cornerstone of our faith, the foundation upon which believers are built into a spiritual house (1 Peter 2:4-6).

2. Rejection and Exaltation: Though rejected by men, Jesus was chosen by God and exalted, demonstrating that God's purposes prevail despite human opposition (Acts 4:11-12).

Theological Significance

The Fulfillment of Prophecy

The Psalms provide numerous prophecies that find their fulfillment in Jesus Christ. These fulfillments underscore the divine inspiration of Scripture and the coherence of God's redemptive plan.

1. Messianic Prophecies: The prophecies in the Psalms about the Messiah's birth, suffering, resurrection, and reign are fulfilled in Jesus, affirming His identity and mission (Luke 24:44).

2. Divine Plan: The fulfillment of these prophecies illustrates God's sovereign control over history and His

commitment to redeeming humanity through His Son (Romans 1:2-4).

The Revelation of God's Character

Through the Psalms, we gain a deeper understanding of God's character as revealed in Jesus Christ. The Psalms highlight aspects of God's nature that Jesus embodies and reveals.

1. God's Love and Mercy: The Psalms frequently speak of God's steadfast love and mercy, qualities perfectly demonstrated in Jesus' life and sacrifice (John 3:16).

2. God's Justice and Righteousness: Jesus embodies God's justice and righteousness, fulfilling the law and establishing God's righteous rule (Matthew 5:17-18).

The Call to Worship and Obedience

The Psalms call believers to worship God and live in obedience to His commands. Jesus reiterates and fulfills these calls, inviting us to follow Him.

1. Worship: The Psalms emphasize worship as a response to God's greatness and goodness. Jesus teaches that true worshipers worship in spirit and truth (John 4:23-24).

2. Obedience: The Psalms highlight the blessings of obedience to God's Word. Jesus calls us to obey His teachings and live according to His example (John 14:15).

Practical Applications for Believers

1. Recognize Jesus as Lord and King: Acknowledge Jesus' authority and sovereignty in your life. Submit to His rule and seek to live according to His will (Philippians 2:9-11).

2. Trust in Jesus During Trials: Follow Jesus' example of trusting God in the midst of suffering. Rely on His presence and promises for strength and comfort (Hebrews 12:1-2).

3. Follow Jesus, the Good Shepherd: Let Jesus guide you in your daily walk. Trust in His provision, protection, and direction (John 10:14-15).

4. Build Your Life on Jesus, the Cornerstone: Establish your faith and life on the foundation of Jesus' teachings and person. Allow Him to be the central focus of your spiritual journey (1 Corinthians 3:11).

5. Engage in Worship and Obedience: Worship God with a sincere heart and live in obedience to His commands. Reflect His love, justice, and mercy in your interactions with others (Romans 12:1-2).

Conclusion

Throughout the Psalms, we see vivid portrayals and prophetic insights that point to Jesus Christ. From His role as the Anointed One and Suffering Servant to the Good Shepherd, Priestly King, and Cornerstone, Jesus fulfills the expectations and promises found in these ancient songs. His life, death, and resurrection bring these Scriptures to their fullest meaning, revealing the depth of God's love and the scope of His redemptive plan.

By understanding and reflecting on Jesus' fulfillment of the Psalms, believers are encouraged to deepen their faith, strengthen their commitment to God's Word, and live out the principles of worship, obedience, and trust. The lessons of Jesus in the Psalms offer timeless guidance and profound inspiration for our journey of faith, reminding us of the eternal truth and unchanging nature of God's Word.

The Significance of His Divinity

The divinity of Jesus Christ is a cornerstone of Christian faith. It signifies His identity as God incarnate, His authority, and His role in the redemption of humanity. Throughout the Psalms, we find prophetic declarations and typological references that highlight the divine nature of the Messiah. This chapter explores the significance of Jesus' divinity as revealed in the Psalms and affirmed in the New Testament, and its implications for believers today.

The Divinity of Jesus in the Psalms

Psalm 2: The Divine Son

Psalm 2:7: "I will declare the decree: The LORD has said to Me, 'You are My Son, today I have begotten You.'"

- "Son" (בֵּן, ben) indicates a unique relationship with God.

This verse prophetically speaks of Jesus as the Son of God, a title that signifies His divine nature and authority. The New Testament writers affirm this understanding, recognizing Jesus as the begotten Son of God (Hebrews 1:5).

Psalm 110: The Divine King and Priest

Psalm 110:1: "The LORD said to my Lord, 'Sit at My right hand, till I make Your enemies Your footstool.'"

- "Lord" (אָדוֹן, adon) implies divine authority.

Psalm 110:4: "The LORD has sworn and will not relent, 'You are a priest forever according to the order of Melchizedek.'"

- "Priest forever" indicates an eternal and divine priesthood.

These verses highlight the dual role of Jesus as both King and Priest. His position at God's right hand signifies His divine authority and eternal reign. The reference to Melchizedek, a priestly figure without beginning or end, underscores Jesus' eternal priesthood.

Psalm 45: The Divine Bridegroom

Psalm 45:6: "Your throne, O God, is forever and ever; a scepter of righteousness is the scepter of Your kingdom."

- "O God" (אֱלֹהִים, Elohim) directly addresses the Messiah as God.

This verse directly addresses the Messiah as God, affirming His divine nature. The eternal throne and righteous scepter signify His everlasting kingdom and perfect justice.

New Testament Affirmations of Jesus' Divinity

The Incarnation

John 1:1, 14: "In the beginning was the Word, and the Word was with God, and the Word was God... And the Word became flesh and dwelt among us, and we beheld His glory, the glory as of the only begotten of the Father, full of grace and truth."

- "Word" (λόγος, logos) indicates divine reason and communication.

The opening of John's Gospel declares the divinity of Jesus, identifying Him as the Word who was with God and was God. His incarnation, becoming flesh, is a profound demonstration of His divinity and His mission to reveal God to humanity.

The Son of God

Matthew 3:17: "And suddenly a voice came from heaven, saying, 'This is My beloved Son, in whom I am well pleased.'"

- "Beloved Son" signifies a unique and divine relationship.

At Jesus' baptism, God the Father affirms Jesus' divine sonship, declaring Him as His beloved Son. This declaration confirms His divine identity and mission.

The Eternal Priesthood

Hebrews 7:24-25: "But He, because He continues forever, has an unchangeable priesthood. Therefore He is also able to save to the uttermost those who come to God through Him, since He always lives to make intercession for them."

- "Continues forever" underscores His eternal nature.

Jesus' eternal priesthood, according to the order of Melchizedek, signifies His unending role as intercessor and mediator between God and humanity. This eternal priesthood is a key aspect of His divinity.

The Divine Authority

Philippians 2:9-11: "Therefore God also has highly exalted Him and given Him the name which is above every name, that at the name of Jesus every knee should bow, of those in heaven, and of those on earth, and of those under the earth, and that every tongue should confess that Jesus Christ is Lord, to the glory of God the Father."

- "Exalted" (ὑπερύψωσεν, hyperypsosen) signifies supreme elevation.

Jesus' exaltation to the highest place and the universal acknowledgment of His lordship affirm His divine authority. His name, above every name, signifies His supreme position in the divine order.

Theological Significance

The Foundation of Christian Faith

1. Central to the Gospel: The divinity of Jesus is central to the Christian gospel. It validates His authority to forgive sins, perform miracles, and offer salvation (John 20:31).

2. Source of Eternal Life: Belief in Jesus' divinity is essential for receiving eternal life. Jesus' divine nature enables Him to conquer death and offer eternal life to all who believe in Him (John 3:16).

The Fulfillment of Prophecy

1. Divine Messiah: The Psalms and other Old Testament prophecies speak of a divine Messiah. Jesus' fulfillment of these prophecies confirms His identity and mission (Luke 24:44).

2. Coherence of Scripture: The fulfillment of divine prophecies in Jesus demonstrates the coherence and divine inspiration of Scripture. It shows that God's plan for redemption is consistent and trustworthy (2 Timothy 3:16-17).

The Revelation of God's Nature

1. Incarnation: Jesus' divinity reveals the nature of God in a tangible way. Through Jesus, we see God's love,

grace, truth, and holiness embodied in human form (John 1:14).

2. Mediator: As both God and man, Jesus is the perfect mediator who reconciles humanity to God. His divine nature enables Him to bridge the gap between a holy God and sinful humanity (1 Timothy 2:5).

Practical Implications for Believers

Worship and Adoration

1. Recognize His Lordship: Acknowledge Jesus' divine authority and submit to His lordship. Worship Him not only as Savior but also as Lord and King (Philippians 2:10-11).

2. Adoration: Engage in heartfelt worship and adoration, recognizing Jesus' divine nature and expressing gratitude for His redemptive work (Revelation 5:12-13).

Trust and Confidence

1. Confidence in Salvation: Trust in Jesus' ability to save completely. His divine nature assures us that His sacrifice is sufficient and His intercession is effective (Hebrews 7:25).

2. Dependence on His Promises: Rely on the promises of Jesus, knowing that they are backed by His divine authority. His words are true and unchanging, offering a secure foundation for faith (Matthew 24:35).

Obedience and Discipleship

1. Follow His Teachings: Commit to following the teachings of Jesus, recognizing their divine origin. His commands are authoritative and life-giving, leading to true discipleship (John 14:15).

2. Imitate His Life: Strive to imitate Jesus in character and conduct. His divine nature is the model for holiness, compassion, and love (1 Peter 2:21).

Proclamation and Mission

1. Proclaim His Divinity: Boldly proclaim the divinity of Jesus as central to the gospel message. Share the truth of

His divine nature and redemptive work with others (Acts 2:36).

2. Engage in Mission: Participate in the mission of the church to make disciples of all nations, teaching them to observe all that Jesus commanded. His divine authority commissions and empowers this mission (Matthew 28:18-20).

Comprehensive Commentary

Theological and Messianic Implications

1. Psalm 2:7: The declaration of the Messiah as God's Son emphasizes His unique and divine relationship with the Father. This title affirms Jesus' divinity and His role in God's redemptive plan (Hebrews 1:5).

2. Psalm 110:1, 4: The dual role of Jesus as King and Priest highlights His divine authority and eternal priesthood. His position at God's right hand signifies His supreme authority and ongoing intercession (Hebrews 7:24-25).

3. Psalm 45:6: Addressing the Messiah as God underscores His divine nature. His eternal throne and righteous rule affirm His sovereignty and justice (Hebrews 1:8).

Exegetical Insights

1. John 1:1, 14: The identification of Jesus as the Word who was with God and was God highlights His preexistence and divine nature. The incarnation demonstrates His willingness to enter into human history to reveal God and accomplish salvation.

2. Matthew 3:17: The Father's declaration of Jesus as His beloved Son at His baptism affirms His divine sonship and mission. This public affirmation underscores His identity and authority.

3. Hebrews 7:24-25: The eternal priesthood of Jesus according to the order of Melchizedek emphasizes His unending intercessory role. His divinity ensures the efficacy and permanence of His priestly work.

4. Philippians 2:9-11: The exaltation of Jesus to the highest place and the universal acknowledgment of His lordship affirm His divine authority. This passage highlights the ultimate recognition of Jesus' divinity and its implications for worship and submission.

Conclusion

The divinity of Jesus Christ is a profound and essential truth that permeates both the Psalms and the New Testament. Through various Psalms, we see prophetic glimpses of the divine Messiah who would come to rule, suffer, redeem, and intercede for humanity. The New Testament confirms and fulfills these prophecies, revealing Jesus as the incarnate Word of God, the eternal Son, and the exalted Lord.

Understanding the significance of Jesus' divinity deepens our appreciation of His redemptive work and compels us to respond with worship, trust, obedience, and proclamation. As believers, we are called to recognize and submit to His divine authority, trust in His promises, follow His teachings, and share the good news of His divine nature with others. In doing so, we reflect the glory of the divine Savior and participate in His mission to bring salvation to the world.

Encouragement for Believers to Delve Deeper into the Psalms

The Book of Psalms is a treasure trove of spiritual wisdom, rich with insights that have nourished the faith of believers for centuries. Within its pages, the Psalms reveal the heart of God, the human experience, and profound prophecies pointing to Jesus Christ. This concluding chapter seeks to encourage believers to delve deeper into the Psalms, exploring their depth, relevance, and the transformative power they hold.

The Importance of the Psalms

Spiritual Nourishment

The Psalms provide spiritual nourishment, offering words of praise, lament, thanksgiving, and petition that resonate with the full spectrum of human emotions. They teach us how to approach God in every season of life, from moments of joy to times of deep despair.

Psalm 23:1: "The LORD is my shepherd; I shall not want."

- This beloved Psalm reminds us of God's provision and care, offering comfort and reassurance.

Psalm 42:1: "As the deer pants for the water brooks, so pants my soul for You, O God."

- This verse expresses a deep longing for God, encouraging us to seek Him earnestly.

Deepening Understanding of God

The Psalms reveal the character of God—His holiness, justice, mercy, and faithfulness. By meditating on the Psalms, believers can gain a deeper understanding of who God is and how He interacts with His creation.

Psalm 145:8-9: "The LORD is gracious and full of compassion, slow to anger and great in mercy. The LORD is good to all, and His tender mercies are over all His works."

- These verses highlight God's compassionate nature and His goodness towards all creation.

Psalm 19:1: "The heavens declare the glory of God; and the firmament shows His handiwork."

- This verse calls us to recognize God's glory displayed in creation, deepening our awe and reverence for Him.

Guidance for Worship and Prayer

The Psalms serve as a guide for worship and prayer, providing words that help us express our adoration, confession, thanksgiving, and supplication. They model a heart posture of humility, dependence, and trust in God.

Psalm 95:1-2: "Oh come, let us sing to the LORD! Let us shout joyfully to the Rock of our salvation. Let us come before His presence with thanksgiving; let us shout joyfully to Him with psalms."

- This Psalm encourages joyful and thankful worship, leading us into God's presence with praise.

Psalm 51:10: "Create in me a clean heart, O God, and renew a steadfast spirit within me."

- This prayer for purification and renewal teaches us how to seek God's forgiveness and transformation.

Prophetic Insights

The Psalms contain prophetic insights that point to Jesus Christ, revealing aspects of His life, suffering, death, and resurrection. Studying these prophecies can deepen our understanding of the Messiah and strengthen our faith in God's redemptive plan.

Psalm 22:16: "For dogs have surrounded Me; the congregation of the wicked has enclosed Me. They pierced My hands and My feet."

- This verse prophetically describes the crucifixion of Jesus, offering a vivid picture of His suffering.

Psalm 110:1: "The LORD said to my Lord, 'Sit at My right hand, till I make Your enemies Your footstool.'"

- This Messianic Psalm speaks of Jesus' exaltation and reign, affirming His divine authority.

Encouragement for Personal Study

Approach with Prayer

Begin your study of the Psalms with prayer, asking God to open your eyes and heart to the truths contained in His Word. Pray for understanding, insight, and the ability to apply what you learn to your life.

Psalm 119:18: "Open my eyes, that I may see wondrous things from Your law."

- This prayer for spiritual illumination sets the tone for a heart ready to receive God's Word.

Reflect and Meditate

Take time to reflect and meditate on the Psalms, allowing their words to sink deeply into your heart and mind. Consider their meaning, context, and how they apply to your life.

Psalm 1:2: "But his delight is in the law of the LORD, and in His law he meditates day and night."

- This verse highlights the blessedness of meditating on God's Word continually.

Journal Your Insights

Keep a journal to record your insights, reflections, and prayers as you study the Psalms. Writing down your thoughts can help you process and remember what God is teaching you.

Psalm 77:11-12: "I will remember the works of the LORD; surely I will remember Your wonders of old. I will also meditate on all Your work, and talk of Your deeds."

- Journaling can be a way to remember and meditate on God's works and faithfulness.

Use Study Aids

Utilize study aids such as commentaries, Bible dictionaries, and concordances to deepen your understanding of the Psalms. These resources can provide historical background, cultural context, and theological insights.

Proverbs 4:7: "Wisdom is the principal thing; therefore get wisdom. And in all your getting, get understanding."

- Seeking wisdom and understanding through study aids can enrich your study of the Psalms.

Engage in Group Study

Consider studying the Psalms with a group of fellow believers. Group study can provide diverse perspectives, encourage discussion, and foster community.

Hebrews 10:24-25: "And let us consider one another in order to stir up love and good works, not forsaking the assembling of ourselves together, as is the manner of some, but exhorting one another, and so much the more as you see the Day approaching."

- Studying the Psalms in community can help us exhort and encourage one another in our faith.

The Transformative Power of the Psalms

Strengthening Faith

The Psalms can strengthen your faith by reminding you of God's faithfulness, power, and promises. They encourage trust in God's character and His ability to fulfill His Word.

Psalm 37:3-5: "Trust in the LORD, and do good; dwell in the land, and feed on His faithfulness. Delight yourself also in the LORD, and He shall give you the desires of your heart. Commit your way to the LORD, trust also in Him, and He shall bring it to pass."

- Trusting in God's faithfulness and committing our ways to Him can strengthen our faith.

Providing Comfort and Hope

The Psalms offer comfort and hope in times of trouble, reminding us that God is our refuge and strength. They assure us of His presence and care, even in the darkest moments.

Psalm 46:1: "God is our refuge and strength, a very present help in trouble."

- This verse provides reassurance of God's presence and support in times of need.

Psalm 121:1-2: "I will lift up my eyes to the hills—from whence comes my help? My help comes from the LORD, who made heaven and earth."

- Looking to God for help can bring hope and encouragement.

Encouraging Righteous Living

The Psalms call us to live righteously, following God's commandments and walking in His ways. They provide practical guidance for living a life that honors God.

Psalm 119:9-11: "How can a young man cleanse his way? By taking heed according to Your word. With my whole heart I have sought You; oh, let me not wander from Your commandments! Your word I have hidden in my heart, that I might not sin against You."

- Hiding God's Word in our hearts helps us live righteously and avoid sin.

Inspiring Worship

The Psalms inspire heartfelt worship, encouraging us to praise God for His greatness, goodness, and mercy. They provide words to express our adoration and thanksgiving.

Psalm 100:1-2: "Make a joyful shout to the LORD, all you lands! Serve the LORD with gladness; come before His presence with singing."

- Joyful worship and service are responses to God's goodness and faithfulness.

Fostering a Deep Relationship with God

Studying the Psalms fosters a deeper relationship with God, as they reveal His heart and invite us into intimate communion with Him. They encourage us to pour out our hearts to God and to listen for His voice.

Psalm 63:1: "O God, You are my God; early will I seek You; my soul thirsts for You; my flesh longs for You in a dry and thirsty land where there is no water."

- Seeking God earnestly deepens our relationship with Him.

Conclusion

The Psalms offer a rich and multifaceted portrait of the life of faith, providing guidance, comfort, and profound insights into the nature of God and our relationship with Him.

Delving deeper into the Psalms can transform our lives, strengthen our faith, and draw us closer to God.

As you continue your journey of faith, let the Psalms be a constant companion, guiding your worship, shaping your prayers, and enriching your understanding of God's Word. Approach them with an open heart, ready to receive the treasures they hold, and let them lead you into a deeper, more intimate relationship with your Creator and Savior.

CHAPTER 15

STUDY GUIDE AND REFLECTION QUESTIONS

Studying the Psalms and understanding their fulfillment in the life and ministry of Jesus Christ can be a deeply enriching experience. To aid in this process, this chapter provides study and reflection questions for each chapter of this book. These questions are designed to deepen your understanding, encourage personal reflection, and facilitate group discussions.

Chapter 1: Introduction to the Psalms and Jesus

1. What is the significance of the Psalms in understanding the nature and character of God?

2. How do the Psalms contribute to our understanding of Jesus as the Messiah?

3. What themes in the Psalms resonate most with you in your current spiritual journey?

4. How does the structure and poetic nature of the Psalms enhance their message?

Chapter 2: Messianic Prophecies in the Psalms

1. What are the key Messianic prophecies found in the Psalms?

2. How do these prophecies point to the life and mission of Jesus?

3. Why is it important to understand the context of these prophecies within the Psalms?

4. In what ways do these prophecies strengthen your faith in Jesus as the Messiah?

Chapter 3: Jesus' Divinity in Psalm 2

1. How does Psalm 2 describe the relationship between God the Father and the Son?

2. What are the implications of Jesus being referred to as God's Anointed One?

3. How does Psalm 2 affirm the divinity and authority of Jesus?

4. How can believers today respond to the call to serve and honor the Son as presented in Psalm 2?

Chapter 4: The Suffering and Triumph of Jesus in Psalm 22

1. How does Psalm 22 foreshadow the crucifixion of Jesus?

2. What specific verses in Psalm 22 are fulfilled in the New Testament accounts of Jesus' suffering?

3. What does Psalm 22 reveal about the depth of Jesus' suffering and His trust in God?

4. How does the triumph and hope expressed in Psalm 22 encourage you in your own faith journey?

Chapter 5: The Eternal Priesthood of Jesus in Psalm 110

1. What is the significance of Jesus being a priest forever in the order of Melchizedek?

2. How does Psalm 110 depict Jesus' authority and eternal priesthood?

3. In what ways does Jesus fulfill the role of both King and Priest as described in Psalm 110?

4. How can understanding Jesus' eternal priesthood impact your prayer life and relationship with God?

Chapter 6: The Shepherd King in Psalm 23

1. What attributes of God as the Shepherd are highlighted in Psalm 23?

2. How does Jesus fulfill the role of the Good Shepherd as described in Psalm 23?

3. In what ways does Psalm 23 provide comfort and assurance during difficult times?

4. How can you apply the truths of Psalm 23 to your daily life and relationship with Jesus?

Chapter 7: The Cornerstone in Psalm 118

1. How is Jesus described as the cornerstone in Psalm 118?

2. What is the significance of the rejection and exaltation of the cornerstone?

3. How does the fulfillment of Psalm 118 in the New Testament affirm Jesus' identity and mission?

4. How can you build your life on Jesus as the cornerstone?

Chapter 8: Trust and Faith in Psalm 27

1. What does Psalm 27 teach about trusting God in the face of fear and adversity?

2. How did Jesus exemplify trust and faith in God during His earthly ministry?

3. In what ways does Psalm 27 encourage you to seek God's presence and guidance?

4. How can you strengthen your trust and faith in God through the truths expressed in Psalm 27?

Chapter 9: The Righteous King in Psalm 45

1. What characteristics of the righteous king are described in Psalm 45?

2. How does Psalm 45 foreshadow the kingship and bridegroom imagery of Jesus?

3. What does the royal wedding song in Psalm 45 reveal about Jesus' relationship with His Church?

4. How can you reflect the righteousness and beauty of the King in your own life?

Chapter 10: The Eternal Reign in Psalm 89

1. How does Psalm 89 describe the Davidic covenant and its fulfillment in Jesus?

2. What promises of God are highlighted in Psalm 89, and how are they fulfilled in Jesus?

3. In what ways does the eternal reign of Jesus provide hope and assurance for believers?

4. How can you live in light of Jesus' eternal reign and the promises of God?

Chapter 11: The Lord's Deliverance in Psalm 34

1. What aspects of God's deliverance and protection are highlighted in Psalm 34?

2. How does Jesus fulfill the role of deliverer from all fears and troubles as described in Psalm 34?

3. What promises of protection and salvation are found in Psalm 34, and how do they apply to your life?

4. How can you seek and trust in God's deliverance in your daily challenges?

Chapter 12: The Heart of Worship in Psalm 40

1. How does Psalm 40 describe the heart of worship and obedience to God?

2. In what ways did Jesus exemplify obedience and worship during His ministry?

3. What are the theological implications of Jesus' perfect obedience as revealed in Psalm 40?

4. How can you cultivate a heart of worship and obedience in your own life?

Chapter 13: Jesus as the Living Word of God

1. How does John 1:1-14 describe Jesus as the living Word of God?

2. What significance does Jesus' divinity and incarnation hold for believers?

3. In what ways does Jesus' role as the living Word affirm the authority and relevance of Scripture?

4. How can you deepen your relationship with Jesus, the living Word, through the study of Scripture?

Chapter 14: Encouragement to Delve Deeper into the Psalms

1. What are the benefits of studying the Psalms for spiritual growth and understanding?

2. How do the Psalms provide guidance for worship, prayer, and righteous living?

3. What practical steps can you take to delve deeper into the Psalms and apply their truths to your life?

4. How can studying the Psalms transform your relationship with God and strengthen your faith?

Conclusion

Studying the Psalms and their fulfillment in Jesus Christ offers profound insights and transformative power for believers. These study and reflection questions are designed to help you engage more deeply with the Psalms, understand their theological significance, and apply their truths to your daily life. As you explore these questions, may you grow in your knowledge of God, deepen your relationship with Jesus, and be inspired to live out your faith with greater passion and commitment.

CHAPTER 16

REFLECTION PROMPTS FOR PERSONAL APPLICATION

Reflection is a vital part of studying Scripture, allowing us to internalize its truths and apply them to our lives. The Book of Psalms, with its rich tapestry of human emotion and divine revelation, offers numerous opportunities for personal reflection and spiritual growth. This chapter provides reflection prompts for personal application, designed to help you engage more deeply with the Psalms and their fulfillment in Jesus Christ.

Reflection Prompts for Each Chapter

Chapter 1: Introduction to the Psalms and Jesus

1. Personal Connection: How do the themes of the Psalms resonate with your current spiritual journey? Reflect on specific Psalms that have spoken to you personally.

2. God's Character: What aspects of God's character are most evident in the Psalms? How do these attributes influence your view of God and your relationship with Him?

3. Prayer and Worship: How can the Psalms guide your prayer life and worship practices? Choose a Psalm to incorporate into your daily devotions.

Chapter 2: Messianic Prophecies in the Psalms

1. Jesus in the Psalms: How do the Messianic prophecies in the Psalms enhance your understanding of Jesus' mission and identity? Reflect on specific prophecies that have deepened your faith.

2. Fulfillment and Faith: How does seeing the fulfillment of these prophecies in Jesus strengthen your trust in God's Word? Consider ways you can share these insights with others.

3. Personal Application: How can the anticipation and fulfillment of these prophecies inspire hope in your own life? Reflect on areas where you need to trust in God's promises.

Chapter 3: Jesus' Divinity in Psalm 2

1. Divine Authority: Reflect on Jesus' authority as described in Psalm 2. How does acknowledging His lordship impact your daily decisions and actions?

2. Reverence and Worship: How does Psalm 2 encourage you to approach Jesus with reverence and worship? Spend time in worship, focusing on His sovereignty.

3. Submission to Christ: Are there areas of your life where you need to submit more fully to Jesus' authority? Reflect on practical steps you can take to align with His will.

Chapter 4: The Suffering and Triumph of Jesus in Psalm 22

1. Identifying with Suffering: Reflect on the suffering described in Psalm 22 and Jesus' fulfillment of it. How does this deepen your understanding of His sacrifice?

2. Trust in Trials: How can Jesus' example of trusting God in the midst of suffering encourage you in your own trials? Reflect on ways to cultivate trust in God's plan.

3. Hope in Resurrection: How does the triumph expressed in Psalm 22 give you hope for the future? Reflect on how this hope can sustain you in difficult times.

Chapter 5: The Eternal Priesthood of Jesus in Psalm 110

1. Priestly Intercession: Reflect on Jesus' role as your eternal High Priest. How does His intercession affect your confidence in approaching God?

2. Kingly Authority: How does understanding Jesus as both King and Priest influence your view of His reign in your life? Reflect on ways to honor His kingship.

3. Living in Light of His Priesthood: How can you live in light of Jesus' eternal priesthood? Consider incorporating prayers of thanksgiving for His ongoing intercession.

Chapter 6: The Shepherd King in Psalm 23

1. Experiencing God's Guidance: Reflect on times when you have experienced God's guidance and provision as described in Psalm 23. How can you trust Him more fully?

2. Comfort in God's Presence: How does the assurance of God's presence in Psalm 23 provide comfort in your current circumstances? Reflect on ways to seek His presence daily.

3. Following the Good Shepherd: How can you more faithfully follow Jesus as your Good Shepherd? Consider practical steps to align your life with His guidance.

Chapter 7: The Cornerstone in Psalm 118

1. Building on the Cornerstone: Reflect on Jesus as the cornerstone of your faith. How is your life built on His teachings and person?

2. Dealing with Rejection: How does Jesus' experience of rejection and exaltation in Psalm 118 encourage you when

you face rejection? Reflect on ways to remain steadfast in your faith.

3. Foundation of Faith: How can you strengthen your foundation in Jesus? Consider specific practices or disciplines to deepen your relationship with Him.

Chapter 8: Trust and Faith in Psalm 27

1. Confidence in God: Reflect on the confidence and trust expressed in Psalm 27. How can this Psalm help you cultivate a similar trust in God?

2. Seeking God's Presence: How does Psalm 27 inspire you to seek God's presence more intentionally? Reflect on ways to make this a priority in your life.

3. Facing Adversity: How can the truths in Psalm 27 help you face current challenges with faith and courage? Reflect on God's promises and His faithfulness.

Chapter 9: The Righteous King in Psalm 45

1. Attributes of the King: Reflect on the attributes of the righteous king in Psalm 45. How can you emulate these qualities in your own life?

2. Jesus as Bridegroom: How does the imagery of Jesus as the bridegroom in Psalm 45 deepen your understanding of His relationship with the Church? Reflect on your role as part of His bride.

3. Living Righteously: How can you live a life that reflects the righteousness and beauty of Jesus, the King? Consider practical ways to pursue holiness.

Chapter 10: The Eternal Reign in Psalm 89

1. God's Faithfulness: Reflect on the faithfulness of God as described in Psalm 89. How have you experienced His faithfulness in your life?

2. Jesus' Eternal Reign: How does the eternal reign of Jesus impact your perspective on the future? Reflect on the hope and assurance this provides.

3. Living in Light of Eternity: How can you live with an eternal perspective, focusing on Jesus' reign and the fulfillment of God's promises? Consider ways to prioritize eternal values.

Chapter 11: The Lord's Deliverance in Psalm 34

1. Experiencing Deliverance: Reflect on times when you have experienced God's deliverance as described in Psalm 34. How does this shape your trust in Him?

2. Seeking God in Prayer: How does Psalm 34 encourage you to seek God in prayer and trust Him for deliverance? Reflect on ways to deepen your prayer life.

3. Living in Gratitude: How can you cultivate a heart of gratitude for God's protection and salvation? Consider specific ways to express your thankfulness.

Chapter 12: The Heart of Worship in Psalm 40

1. Worship and Obedience: Reflect on the connection between worship and obedience in Psalm 40. How can you live a life that honors God in both areas?

2. Jesus' Example: How does Jesus' perfect obedience and worship inspire you? Reflect on ways to follow His example more closely.

3. Cultivating Worship: How can you cultivate a heart of worship in your daily life? Consider practical steps to make worship a central part of your routine.

Chapter 13: Jesus as the Living Word of God

1. Engaging with the Word: Reflect on the significance of Jesus as the living Word of God. How can this truth deepen your engagement with Scripture?

2. Living by the Word: How does understanding Jesus as the living Word influence your daily decisions and actions? Reflect on ways to apply His teachings in your life.

3. Relationship with Jesus: How can you deepen your relationship with Jesus, the living Word? Consider specific practices to foster intimacy with Him through Scripture.

Chapter 14: Encouragement to Delve Deeper into the Psalms

1. Personal Study: Reflect on the benefits of studying the Psalms for your spiritual growth. How can you incorporate regular study of the Psalms into your spiritual practices?

2. Application to Life: How can the truths of the Psalms be applied to your daily life? Reflect on specific ways to live out the principles found in the Psalms.

3. Sharing Insights: How can you share the insights gained from studying the Psalms with others? Consider opportunities for teaching, mentoring, or group study.

Conclusion

The Book of Psalms offers profound insights and transformative power for believers. By engaging deeply with the Psalms and reflecting on their application to your life, you can grow in your faith, deepen your relationship with God, and live out the truths of Scripture more fully. Use these reflection prompts to guide your study and application of the Psalms, allowing their rich and timeless truths to shape your spiritual journey.

CHAPTER 17

GROUP DISCUSSION TOPICS

Group discussions can enhance the study of the Psalms by providing diverse perspectives, fostering community, and deepening understanding. This chapter provides a range of discussion topics for each chapter of this book, designed to facilitate meaningful conversations and collective growth in faith. Use these topics to guide your group discussions, encouraging participants to engage deeply with the Psalms and their fulfillment in Jesus Christ.

Chapter 1: Introduction to the Psalms and Jesus

1. The Role of the Psalms: Discuss the significance of the Psalms in the overall narrative of Scripture. How do they contribute to our understanding of God and His relationship with humanity?

2. Themes in the Psalms: What themes in the Psalms resonate most with your personal experiences? Share specific Psalms that have impacted you and why.

3. Jesus in the Psalms: How do the Psalms foreshadow Jesus Christ? Discuss specific examples and their implications for understanding Jesus' mission and identity.

Chapter 2: Messianic Prophecies in the Psalms

1. Identifying Prophecies: Review key Messianic prophecies in the Psalms. How do these prophecies point to Jesus, and what is their significance for believers?

2. Fulfillment in Jesus: How does Jesus fulfill these prophecies? Discuss the importance of understanding these fulfillments in strengthening your faith.

3. Prophetic Significance: Why is it important for Christians to study and understand Messianic prophecies in the Psalms? How do they enhance our appreciation of the Bible's coherence?

Chapter 3: Jesus' Divinity in Psalm 2

1. Divine Authority: Discuss the portrayal of Jesus' divinity and authority in Psalm 2. How does this Psalm shape your understanding of Jesus as Lord and King?

2. Application of Authority: How should the recognition of Jesus' authority influence our lives and actions? Share practical examples of living under Jesus' lordship.

3. Worship and Submission: How does Psalm 2 encourage us to worship and submit to Jesus? Discuss ways to incorporate this attitude into your daily life.

Chapter 4: The Suffering and Triumph of Jesus in Psalm 22

1. Understanding Suffering: How does Psalm 22 help us understand the suffering of Jesus? Discuss the emotional and spiritual aspects of His suffering.

2. Trust in Adversity: How does Jesus' example of trusting God in suffering encourage you in your own trials? Share personal experiences of finding strength in this example.

3. Hope and Triumph: Discuss the themes of hope and triumph in Psalm 22. How do these themes provide comfort and assurance for believers?

Chapter 5: The Eternal Priesthood of Jesus in Psalm 110

1. Priestly Role: What is the significance of Jesus' eternal priesthood according to the order of Melchizedek? Discuss how this role affects your understanding of His ministry.

2. Jesus as King and Priest: How does Jesus fulfill the dual roles of King and Priest as described in Psalm 110? What are the implications for our faith?

3. Impact on Prayer Life: How does Jesus' eternal priesthood influence your prayer life? Discuss ways to deepen your reliance on His intercession.

Chapter 6: The Shepherd King in Psalm 23

1. God as Shepherd: Discuss the attributes of God as the Shepherd in Psalm 23. How have you experienced His guidance and provision in your life?

2. Jesus the Good Shepherd: How does Jesus fulfill the role of the Good Shepherd? Share ways in which you can follow His guidance more closely.

3. Comfort in Psalm 23: How does Psalm 23 provide comfort and reassurance? Discuss ways to apply its truths in difficult times.

Chapter 7: The Cornerstone in Psalm 118

1. Jesus the Cornerstone: What does it mean for Jesus to be the cornerstone of our faith? Discuss the implications for personal and communal faith practices.

2. Rejection and Exaltation: How does Jesus' experience of rejection and exaltation in Psalm 118 relate to our own experiences? Share insights and applications.

3. Building on the Cornerstone: How can we build our lives on Jesus as the cornerstone? Discuss practical steps to strengthen this foundation.

Chapter 8: Trust and Faith in Psalm 27

1. Confidence in God: How does Psalm 27 inspire confidence and trust in God? Share personal stories of finding strength in this Psalm.

2. Seeking God's Presence: Discuss the importance of seeking God's presence as emphasized in Psalm 27. How can we make this a priority in our lives?

3. Facing Adversity: How can the truths in Psalm 27 help us face challenges with faith and courage? Share practical ways to apply this Psalm in difficult situations.

Chapter 9: The Righteous King in Psalm 45

1. Attributes of the King: Discuss the characteristics of the righteous king in Psalm 45. How can we reflect these attributes in our own lives?

2. Jesus as Bridegroom: How does the imagery of Jesus as the bridegroom in Psalm 45 deepen our understanding of His relationship with the Church? Share insights and applications.

3. Living Righteously: What does it mean to live a life that reflects the righteousness and beauty of Jesus, the King? Discuss practical ways to pursue this.

Chapter 10: The Eternal Reign in Psalm 89

1. God's Promises: How does Psalm 89 highlight God's promises and faithfulness? Discuss the impact of these promises on your faith.

2. Jesus' Eternal Reign: How does the eternal reign of Jesus affect your perspective on the future? Share how this hope influences your daily life.

3. Living with an Eternal Perspective: How can we live with an eternal perspective, focusing on Jesus' reign and the

fulfillment of God's promises? Discuss practical ways to prioritize eternal values.

Chapter 11: The Lord's Deliverance in Psalm 34

1. Experiencing Deliverance: Share experiences of God's deliverance as described in Psalm 34. How does this shape your trust in Him?

2. Seeking God in Prayer: Discuss how Psalm 34 encourages us to seek God in prayer and trust Him for deliverance. How can we deepen our prayer lives?

3. Living in Gratitude: How can we cultivate a heart of gratitude for God's protection and salvation? Discuss specific ways to express thankfulness.

Chapter 12: The Heart of Worship in Psalm 40

1. Worship and Obedience: How does Psalm 40 connect worship and obedience? Discuss ways to live a life that honors God in both areas.

2. Jesus' Example: How does Jesus' perfect obedience and worship inspire you? Share ways to follow His example more closely.

3. Cultivating Worship: How can we cultivate a heart of worship in our daily lives? Discuss practical steps to make worship central to our routine.

Chapter 13: Jesus as the Living Word of God

1. Engaging with the Word: Discuss the significance of Jesus as the living Word of God. How can this truth deepen our engagement with Scripture?

2. Living by the Word: How does understanding Jesus as the living Word influence our daily decisions and actions? Share practical ways to apply His teachings.

3. Relationship with Jesus: How can we deepen our relationship with Jesus, the living Word? Discuss specific practices to foster intimacy with Him through Scripture.

Chapter 14: Encouragement to Delve Deeper into the Psalms

1. Personal Study: Discuss the benefits of studying the Psalms for spiritual growth. How can we incorporate regular study of the Psalms into our spiritual practices?

2. Application to Life: How can the truths of the Psalms be applied to our daily lives? Share specific ways to live out the principles found in the Psalms.

3. Sharing Insights: How can we share the insights gained from studying the Psalms with others? Discuss opportunities for teaching, mentoring, or group study.

Conclusion

Group discussions can greatly enhance the study of the Psalms, providing a platform for sharing insights, encouraging one another, and growing together in faith. Use these discussion topics to guide your conversations, fostering a deeper understanding and application of the Psalms and their fulfillment in Jesus Christ. Through these discussions, may you and your group be enriched, strengthened, and inspired to live out the truths of God's Word more fully.

LIST OF MESSIANIC PSALMS

The Book of Psalms contains numerous passages that are prophetic and point to the Messiah, Jesus Christ. These Messianic Psalms provide insights into His life, suffering, death, resurrection, and eternal reign. This appendix lists key Messianic Psalms, along with brief explanations of their significance and the corresponding New Testament fulfillments.

List of Messianic Psalms

Psalm 2: The Reign of the LORD's Anointed

- Significance: Prophesies the divine sonship and kingship of the Messiah.

- Key Verses: "You are My Son, today I have begotten You." (Psalm 2:7)

- New Testament Fulfillment: Affirmed in Acts 13:33 and Hebrews 1:5, identifying Jesus as the Son of God.

Psalm 8: The Glory of the Messiah and His Creation
- Significance: Speaks of the dominion of the Son of Man over creation.
- Key Verses: "What is man that You are mindful of him, and the son of man that You visit him?" (Psalm 8:4)
- New Testament Fulfillment: Referenced in Hebrews 2:6-8, applying the dominion of creation to Jesus.

Psalm 16: The Hope of the Faithful, the Messiah's Resurrection
- Significance: Foretells the resurrection of the Messiah.
- Key Verses: "For You will not leave my soul in Sheol, nor will You allow Your Holy One to see corruption." (Psalm 16:10)
- New Testament Fulfillment: Quoted in Acts 2:25-28 and Acts 13:35-37, affirming Jesus' resurrection.

Psalm 22: The Suffering and Praise of the Messiah
- Significance: Describes the suffering and subsequent exaltation of the Messiah.
- Key Verses: "My God, My God, why have You forsaken Me?" (Psalm 22:1); "They pierced My hands and My feet." (Psalm 22:16)
- New Testament Fulfillment: Jesus quotes this Psalm on the cross (Matthew 27:46), and it describes the crucifixion (John 19:24).

Psalm 23: The Good Shepherd
- Significance: Portrays the Messiah as the Shepherd who provides and protects.
- Key Verses: "The LORD is my shepherd; I shall not want." (Psalm 23:1)
- New Testament Fulfillment: Jesus identifies Himself as the Good Shepherd (John 10:11-14).

Psalm 24: The King of Glory

- Significance: Declares the coming of the King of glory.

- Key Verses: "Who is this King of glory? The LORD strong and mighty." (Psalm 24:8)

- New Testament Fulfillment: Jesus' ascension and return are seen as the entry of the King of glory (Acts 1:9-11).

Psalm 34: The LORD, a Provider and Deliverer

- Significance: Expresses trust in the LORD's deliverance.

- Key Verses: "He guards all his bones; not one of them is broken." (Psalm 34:20)

- New Testament Fulfillment: This verse is applied to Jesus on the cross (John 19:36).

Psalm 40: The Messiah's Obedience and Sacrifice

- Significance: Highlights the Messiah's willingness to do God's will.

- Key Verses: "Behold, I come; in the scroll of the book it is written of me." (Psalm 40:7-8)

- New Testament Fulfillment: Quoted in Hebrews 10:5-7, affirming Jesus' mission.

Psalm 45: The Messiah's Throne and Reign

- Significance: Describes the beauty and eternal throne of the Messiah.

- Key Verses: "Your throne, O God, is forever and ever." (Psalm 45:6)

- New Testament Fulfillment: Referenced in Hebrews 1:8, confirming Jesus' eternal kingship.

Psalm 68: The Messiah's Victory and Ascension

- Significance: Proclaims the Messiah's victory and gifts to men.

- Key Verses: "You have ascended on high, You have led captivity captive." (Psalm 68:18)

- New Testament Fulfillment: Applied to Jesus' ascension in Ephesians 4:8.

Psalm 69: The Messiah's Zeal and Suffering
- Significance: Speaks of the Messiah's suffering and zeal for God's house.
- Key Verses: "They gave me gall for my food, and for my thirst they gave me vinegar to drink." (Psalm 69:21)
- New Testament Fulfillment: Describes Jesus' crucifixion (John 19:29) and His zeal for the temple (John 2:17).

Psalm 72: The Messiah's Reign of Righteousness and Peace
- Significance: Envisions the righteous and eternal reign of the Messiah.
- Key Verses: "He shall have dominion also from sea to sea, and from the River to the ends of the earth." (Psalm 72:8)
- New Testament Fulfillment: Reflects the universal reign of Christ (Revelation 11:15).

Psalm 89: The Messiah's Covenant and Kingdom
- Significance: Affirms the Davidic covenant and the eternal throne of the Messiah.
- Key Verses: "I have made a covenant with My chosen, I have sworn to My servant David: 'Your seed I will establish forever, and build up your throne to all generations.'" (Psalm 89:3-4)
- New Testament Fulfillment: Confirmed in the angel's announcement to Mary (Luke 1:32-33).

Psalm 102: The Eternal Nature of the Messiah
- Significance: Declares the eternal nature and unchanging character of the Messiah.
- Key Verses: "Of old You laid the foundation of the earth, and the heavens are the work of Your hands." (Psalm 102:25)
- New Testament Fulfillment: Applied to Jesus in Hebrews 1:10-12.

Psalm 110: The Priestly King

- Significance: Describes the Messiah as both King and Priest.

- Key Verses: "The LORD said to my Lord, 'Sit at My right hand, till I make Your enemies Your footstool.'" (Psalm 110:1); "You are a priest forever according to the order of Melchizedek." (Psalm 110:4)

- New Testament Fulfillment: Quoted extensively in the New Testament, including Matthew 22:44 and Hebrews 5:6, affirming Jesus' dual role.

Psalm 118: The Chief Cornerstone

- Significance: Speaks of the Messiah as the cornerstone rejected by men but chosen by God.

- Key Verses: "The stone which the builders rejected has become the chief cornerstone." (Psalm 118:22)

- New Testament Fulfillment: Referenced in Matthew 21:42, Acts 4:11, and 1 Peter 2:7, affirming Jesus as the cornerstone.

Conclusion

The Messianic Psalms provide a rich tapestry of prophecy and revelation, pointing to the life, mission, and divinity of Jesus Christ. By studying these Psalms and their New Testament fulfillments, believers can deepen their understanding of Jesus as the Messiah and the fulfillment of God's redemptive plan. This list serves as a guide to exploring these profound connections, enriching your study of Scripture and strengthening your faith.

REFERENCES

The Messianic Psalms are rich with prophecies and typological references that find their fulfillment in the New Testament. These fulfillments affirm the coherence of Scripture and the divine inspiration of both the Old and New Testaments. This appendix provides cross-references to New Testament passages where these fulfillments are explicitly noted or strongly implied. Understanding these connections deepens our appreciation of Jesus Christ's role as the promised Messiah and strengthens our faith in God's redemptive plan.

Cross-References to New Testament Fulfillments
Psalm 2: The Reign of the LORD's Anointed
- Psalm 2:7: "You are My Son, today I have begotten You."
- New Testament Fulfillment: Acts 13:33, Hebrews 1:5

Psalm 8: The Glory of the Messiah and His Creation

- Psalm 8:4-6: "What is man that You are mindful of him, and the son of man that You visit him? For You have made him a little lower than the angels, and You have crowned him with glory and honor. You have made him to have dominion over the works of Your hands; You have put all things under his feet."
- New Testament Fulfillment: Hebrews 2:6-8

Psalm 16: The Hope of the Faithful, the Messiah's Resurrection
- Psalm 16:10: "For You will not leave my soul in Sheol, nor will You allow Your Holy One to see corruption."
- New Testament Fulfillment: Acts 2:25-31, Acts 13:35-37

Psalm 22: The Suffering and Praise of the Messiah
- Psalm 22:1: "My God, My God, why have You forsaken Me?"
- New Testament Fulfillment: Matthew 27:46, Mark 15:34
- Psalm 22:16: "They pierced My hands and My feet."
- New Testament Fulfillment: John 19:37, Luke 24:39
- Psalm 22:18: "They divide My garments among them, and for My clothing they cast lots."
- New Testament Fulfillment: John 19:23-24

Psalm 23: The Good Shepherd
- Psalm 23:1: "The LORD is my shepherd; I shall not want."
- New Testament Fulfillment: John 10:11-14

Psalm 24: The King of Glory
- Psalm 24:7-10: "Lift up your heads, O you gates! And be lifted up, you everlasting doors! And the King of glory shall come in. Who is this King of glory? The LORD strong and mighty, the LORD mighty in battle."
- New Testament Fulfillment: Revelation 19:11-16

Psalm 34: The LORD, a Provider and Deliverer

- Psalm 34:20: "He guards all his bones; not one of them is broken."

- New Testament Fulfillment: John 19:36

Psalm 40: The Messiah's Obedience and Sacrifice

- Psalm 40:6-8: "Sacrifice and offering You did not desire; My ears You have opened. Burnt offering and sin offering You did not require. Then I said, 'Behold, I come; in the scroll of the book it is written of me. I delight to do Your will, O my God, and Your law is within my heart.'"

- New Testament Fulfillment: Hebrews 10:5-7

Psalm 45: The Messiah's Throne and Reign

- Psalm 45:6-7: "Your throne, O God, is forever and ever; a scepter of righteousness is the scepter of Your kingdom. You love righteousness and hate wickedness; therefore God, Your God, has anointed You with the oil of gladness more than Your companions."

- New Testament Fulfillment: Hebrews 1:8-9

Psalm 68: The Messiah's Victory and Ascension

- Psalm 68:18: "You have ascended on high, You have led captivity captive; You have received gifts among men, even from the rebellious, that the LORD God might dwell there."

- New Testament Fulfillment: Ephesians 4:8

Psalm 69: The Messiah's Zeal and Suffering

- Psalm 69:9: "Because zeal for Your house has eaten me up, and the reproaches of those who reproach You have fallen on me."

- New Testament Fulfillment: John 2:17, Romans 15:3

- Psalm 69:21: "They also gave me gall for my food, and for my thirst they gave me vinegar to drink."

- New Testament Fulfillment: Matthew 27:34, John 19:29

Psalm 72: The Messiah's Reign of Righteousness and Peace

- Psalm 72:8: "He shall have dominion also from sea to sea, and from the River to the ends of the earth."

- New Testament Fulfillment: Revelation 11:15

Psalm 89: The Messiah's Covenant and Kingdom

- Psalm 89:3-4: "I have made a covenant with My chosen, I have sworn to My servant David: 'Your seed I will establish forever, and build up your throne to all generations.'"

- New Testament Fulfillment: Luke 1:32-33, Acts 13:23

Psalm 102: The Eternal Nature of the Messiah

- Psalm 102:25-27: "Of old You laid the foundation of the earth, and the heavens are the work of Your hands. They will perish, but You will endure; yes, they will all grow old like a garment; like a cloak You will change them, and they will be changed. But You are the same, and Your years will have no end."

- New Testament Fulfillment: Hebrews 1:10-12

Psalm 110: The Priestly King

- Psalm 110:1: "The LORD said to my Lord, 'Sit at My right hand, till I make Your enemies Your footstool.'"

- New Testament Fulfillment: Matthew 22:44, Acts 2:34-35, Hebrews 1:13

- Psalm 110:4: "The LORD has sworn and will not relent, 'You are a priest forever according to the order of Melchizedek.'"

- New Testament Fulfillment: Hebrews 5:6, Hebrews 7:17

Psalm 118: The Chief Cornerstone

- Psalm 118:22: "The stone which the builders rejected has become the chief cornerstone."

- New Testament Fulfillment: Matthew 21:42, Acts 4:11, 1 Peter 2:7

Conclusion

The cross-references provided in this appendix demonstrate the profound connections between the Messianic Psalms and their New Testament fulfillments. These connections affirm the divine inspiration of Scripture and the central role of Jesus Christ in God's redemptive plan. By studying these fulfillments, believers can gain a deeper understanding of the coherence and reliability of the Bible, and a greater appreciation for Jesus as the promised Messiah. This comprehensive list serves as a valuable resource for exploring the rich prophetic heritage of the Psalms and its realization in the life and mission of Jesus Christ.

RESOURCES

The study of the Psalms and their fulfillment in Jesus Christ is a rich and rewarding endeavor that can be deepened through the use of various resources. This chapter provides a curated list of books, commentaries, study guides, and online tools to help you explore the Psalms and their Messianic prophecies more thoroughly. These resources are selected to enhance your understanding, provide scholarly insights, and support your spiritual growth.

Books and Commentaries

Books

1. "The Treasury of David" by Charles H. Spurgeon

   - A comprehensive commentary on the Psalms by one of the most revered preachers in history, offering detailed expositions and devotional insights.

2. "The Psalms: An Introduction and Commentary" by Tremper Longman III

- Provides an accessible yet scholarly introduction to the Psalms, exploring their literary structure, themes, and theological significance.

3. "Christ in the Psalms" by Patrick Henry Reardon

- A patristic commentary that explores how the Psalms point to Christ, drawing on the insights of early Church Fathers.

4. "Reflections on the Psalms" by C.S. Lewis

- A collection of essays by C.S. Lewis that reflect on the themes and personal impact of the Psalms.

Commentaries

1. "Word Biblical Commentary: Psalms" by Peter C. Craigie, Marvin E. Tate, and Leslie C. Allen

- A detailed and scholarly commentary series that provides in-depth analysis of the Hebrew text and its theological implications.

2. "The New International Commentary on the Old Testament: The Book of Psalms" by Robert L. Hubbard Jr. and Gerald H. Wilson

- A comprehensive and accessible commentary that examines the Psalms within their historical and literary context.

3. "Psalms: An Exegetical and Theological Exposition of Holy Scripture" by Steven J. Lawson

- Part of the "New American Commentary" series, this volume provides a clear and theological exposition of the Psalms.

Study Guides and Devotionals

1. "A Study of Psalms: A Devotional Commentary" by William S. Plumer

- Combines scholarly insight with devotional application, making it suitable for both study and personal reflection.

2. "Psalms: A 12-Week Study" by J.I. Packer and Dane C. Ortlund

   - Part of the "Knowing the Bible" series, this study guide provides structured lessons and discussion questions.

   3. "Journey Through the Psalms: A 30-Day Bible Study Devotional" by Denise Hughes

   - A month-long devotional that offers daily readings and reflections on selected Psalms.

Online Resources and Tools

   1. Blue Letter Bible (www.blueletterbible.org)

   - An online tool that provides multiple Bible translations, commentaries, concordances, and other study aids.

   2. Bible Gateway (www.biblegateway.com)

   - A comprehensive online Bible resource that offers various translations, study notes, and reading plans.

   3. The Bible Project (www.thebibleproject.com)

   - Features videos and study guides that provide visual and narrative summaries of biblical books, including the Psalms.

   4. Bible Study Tools (www.biblestudytools.com)

   - Offers a wide range of resources including commentaries, dictionaries, lexicons, and reading plans.

   5. Logos Bible Software (www.logos.com)

   - A powerful Bible study software that provides access to a vast library of resources, including commentaries, original language tools, and theological works.

Academic Journals and Articles

   1. "Journal for the Study of the Old Testament"

   - Publishes scholarly articles on various aspects of Old Testament studies, including the Psalms.

   2. "The Biblical Archaeologist"

- Offers insights into the historical and archaeological context of the Bible, including studies on the Psalms.

3. "The Expository Times"

- Provides articles and reviews on biblical studies, theology, and ministry, with frequent contributions on the Psalms.

Educational Courses and Lectures

1. The Psalms Course by Gordon-Conwell Theological Seminary (Available on iTunes U)

- A series of lectures by seminary professors that explore the literary, historical, and theological aspects of the Psalms.

2. "The Psalms" Course by Yale Divinity School (Available on YouTube)

- Lectures by scholars that cover various topics related to the Psalms, including their use in worship and their Messianic significance.

3. BiblicalTraining.org: "The Psalms"

- Offers free online courses and lectures by respected biblical scholars, providing in-depth study of the Psalms.

Conclusion

The study of the Psalms and their fulfillment in Jesus Christ is a journey that can be greatly enriched by the use of these resources. Whether you are a scholar, a student, or a layperson seeking to deepen your understanding, these books, commentaries, study guides, and online tools provide valuable insights and support. As you explore these resources, may your study of the Psalms lead to a deeper appreciation of God's Word, a stronger faith in His promises, and a closer walk with Jesus, the Messiah foretold in these ancient songs.

www.ingramcontent.com/pod-product-compliance
Lightning Source LLC
Chambersburg PA
CBHW051245150726

48001CB00017B/11